The Siren and the Sage

The Siren and the Sage

Knowledge and wisdom in ancient Greece and China

Steven Shankman and Stephen Durrant

CASSELL
London and New York

Cassell
Wellington House, 125 Strand, London WC2R OBB
370 Lexington Avenue, New York, NY 10017-6550

First published 2000

British Library Cataloguing-in-Publication Data
A catalogue record for this book is available from the British Library.

ISBN 0-304-70639-6 (hardback)
      0-304-70640-X (paperback)

Library of Congress Cataloging-in-Publication Data
Shankman, Steven, 1947–
      The siren and the sage : knowledge and wisdom in ancient Greece
         p.   cm.
      Includes bibliographical references and index.
      ISBN 0-304-70639-6—ISBN 0-304-70640-X (pbk.)
      1. Greek literature—History and criticism.   2. Chinese
   literature—To 221 B.C.—History and criticism.   3. Literature,
   Comparative—Greek and Chinese.   4. Literature, Comparative—Chinese
   and Greek.   5. Greece—Intellectual life.   6. China—Intellectual
   life.   7. Philosophy, Ancient.   I. Durrant, Stephen, W., 1944–   .
   II. Title.
   PA3070.S53   2000
   880.9′001—dc21
                                                              99-32296
                                                                   CIP

Typeset by BookEns Ltd, Royston, Herts.
Printed and bound in Great Britain by Biddles Limited,
Guildford and King's Lynn

Contents

Contents

Acknowledgments

We would like to express our sincerest gratitude to the National Endowment for the Humanities, which awarded us a Collaborative Projects Fellowship for the academic year 1996–7. This fellowship freed us from teaching obligations and afforded us the leisure to write a draft of this book. We are extremely grateful for this timely and generous support from the NEH.

Our home institution, the University of Oregon, provided us with travel and research funds that greatly facilitated our writing and research. We are particularly grateful for the generous support of Steadman Upham, now President of the Claremont Graduate University, who was then Vice Provost for Research and Dean of the Graduate School at the University of Oregon. The staff of the Oregon Humanities Center provided timely help with photocopying and mailings relating to our research.

We owe a significant debt, as well, to Esther Jacobson, Maude I. Kerns Professor of Oriental Art at the University of Oregon. It was Esther who organized an NEH Institute for University of Oregon humanities faculty, in the summer of 1991, with the goal of integrating Asian materials into the curriculum. It was in the course of this stimulating seminar that the authors of this book became acquainted and it was out of the many lively discussions we had during that delightful summer that the idea of this book first emerged.

We are also extremely grateful to the University of Oregon for supporting a conference entitled "Thinking Through Comparisons: Ancient Greece and China" in the spring of 1998, organized by the Oregon Humanities Center. This conference enabled us to bring to Eugene many of the world's experts and pioneers in the field of classical Sino-Hellenic studies and to share and test our ideas.

Special thanks are due to David Stern and Nancy Guitteau, whose generosity, vision, and selfless concern for higher education made possible the Coleman-Guitteau Endowed Professorship at the Oregon Humanities Center, which we held in 1994–5. This professorship allowed us to team-teach a course, entitled "Knowledge and Wisdom in Ancient Greece and China," that laid the foundations for this book. Generous thanks as well to Jim and Shirley Rippey. A Rippey Award for Innovative Teaching allowed one of us (Steven Shankman) to travel to China and to develop some of the expertise needed to teach a version of this course on his own. We would like to thank Professor Mineke Schipper of the University of Leiden for urging us to send our manuscript to Cassell; Janet Joyce and Sandra Margolies for so cheerfully and efficiently seeing the book through to publication; and Stephanie Rowe for preparing the index with such meticulous care and thoughtfulness.

Friends and colleagues were kind enough to read sections of this manuscript – and in some cases the entire book – and offered encouragement as well as useful suggestions for revision. Particular thanks are due to Claudia Baracchi, Ian Duncan, James W. Earl, Jeffrey Hurwit, Glenn Hughes, Don Levi, Massimo Lollini, Louis Orsini, Henry Rosemont, William H. Race, Lisa Raphals, and Haun Saussy. Needless to say, these wise counselors bear no responsibility whatsoever for the inevitable shortcomings of this book.

We would also like to thank Wang Gongyi for allowing us to use one of her lithographs for the cover of this book and Lin Hue-ping for facilitating this arrangement.

IN MEMORIAM
MARSHALL AND EMILY WELLS

Filial Piety

I

Odysseus loved his father, it is true,
But when he saw him after twenty years,
Did he embrace him, giving him his due
Of filial affection, shedding tears
Of pity for the old man's ceaseless grieving,
Soothing a father's pangs for a son's leaving?

II

He pondered tender thoughts but in the end
Chose to conceal himself so as to observe,
Coolly detached, Laertes' grief and bend
A son's compassion to the explorer's nerve.
So curious Odysseus put his men
At fatal risk to see the Cyclops' den.

III

Child of Odysseus, aching to explore
Distant locales beyond the cozy West,
I am poised to leave for China. But what for?
To ensure that old Laertes gets no rest?
Confucius says you must not travel far
From parents but remain near where they are.

IV

Reluctantly, because Laertes ails,
I choose to stay. The exotic names now sting,
Ringing of thrills just vanished. Not one fails
To evoke regret: Baotou; Hohhot; Beijing;
Shangdu, the summer palace of great Khan;
Xian; Taroko Gorge; Hualien; Yinchuan.

V

Odysseus crossed the seas. Although I feel
His fabled urge to hear the Sirens' song,
When fathers ail I heed the tough appeal
Of sage Confucius saying sons belong
At home with family, that one must be
Princely, observing filial piety.

Steven Shankman

Introduction

Preamble

In today's global village, we are constantly aware of what is going on in remote regions of the world, even if we are frustrated at not being able to resolve crises that we view on our television sets and can instantaneously discuss with others, sometimes thousands of miles away, on our telephones or computer screens. This was not, of course, the rule in the history of civilizations. In antiquity, for example, impressive civilizations existed and produced great artists and thinkers who had little or no awareness that other artists and thinkers, thousands of miles away, were at that very moment producing equally great works of poetry and philosophy. Such is the relation of ancient Chinese to ancient Greek culture.

Seemingly unaware of each other's presence, the cultures of ancient China and ancient Greece stand as two major influences on the course of world civilization. The texts and cultural values of classical China spread throughout East Asia and became the basis of learning in such countries as Korea, Japan, and Vietnam. Even today, some scholars speak of a "Confucian East Asia" and attribute the startling rise of Pacific Rim economic power to a Chinese style.[1] Likewise, Greek civilization is credited with creating many of the intellectual paradigms of the West. Modern philosophy, science, and technology, many argue, occur at the end of the track first laid down in ancient Athens. Both of these cultures are products of what Karl Jaspers calls the "Axial Age,"[2] a time that extends from approximately 800 to 200 BCE when creative thinkers seem "everywhere to have sprung up amid the variety and instability of small competing states."[3]

1

We are intrigued by evidence that ancient China and ancient Greece may have actually been aware of each other's presence, even though that knowledge was presumably indirect and mediated by nomadic peoples in Central Asia. Quite recently, for example, Chinese silks were found in a fifth-century BCE Athenian grave, a startling discovery that argues for the existence of connections between the West and the Far East several centuries before the known existence of the Silk Routes.[4] Certainly Indo-European peoples were in close contact with the Chinese from as early as the second millennium BCE and may have acted as a bridge between East and West.[5] If comparative work on ancient Chinese and Greek literature were limited to such historically demonstrable incidents of interconnectedness, however, then comparatists would have closed up shop long ago. Perhaps the essence of at least one central meaning of "comparative literature" is contained in Aristotle's observation that it is the mark of a naturally lively mind to create metaphors and thereby to see connections between things (*Poetics* 1459a), sometimes between things that on the surface might appear quite disparate and unrelated. To the question, "Why compare Greece and China?" we would reply, "How is it possible *not* to compare them?" In our increasingly multicultural world, if we are to avoid isolationism and the Balkanization of humanity into discrete cultural entities, it seems to us that we must all be comparatists.

The ancient Chinese and Greek fields offer a rich and even representative terrain in this regard. In what sense "representative"? Let us briefly consider the related matters of language and script. Chinese is the oldest attested written language of the Sino-Tibetan language family and is spoken today by more people than any of the world's languages. Classical Greek is one of the oldest written languages of Indo-European, the language family with the most native speakers. In fact, speakers of the Sino-Tibetan and Indo-European language groups together account for about three-quarters of the world's population.

The ancient Greek and Chinese languages work in very different ways. Classical Chinese, the literary language of China in the period from roughly 500 to 100 BCE, is primarily monosyllabic;[6] the word most often corresponds to a single syllable, which in turn is written by a single Chinese character. Because classical Chinese, like most forms of modern Chinese, is uninflected, there is no way to determine what we often call "parts of speech" from the form of the word itself. Instead, linguistic function depends upon word order or occasional grammatical particles. Ancient Greek, in contrast, is a highly inflected language that fashions words, through extensive verbal morphology, into complex patterns of relationships. This linguistic distinction, stated all too simply here, parallels a whole array of differences that can be traced in early literature (the Greek epic and the Chinese lyric), history (Greek history as unified story and Chinese history as a "fragmented" presentation), and philosophy (Greek tendency to systematize and Chinese emphasis upon situational response).[7]

The written form of these two languages also stands in sharp contrast. Ancient Greek is written with an alphabet that derives from the early Phoenician script and probably appeared, at the latest, by the tenth century BCE. Some have gone so far as to argue that "the decisive step towards acquiring individuality is not writing as such, but alphabetic writing ... [i.e.] the principle of representing the individual sounds which are relevant in a language."[8] Chinese writing, as is well known, is perhaps the most striking, and certainly the most tenacious, system of nonalphabetic writing in world history. The origin of Chinese script is a subject of dispute, but it is clearly attested as a fully developed system in the oracle-bone script of the thirteenth century BCE. Chinese graphs presumably had a pictographic origin, but, by the time of the oracle bones, most had become stylized in ways that obscured their pictographic or ideographic origins. Phonetic principles were used extensively as the script developed, and were fundamental to the elaboration of a full-fledged writing system.

It is not our intention here to become embroiled in the issue of whether or not reading Chinese involves a fundamentally different psychology than reading Greek or any other alphabetic script. What is important for us is that the Chinese themselves have traditionally seen a relationship between their script and the natural world that the script represents and in which it was often felt to participate. Xu Shen (30?–124?), the author of the first etymological dictionary of Chinese characters, says that the first steps toward writing were taken when the mythological emperor Bao Xi (= Fu Xi, traditional dates *c*. 2800 BCE) "lifted his head up and observed the images in the sky; bowed his head down and saw the formations of the earth; and then looked out at the patterns on birds and beasts and the veins of the earth." Later, Xu Shen goes on to say, the Yellow Emperor's wise minister Cang Jie (traditional dates *c*. 2500 BCE) invented written characters when he "saw the tracks of birds and beasts and understood that one can perceive differences in their distinctive patterns."[9]

This notion of the natural origins of Chinese, whether ultimately right or wrong, is reinforced by the strong emphasis in China upon calligraphic art and the link between the strokes of the written text and those of the artist's brush that depict bamboo, flowers, mountains, and other aspects of the natural world. Surely, it is more difficult to break the link, which some would call arbitrary, between the written word and the world it represents in a script like Chinese than in Greek, where the units of the script represent units of sound and nothing more. With Chinese writing there is, at the least, a tenacious *illusion* of direct and natural participation in the world of those things and ideas writing is meant to depict.

Previous comparative studies of ancient Greece and China

A considerable body of scholarship comparing ancient Greece and ancient China now exists. Despite occasional attacks upon broadly comparatist endeavors and upon the allegedly simplistic ways in which they have sometimes proceeded, the numbers of such comparative studies are increasing and are yielding valuable results. One might argue that the work of Western sinology, which has primarily been conducted in languages profoundly influenced by the very vocabulary and categories of the Greeks, is innately comparative and has sometimes labored under an anxiety generated by Greek literature and philosophy. Certainly many of the most influential works of sinological study frequently mention classical Greece and regard it as a crucial and perhaps even dominant point of reference for all educated Western readers. The second volume of Joseph Needham's multivolumed *Science and Civilisation in China,* which is surely one of the most valuable sinological works of the century, is a case in point.[10] Needham makes hundreds of references to Greek thought in this text, including over forty references to Aristotle alone. Benjamin Schwartz's masterful study of traditional Chinese philosophy, *The World of Thought in Ancient China,*[11] is a more recent example. Ancient Greek philosophy is mentioned in his work more than thirty times, even though Schwartz's subject, as the title indicates, is ancient China.

Many native Chinese scholars, sometimes fresh from graduate study in the West, often use Greek philosophy as a touchstone for their own tradition and even may be said to have labored under an anxiety induced by the Greek model. Hu Shi's *The Development of the Logical Method in Ancient China* is a splendid example.[12] Hu's work, which was first submitted as a dissertation at Columbia University in 1917, is filled with a spirit of advocacy, which was not unusual among Chinese intellectuals of his generation. Hu wished to resuscitate "logical methods" that he believed existed in ancient China but had been fettered by the dominance of a moralistic Confucian tradition. His purpose was "to make my own people see that these methods of the West are not totally alien to the Chinese mind" (p. 9). The predominance of logic is, to him, the most admirable characteristic of the West. Comparative studies, such as his own implicitly is, should, he

4

believes, attempt to uncover those aspects of the Chinese tradition that have the potential of directing China toward Western-style science and technology. Even a scholar like Kung-chuan Hsiao, who is much less inclined to refer to Greek comparisons or to advocate emulating Western ideas, cannot help but conjecture, in the last words of a long and highly useful volume, that if Greek philosophy or Roman law rather than Buddhism had been introduced into China during the third century BCE, "one can at least safely conclude that political thought and institutions would have displayed a more positive content, and more rapid change, or advance."[13]

Specialists in Western philosophy and classical Greece largely ignore China. There have been noteworthy exceptions, including two we shall note briefly here: F. S. C. Northrop and G. E. R. Lloyd. Northrop is a philosopher who published a book in 1946 entitled *The Meeting of East and West: An Inquiry into World Understanding.*[14] In this book, the author establishes a sweeping contrast between a Western knowledge that is expressed in "logically developed, scientific and philosophical treatises" and an Eastern knowledge in which an individual concentrates "attention upon the immediately apprehended aesthetic continuum of which he is a part" (p. 318). Elsewhere, he explains that the former derives "concepts by postulation" and the latter "concepts by intuition."[15]

Such a sweeping comparison as that presented by Northrop comes perilously close to positing the existence of the very kinds of "mentalities" that the distinguished historian of Greek science G. E. R. Lloyd would like to "demystify." Lloyd's extraordinarily lucid and provocative study *Demystifying Mentalities*[16] is an attack upon the theory of distinct cultural mentalities such as Lévy-Bruhl's belief in a "primitive mentality" or James Frazier's notion of magic, religious, and scientific mentalities as the three progressive stages through which a civilization truly worthy of the name must ascend. Lloyd's criticisms of the idea of mentalities are convincing. He compares certain aspects of ancient Greek and ancient Chinese thought that may appear to represent essentially distinct mentalities. He contrasts "a Greek preoccupation with foundational questions and a readiness to countenance extreme or radical solutions" with Chinese "well-developed pragmatic tendencies, with a focus on practicalities, on what works or can be put to use" (p. 124). Lloyd then explains this contrast not by inferring the existence of an essential Hellenic and an essential Chinese mentality. He sees the contrast as deriving, instead, from concrete differences in the sociopolitical contexts of the two cultures. There is nothing in Warring States China, he notes, equivalent to the plurality of constitutions and political organizations of the Greek city-states, circumstances that promoted intellectual competition. Moreover, in China philosophical argument seems always to have been articulated as an attempt to persuade an emperor, king, or duke, a situation that Lloyd believes inhibited certain types of argumentation. Lloyd's ideas on the distinctions in Greek and Chinese thought and their respective political contexts are extremely useful.

In a more recent book, *Adversaries and Authorities: Investigations into Ancient Greek and Chinese Science* (1996), Lloyd continues his criticism of the tendency of some scholars to identify distinct Greek and Chinese mentalities, and he notes that his primary objection to such an approach is that "it provides not even the beginnings of an explanation, but at most a statement of what has to be explained."[17] What he believes comparatists must do is to seek out what *questions* each side of the comparison were actually trying to answer. Such examination, he attempts to demonstrate in this book, sometimes reveals that the Greeks and the Chinese were addressing entirely different problems and that apparent equivalences between the two often prove, when examined in this light, to be illusory.

In the past few years, a number of other important works have appeared in the area of Sino-Hellenic comparative studies. Most of these new works come primarily from the sinological community and they tend to focus on the allegedly distinctive features of Chinese culture, a culture which the authors of these books often view as the West's "other." We have benefited from many of these studies, which we frequently cite in our notes. Limitations of space will not permit us to discuss all of them here. Three recent comparative projects are, however, particularly relevant to *The Siren and the Sage* and we wish to acknowledge them now.

Perhaps the most sweeping comparative study currently under way is, like the present book, a collaborative project. The sinologist Roger T. Ames and the philosopher David L. Hall have coauthored three provocative books. The first of these, *Thinking Through Confucius*, is an exercise in rethinking Confucius (Hall and Ames might say "unthinking" Confucius) in the light of certain issues in contemporary Western philosophy. In their second and more sweeping work, *Anticipating China: Thinking Through the Narratives of Chinese and Western Culture*, Hall and Ames pursue a contrast between what they call "second problematic thinking," which can also be labeled "causal thinking," and "first problematic thinking," which they associate with "analogical or correlative thinking." Their book establishes a very strong contrast between a classical Western emphasis upon transcendence, order, and permanence and a Chinese preoccupation with pragmatism, vagueness, and change. At each stage of their comparison, Hall and Ames acknowledge the presence of philosophical countertrends in each civilization, thus blunting the criticism that they have overessentialized the two sides of their comparison. Their third book, *Thinking from the Han: Self, Truth, and Transcendence in Chinese and Western Culture*,[18] centers upon three topics – self, truth, and transcendence – that they believe "permit the most efficient advertisement of the barriers existing between Chinese and Western interlocutors."[19] While we reach certain conclusions similar to those of Hall and Ames and owe a debt to their research, our comparative work has a different focus. Our goal is to investigate equivalent figurations or symbolisms rather than to produce a sweeping set of contrasts between East and West.[20] We shall suggest certain patterns of similarity and difference that emerge from a close investigation of a select number of texts, texts that we mainly approach from a literary perspective.

Lisa Raphals's suggestive *Knowing Words: Wisdom and Cunning in the Classical Traditions of China and Greece* is a comparative study that is, like ours, more strictly literary than that of Hall and Ames. Her work is, however, both more narrowly focused and more technical than *The Siren and the Sage*. Raphals's theme is "the provenance of metic intelligence"[21] in classical Greece and China, a topic she derives from the famous study of the French classicists Marcel Detienne and Jean-Pierre Vernant,[22] and whose fortunes she traces forward into such postclassical Chinese novels as *Romance of the Three Kingdoms* (*c.* 1500) and *Journey to the West* (*c.* 1600). Our study, in contrast to that of Professor Raphals, is confined to the classical period of these two cultures: in Greece we end with Aristotle (384–322), in China with Sima Qian (145–86 BCE). While our themes and focus differ from hers, we nevertheless share Professor Raphals's belief that comparison, if it is to proceed at all, must first attempt to understand each intellectual tradition in its own terms.[23]

François Jullien, in several recent books, has attempted to do just this.[24] Rejecting "naive assimilation, according to which everything can be directly transposed from one culture to another,"[25] Jullien, it seems to us, tries to identify distinctive terms or tendencies of traditional Chinese culture that have rarely been discussed precisely because they are so thoroughly and naturally embedded in Chinese discourse. These features, such as a privileging of indirect expression or an emphasis upon the "deployment" or "situation" of a thing rather than its inherent quality, to give two examples, become for Jullien a wellspring from which to explain Chinese "difference" as well as a foundation upon which productive comparison with Western culture can be built. There is little doubt that his comparisons are driven by the Chinese side of the equation, which he argues provides a perspective that enables us "to envisage our thought from without" (*pour envisager notre pensée au dehors*).[26] This has invited the criticism that Jullien establishes an "other" (i.e. China) without having first explicitly defined and clarified his principal point of reference (i.e. Greece and the West).[27] While Jullien argues persuasively and often brilliantly for the predominance, in Chinese thought, of obliqueness or indirectness, in contrast to what he sees as the straightforwardness of Western discourse, he is not insensitive to the occasional indirectness of the Western philosophical tradition, as he suggests in his remarks on Plato's seventh letter.[28] From our perspective, however, the contrast is not as stark as Jullien would have us believe. We shall argue, moreover, that Plato's texts are far more oblique and suggestive than conventional wisdom allows or than Jullien – even when seen in the light of his more nuanced reading of Plato – suggests.

Whether our presentation of the two sides of the Greece–China comparison is properly balanced remains to be seen. Certainly we agree that each of these traditions is enormously rich and complex. It seems to us that any comparative study will almost of necessity flatten and oversimplify one or the other (or both!) of these two great traditions. Perhaps this should not overly concern us. Progress in this difficult comparative endeavor will perhaps best come from a variety of approaches and studies. No one scholarly work can ever hope to say all that might be interestingly said in comparing the literary productions of two cultures as vast and diverse as those of ancient Greece and ancient China.

The sage

Sage (*sheng ren*) is a term that appears throughout ancient Chinese texts to designate the person of ideal wisdom and understanding. The first Chinese etymological dictionary, written in approximately 100 CE, associates sageness with the ability "to penetrate" or "to comprehend."[29] In one of the earliest occurrences of "sage" in a Chinese text, *The Book of Historical Documents* (*Shu jing, c.* 300 BCE), it is glossed as follows: "Sageness is to understand all things." This is a notion of the sage as possessor of knowledge in the sense of encyclopedic comprehensiveness, a meaning that can be found in Confucius (e.g. *Analects* 7.34), who with characteristic modesty wisely denies that he has achieved such lofty status: "How would I dare to claim either sageness [*sheng*] or humaneness [*ren*]?" In the *Dao de jing*, Laozi transforms the ideal of sageness from encyclopedic knowledge into the wisdom that would allow a person to participate in the oneness that is the *dao*: "By embracing oneness [*bao yi*], the sage [*sheng ren*] acts on behalf of all under heaven" (22.7–8).[30]

We wish to equate the "knowledge" of our subtitle with the ideal of encyclopedic comprehensiveness. But what do we mean by the "wisdom" of the sage? Let us look closely at the first chapter of the *Dao de jing*:

> If a way can be spoken (or followed), it is not the constant way.
> If a name can be named, it is not the constant name.
> Nameless is the beginning of heaven and earth.
> Named is the mother of the ten thousand things.
> Therefore,
>   constantly have no intention (*wu yu*) to observe its wonders;
>   constantly have an intention (*you yu*) to observe its manifestations.
> These two come forth together but are differently named.
> Coming forth together they are called mystery.
> Mystery upon mystery,
> Gateway to many wonders.[31]

This passage has been more often translated, read, and commented upon in the West than any passage of ancient Chinese literature.

The *Dao de jing*, sometimes translated as "The Classic of the Way and Its Power," is a small book traditionally ascribed to an enigmatic figure named Laozi (*c.* sixth century BCE) or "the Old Master" but surely written several centuries after the time in which Laozi is said to have lived. The opening chapter quoted above functions as a sort of epitome of the work as a whole, as Laozi addresses both the inadequacy and the necessity of language. Names, which cut the world of thought and thing into discrete units – and are, moreover, subject to constant change – can never adequately articulate one's experience of unity and origin. We would argue that it is impossible to express, at least in any strictly referential or purely discursive fashion, such experiences of unity or origin. "Nameless is the beginning of heaven and earth": why is the beginning [*shi*] nameless? Could it be that it is nameless, in part, because the beginning of all things cannot be conceptualized and therefore cannot be named? What was there *before* the beginning of heaven and earth (*tian di*)?[32] Nothing? But isn't that nothing still something?[33] It appears that, when we name, we name things in a referential manner. We live in a world of "the ten thousand things" (*wan wu*) and naming is the "mother" (*mu*) of these things in the sense that naming brings them into conceptual existence, allowing us to differentiate one thing from another, to communicate, and to manipulate reality as we must if we are to survive. But naming, while necessary, can also cut us off from the very experiences that the naming – such as the naming of the beginning, or the naming of the experience of oneness with the *dao* – is attempting to describe and thus name. The author of the *Dao de jing* lives in this tension between "the nameless" and "the named."

The author also lives in the tension between the experiences of "having no intention" and "having an intention." Intention (*yu*), for the author of the first chapter of the *Dao de jing*, appears to refer specifically to the desire to conceptualize and manipulate reality. It is the muting of such a willful intentionalism that characterizes – so far as we can so characterize it in language – the wondrous experience of participation in the total process that is the *dao*. "These two come forth together but are differently named. / Coming forth together they are called mystery." Which two? "These two" (*liang zhe*) refers, most immediately, to "not having an intention" (*wu yu*) and "having an intention" (*you yu*), which is parallel to the previously mentioned pairing of "the nameless" and "the named."

There is, the author is suggesting, no difference between "not having an intention" and "having an intention"; and yet there is a difference. There is no difference between "the nameless and the named"; and yet there is a difference. This is a paradoxical truth – a mystery (*yuan*), if you will – because the necessary linguistic act of separating "constantly [*chang*] not having an intention" from "constantly having an intention" or "the nameless" from "the named" makes it *appear* as if each member of these two pairs is in fact a distinct entity. But it is not. From a purely logical perspective, we can name the named but we obviously cannot name the nameless, for then it would not be nameless. And this thinker wants to name the nameless while at the same time suggesting that the nameless cannot be named. Language itself, perhaps because it is traditionally used to describe things and concepts, cannot adequately express the experience of participation in the *dao* – for this experience, in its fullness, obliterates one's individuality, one's separateness, one's need for the distinguishing acts of language. To the author of the first chapter of the *Dao de jing*, it now appears that language may *both* refer to external reality, to the world of things, *and* be an evocation of the experience of a person's mysteriously inchoate participation in the *dao*.

To borrow Eric Voegelin's terminology, language both reflects and participates in the paradox of consciousness. Consciousness must be understood in both its *intentionalist* and *participatory* modes.[34] Consciousness intends objects, and in this capacity of intentionality, reality consists of the "things" intended by this aspect of consciousness, of what Voegelin calls "thing-reality" (Laozi's "ten thousand things"). But a thinker will be engaging in an act of imaginative oblivion if she or he takes thing-reality for the whole picture. For consciousness has its participatory dimension as well. Consciousness is not only a subject intending objects, but it is a participant in what Voegelin calls "It-reality"[35] (one crucial aspect of Laozi's *dao*). Intentional acts always occur within a comprehending structure of reality.[36]

What is the distinction between the "knowledge" and "wisdom" of our subtitle and how does this distinction relate to the paradox of consciousness? We all desire to know, and yet the intensity of this very desire to know and to control reality can cause a serious imbalance in the human psyche. We may forget that this desire to know takes place within a comprehensive structure of reality (*dao*) of which the human consciousness is itself a part and which can never be mastered. In our desire to know, we may forfeit the wisdom of the sage. Knowledge and wisdom will be at odds.

The preceding analysis of language and of consciousness is our own way of "naming" the concerns and approach of this book. The first chapter of the *Dao de jing* implies a theory of the structure of consciousness, of the relation between language and reality, that we find particularly illuminating for a comparison between ancient Chinese and ancient Greek literature. We find an equivalent figuration in Diotima's remarks made to Socrates in Plato's *Symposium* (203b–204a), when the prophetess relates a myth that describes the erotic experience of the philosophical quest as a combination of intentionalist seeking (*poros*), on the one hand, and of needy receptivity (*penia*), on the other. Both the Chinese sage and the Greek philosopher articulate the nature of that wisdom – which had been expressed by earlier authors, such as the poets, but with less decisive analytic precision and conciseness – that might allow them to live in the tension between the nameless and the named, between the experience of participation in oneness and the necessary sense of their own individuality. *The Siren and the Sage: Knowledge and Wisdom in Ancient Greece and China* is a comparative exploration of this tension in selected works of Chinese and Greek authors from the time of the composition of the *Classic of Poetry* (*c*. 1000–500 BCE) and Homer (*c*. 900–700 BCE) through to that of Sima Qian (145–86 BCE).

In Part I, we will compare and contrast two of the earliest works in Chinese and Greek literature, works composed at approximately the same time: the *Odyssey* and the *Classic of Poetry*. Part II will juxtapose the works of two historians, Thucydides (*c*. 460–398) and Sima Qian. Part III will draw comparisons between some central figures of Chinese (Confucius, Laozi, and Zhuangzi) and Greek philosophy (Plato). We will be suggesting that Greek authors have often stressed intentionality while Chinese thinkers have perhaps been more responsive to the participationist dimension. This does not mean, however, that we do not find a strong intentionalist strain in China or a participationist tradition in Greece. It was, in fact, the intentionalism of Huizi and others that elicited the participationist critique of Zhuangzi, as we will discuss in Part III. It was Plato, moreover, who coined the philosophical term "participation" (*methexis*).

It should be noted that the Plato we present here is not the unbending metaphysical absolutist so often pictured in the conventional understandings, but rather an open and tentative enquirer who has much in common with Laozi and Zhuangzi. The Daoist sage might appear, at first glance, to have more in common with the withdrawal from politics characteristic of the thought of Pyrrho of Elis (*c*. 365–275 BCE), the official founder of Greek skepticism, or with the Epicureans or Stoics, than with the philosopher Plato. We see many parallels worth noting, however, between the thought of Plato, on the one hand, and of Laozi and Zhuangzi, on the other. And it is Plato, rather than Pyrrho or the Epicureans or the Stoics, who has had the most decisively powerful influence on Western thought, as Whitehead observed in his now famous remark, "The safest generalization of the European philosophical tradition is that it consists of a series of footnotes to Plato."[37]

The siren

The Daoist sage (*sheng ren*), as we have suggested, attempts to live in the tension between the nameless and the named, between the experience of participation in oneness and his own necessary sense of individuality. So, we shall argue, does the Greek philosopher, as represented by Plato. So much for the "sage" of our title. But what of the siren? On his arduous return home from Troy, Odysseus must endure many trials and temptations. One of these – the first he meets after escaping from the seductive clutches of the beautiful witch Kirkê – is his encounter with the Sirens.[38] Homer does not describe what these two Sirens look like. Visual artists will depict them as creatures having the heads of women and the bodies of birds. While what the Siren represented for the ancient Greeks is not precisely clear, what is "certain," according to Alfred Heubeck and Arie Hoekstra, editors of the recent Oxford commentary on the *Odyssey*, is that "both the conception and the portrayal of man–beast hybrids ... are influenced by oriental models,"[39] probably from the ancient Near East.

When Odysseus approaches the island of the Sirens, his ship is suddenly becalmed. Scrupulously following Kirkê's directions (XII.47–54), he then orders his men to plug their ears with wax. He asks that they tie him to the mast, with his ears unplugged, so that he can listen to the Sirens' song. And he warns them that, despite his supplications, they must ignore his commands to untie him. Rather, they must fasten him all the more tightly to the mast if he demands that they untie him. And what is this Siren-song, so compelling that it has resulted in the deaths of all who have listened to its beauties?

> Over here, praiseworthy Odysseus, great glory of the Greeks!
> Anchor your ship so that you can hear our voices.
> For no one has ever steered his black ship past us
> Without hearing the honey-toned voices issuing from our lips.
> He who experiences the rapture of our song leaves us knowing even more
>   than he did before he came.
> For we know everything that the Greeks and Trojans
> Suffered – it was the gods' will – in broad Troy.
> We know everything that happens on the much-nourishing earth.
>
> (XII.184–91)

The Sirens offer Odysseus comprehensive and absolute knowledge that will obviate the need for further seeking, for they know everything (*idmen gar toi panth'*, 189). This is the very comprehensiveness that Confucius (7.34) had the wisdom to deny that he could ever possess. The Sirens promise a dissolving of the difficult but necessary tension that will be articulated by the sage who composed the first chapter of the *Dao de jing*. They offer an increase of intentional knowing to the point of all-knowingness, such as Hegel promises in the preface to *The Phenomenology of Mind* when he says that his work will "help bring philosophy nearer to the form of science – that goal where it can lay aside the name of *love* of knowledge and be actual *knowledge*" since "the systematical development of truth in scientific form ... can alone be the true shape in which truth exists."[40] What the Sirens offer, in other words, is the *knowledge* that will make the *wisdom* of the sage unnecessary. Those who succumb and short-circuit their journeys become part of the large heap (*polus this*, XII.45) of human bones covered with shriveled skin that lies at the Sirens' feet.

Homer presents us with a powerful image of Odysseus, tied rigidly to the mast of his ship and listening to the Sirens' song surrounded by his men, whose ears have been plugged with wax. This scene vividly portrays the tension between the desire to experience a (finally illusory) sense of total immersion in "being" (as the Greek philosophers will later express it), on the one hand, and the will to retain one's sense of bounded individuality, on the other. Odysseus – alone of men – has it both ways, but the tension is unbearable. This scene, then, pulls in two directions at once: it represents Odysseus' desire to yield to the illusion of absolute knowledge, on the one hand; and, on the other, it registers the Greek hero's struggle to retain a necessary awareness of the truth that the intentionalist knower always remains no more than an embodied participant in the never-ending journey or search for wisdom. Do the poets of the ancient Chinese *Classic of Poetry* express similar desires and insights? In order to address this question, let us turn to a comparative analysis of the *Odyssey* and the roughly contemporary *Classic of Poetry*.

Notes

1. See, for example, G. Rozman, "The Confucian Faces of Capitalism," in *Pacific Century*, ed. M. Borthwick (Boulder, CO: Westview, 1992), pp. 310–18, and the articles in *The East Asian Region: Confucian Heritage and Its Modern Adaptation*, ed. Gilbert Rozman (Princeton, NJ: Princeton University Press, 1991) and in *Confucian Traditions in East Asian Modernity: Moral Education and Economic Culture in Japan and the Four Mini-dragons*, ed. Tu Wei-ming (Cambridge, MA: Harvard University Press, 1996).

2. *The Origin and Goal of History* (New Haven: Yale University Press, 1953).

3. A. C. Graham, *Disputers of the Tao: Philosophical Argument in Ancient China* (La Salle, IL: Open Court, 1989), p. 1.

4. Andrew Stewart, *Greek Sculpture: An Exploration*, 2 vols (New Haven: Yale University Press, 1990), vol. 1, p. 166. These silks, Stewart suggests, may have belonged to the family of Alcibiades, "notorious for his flamboyant extravagance" (*ibid.*). See our discussion of Alcibiades in Parts II and III of this book.

5. On this issue, see Victor H. Mair, "Mummies of the Tarim Basin," *Archaeology* (April/May, 1995): 28–35.

6. A still classic article on the issue of the "monosyllabic" nature of early Chinese that forces us to qualify such a description considerably is George A. Kennedy, "The Monosyllabic Myth," in *The Selected Works of George A. Kennedy*, ed. Tien-yi Li (New Haven: Far Eastern Publications, 1964), pp. 104–18. A most recent and extremely lucid discussion of the nature of the early Chinese language and script, which touches upon the issue of monosyllabism and what he would call the zodiographic form of the earliest Chinese writing is William G. Boltz, "Language and Writing," in Michael Loewe and Edward L. Shaughnessy (eds), *The Cambridge History of Ancient China, from the Origins of Civilization to 221 BC* (Cambridge University Press, 1999), pp. 74–123.

7. For some basic bibliography on these issues, see Stephen Durrant, *The Cloudy Mirror: Tension and Conflict in the Writings of Sima Qian* (Albany: State University of New York Press, 1995), p. 124, p. 179 n.8.

8. See the discussion on this controversy in Florian Coulmas, *The Writing Systems of the World* (Oxford: Blackwell, 1989), pp. 159–62.

9. *Shuo wen jie zi zhu* [A Commentary on Explaining Simple Graphs and Analyzing Compound Characters] (Taipei: Shijie, 1962), 15A.1.

10. Cambridge: Cambridge University Press, 1956. The second volume is entitled *History of Scientific Thought*.

11. Cambridge, MA: Harvard University Press, 1985.

12. 1922; rpt., New York: Paragon, 1963.

13. *History of Chinese Political Thought*, Vol. 1: *From the Beginnings to the Sixth Century A.D.*, trans. F. W. Mote (Princeton, NJ: Princeton University Press, 1979), p. 667.

14. New York: Macmillan, 1946.

15. *The Logic of the Sciences and the Humanities* (New York: Meridian Books, 1947), pp. 77–101.

16. Cambridge: Cambridge University Press, 1990.

17. Cambridge: Cambridge University Press, 1996, p. 3.

18. *Thinking Through Confucius* (Albany: State University of New York, 1987); *Anticipating China: Thinking Through the Narratives of Chinese and Western Culture* (Albany: State University of New York, 1995); *Thinking from the Han: Self, Truth, and Transcendence in Chinese and the Western Culture* (Albany: State University of New York Press, 1998).

19. *Ibid.*, p. xviii.

20. We prefer the term "figuration" to "symbolism" because the "symbol," in Western thought, traditionally is thought to refer to a transcendent realm that we cannot assume in the Chinese case. When we occasionally use the term "symbol" in this book, we mean it in the sense – as in the symbolist poetry of Mallarmé – of that which is suggestive, or indicative, of a meaning beyond itself (with no necessary reference to a superior, "transcendent" level of meaning).

21. Ithaca, NY: Cornell University Press, 1992, p. xiii.

22. *Cunning Intelligence in Greek Culture and Society*, trans. Janet Lloyd (Chicago: University of Chicago Press, 1991).

23. *Ibid.*, pp. 7–8. See also the excellent review of Raphals's book by Benjamin Schwartz in *Harvard Journal of Asiatic Studies*, 56 (2) (December 1996): 229–30.

24. See especially his *The Propensity of Things: Toward a History of Efficacy in China*, trans. Janet Lloyd (1992; New York: Zone Books, 1995) and *Le détour et l'accès: stratégies du sens en Chine, en Grèce* (Paris: Bernard Grasset, 1995).

25. *The Propensity of Things*, p. 20.

26. *Le détour et l'accès*, p. 9.

27. This criticism has been voiced by Jean-Paul Reding, himself a distinguished comparatist, in a review of Jullien's work published in *China Review International*, 3 (1) (Spring, 1996): 160–8.

28. *Le détour et l'accès*, pp. 287–8.

29. *Shuo wen jie zi zhu*, 12A.7.

30. The word *sheng* (sage) appears twenty-three times in *Dao de jing* and only eight times in the somewhat longer *Analects*.

31. This translation and all others that follow, unless otherwise noted, are our own. The *Dao de jing* has been translated into English over one hundred times, and each year new translations appear. We particularly recommend the fairly conservative

translation of D. C. Lau, *Lao Tzu, Tao Te Ching* (Harmondsworth: Penguin, 1963), later revised according to the recently discovered Mawangdui manuscripts and published in Everyman's Library (New York: Albert Knopf, 1994), and the scholarly translation of Robert G. Henricks, *Lao-Tzu, Tao-te ching* (New York: Ballantine Books, 1989), which also takes the Mawangdui manuscripts into careful consideration.

Since there are so many quite different translations of this first chapter, two sections of our own translation deserve brief comment. First, the common translation "The Way that can be spoken ..." perpetuates a grammatical misunderstanding. On this issue, see Chad Hansen, *A Daoist Theory of Chinese Thought: A Philosophical Interpretation* (New York: Oxford University Press, 1992), p. 215. Second, it is tempting to follow many interpreters and break lines 5 and 6 after the Chinese *wu* and *you*, making the contrast one between "not having" and "having" instead of "having no intention" and "having intention." Thus, we might translate:

> Therefore,
>   constantly not having, one would intend to observe its wonders;
>   constantly having, one would intend to observe its manifestations.

Hansen, for one, advocates just such a reading (*ibid.*, p. 221). But the Mawangdui manuscripts, which were unearthed in 1973 and are the earliest extant texts of *Dao de jing*, make such a reading less plausible. On this issue, see A. C. Graham, *Disputers of the Tao: Philosophical Argument in Ancient China* (La Salle, IL: Open Court, 1989), p. 219. See also the comments of Wing-tsit Chan, *The Way of Lao Tzu* (New York: Macmillan, 1963), p. 100.

32. This problem of the inability to know beginnings is raised in a somewhat different way in an Indian Veda, a text probably not too distant in time from *Dao de jing*:

> Who knows it for certain; who can proclaim it here; namely, out of what it was born and wherefrom this creation issued? The gods appeared only later – after the creation of the world. Who knows, then, out of what it has evolved?
> Wherefrom this creation issued, whether he has made it or whether he has not – he who is the superintendent of this world in the highest heaven – he alone knows, or, perhaps, even he does not know.
> *Sources of Indian Tradition*, vol. 1 (New York: Columbia University Press, 1958), p. 16.

33. Cf. *Zhuangzi*, 2.4.

34. See *In Search of Order*, the fifth (posthumous) volume of *Order and History* (Baton Rouge: Louisiana State University Press, 1956–87). On the similarities between the quests of Laozi and Voegelin, see Seon-Hee Suh Kwon, "Eric Voegelin and Lao Tzu: The Search for Order," Ph.D. dissertation, Texas Tech University, 1991. The terms "intentionality" and "participation" have a long pedigree in Western philosophy. Voegelin takes the term "intentionality" from Husserl. This Husserlian "intentionality of consciousness," as Emmanuel Levinas writes, is in turn "a thesis borrowed by Husserl from Brentano. ... Brentano had obtained the thesis from scholastic philosophy" (*The Theory of Intuition in Husserl's Phenomenology*, second edition, trans. André Orianne [Evanston, IL: Northwestern University Press, 1995], p. 42). For a history of the term "participation" (*methexis* or *metalepsis* in Plato and Aristotle) in Western philosophical and theological thought, see M. Annice, "Historical Sketch of the Theory of Participation," *The New Scholasticism*, 26 (1952): 47–79.

35. "The It referred to [in the phrase "It-reality"] is the mysterious 'it' that also occurs in everyday language in such phrases as 'it rains' " (*In Search of Order*, p. 16).

36. In finding analogous terms in Western philosophy to the language of Laozi, we realize that we run the risk of blurring important differences between the two traditions. In the introduction to their translation of the *Analects* (*The Analects of Confucius: A Philosophical Translation* [New York: Ballantine Books, 1998]), for example, Roger Ames and Henry Rosemont persuasively argue that ancient Chinese must be seen more as an event language than as a "thing" language; hence, a term such as Voegelin's "thing-reality" would not be quite true to the spirit of ancient Chinese thought. Yet the point of Voegelin's analysis, which is admittedly conducted in the language of Western philosophy, is precisely to preempt the customary reifications – such as the existence of objectively present and representable "things" – that are often attributed to Western thought; and such preemptive gestures, in Voegelin's analysis, are made in the interests of more faithfully describing the empirical (in the broad sense) process of how the consciousness actually participates in reality.

37. Alfred North Whitehead, *Process and Reality: An Essay in Cosmology* (New York: Macmillan, 1929), p. 63.

38. For a vivid pictorial representation of the Sirens singing to Odysseus as he is tied to the mast of his ship, see the remarkable red-figure stamnos (wine jar), *c.* 475 BCE, depicting this scene, by the Siren Painter, British Museum E 440. For a discussion of other pictorial images of the Sirens in ancient art and their relation to the text of the *Odyssey*, see Diana Buitron, Beth Cohen, Norman Austin *et al., The Odyssey and Ancient Art* (Annandale-on-Hudson, NY: Edith C. Blum Art Institute, 1992), pp. 108–11. For a more strictly literary approach to the significance of the Sirens in Homer's poem, see Lillian Eileen Doherty, *Siren Songs: Gender, Audiences, and Narrators in the Odyssey* (Ann Arbor: University of Michigan Press, 1995). See also Pietro Pucci, *Odysseus Polytropos: Intertextual Readings in the Odyssey and Iliad* (Ithaca, NY: Cornell University Press, 1987), pp. 209–13.

39. *A Commentary on Homer's Odyssey*, 3 vols (Oxford: Clarendon Press, 1988–92), Vol. 2, p. 119. See also M. P. Nilsson, *Geschichte der griechischen Religion* (Munich, 1967), Vol. 1, pp. 228–9, as cited by Heubeck and Hoekstra. Such hybrids are not unknown in early China and are discussed, most recently, in Michael Loewe, "Man and Beast: The Hybrid in Early Chinese Art and Literature," *Divination, Mythology and Monarchy in Han China*, University of Cambridge Oriental Publications 48 (Cambridge: Cambridge University Press, 1994), pp. 38–54.

40. *The Phenomenology of Mind*, trans. J. B. Baillie (New York: Harper Torchbooks, 1967), p. 170.

PART I

Intimations of intentionality: the *Classic of Poetry* and the *Odyssey*

With Homer and the *Classic of Poetry* (*Shi jing*), the Greek and Chinese literary and poetic traditions begin. These works were composed at roughly the same time, but in regard to structure and style they are very different. The *Odyssey* is a sweeping, unified narrative that presents the adventures of a single hero and his search for wisdom and for home. The Chinese *Classic of Poetry* is a collection of 305, often very diverse, short poems.

Although it is preceded by oracle inscriptions, bronze inscriptions, and perhaps by portions of the *Classic of Historical Documents* (*Shu jing*) and the *Classic of Changes* (*Yi jing*), the *Classic of Poetry* appears upon the stage of Chinese literature with a suddenness and power that is hard to explain. Almost assuredly the poetry of this collection is a written redaction of what had been a long and rich oral tradition of song. A four-syllable line predominates throughout these poems, but while most of the poems share this formal characteristic, the content and purpose of the individual pieces vary widely. Some of the oldest poems, particularly those found in the section called "Hymns" (*song*), are of a religious nature and almost certainly were performed in ceremonies at the ancestral shrines. Other poems, particularly those of the "Greater Odes" (*da ya*) section of the text, are relatively long songs in praise of royal ancestors, such as the founders of the Zhou state, Kings Wen and Wu, and might have been sung as a part of court ritual. Still other poems, especially those of the "Airs" (*feng*) section, are simple songs dealing with a wide variety of topics such as romance, marriage, abandonment, warfare, and agriculture. As noted earlier, the poems span a long period of time; some may come from the early years of the Zhou dynasty (*c.* 1045–221 BCE), and others may be as late as the last years of the sixth century BCE.[1] According to a tradition first attested in the writings of the historian Sima Qian (145–*c.* 86 BCE), Confucius was the editor of the collection, selecting the three hundred or so pieces of the current text from a much larger corpus of poetry. While there is reason to doubt this tradition, Confucius probably knew the collection well and may have used it as a primary text for teaching his disciples.[2]

Several of the poems in the Chinese *Classic of Poetry* are narratives, particularly those in praise of royal ancestors, but the majority are lyrical. The earliest definition of the Chinese word *shi* tips it very much in the direction of lyric: "*Shi,*" in the words of an early Zhou text, "articulates what is on the mind intently."[3] A slightly later definition expands this formula: "The *shi* (i.e. "poem") is that to which the intention of the mind is directed."[4] We should note here that there is no distinction, in ancient Chinese, between "mind" and "heart" – thus, the *shi* is the expression of something that is both, and simultaneously, what we modern Westerners might distinguish as thought and feeling. The artistic power of the *Classic of Poetry* derives, in large measure, from the way in which the poet's inner life finds full and authentic expression in the words of the text. Liu Xie (*c.* 465–522), perhaps the greatest Chinese critic, praises the *Classic of Poetry* because of the emotional authenticity of its *shi* poetry: "On account of an emotion," he says, "[the authors] produced a written text."[5] To be successful, then, this type of literature, *shi*, should always be a tasteful and sincere externalization of what already exists within the heart or mind.

The stirring of powerful emotion is a crucial intention of Homer's *Odyssey* as well. Homer's poetic line, the dactylic hexameter, is a relatively long, dignified, and muscular line that aptly conveys its heroic contents. We would hardly characterize Homeric poetry, however, as a "sincere externalization of what already exists within the heart or mind." The emphasis in Homer is on action or plot and the ways in which character is revealed in action. As Aristotle – whose formulations in the *Poetics* are drawn largely from his experience of the Homeric poems – would have it, poetry is an imitation (*mimesis*) of an action.[6] Poetry (*poiêsis*), derived from the verb *poiein*, meaning "to make," is a fabrication, a made thing. Sincerity is often beside the point, for poetry does not necessarily speak truth in a literal or historically accurate sense. Odysseus has many virtues, but "sincerity" surely is not the first that comes to mind. As Achilles famously said to Odysseus when, in the ninth book of the *Iliad*, the latter came to Achilles' tent to try to persuade the disgruntled warrior to join his fellow Greeks and reenter the fighting, "As hateful to me as are the gates of Hades is that man who hides one thing in his mind and says another" (312–13).[7] It is this very Odysseus, whose sincerity is here severely questioned by the greatest of Homer's heroes in one of the best-known scenes of the *Iliad*, who becomes the poet of a significant amount of the *Odyssey*, as he recounts his travels at the court of the Phaiakians. The slippery and insincere Odysseus, who "feigned many falsehoods, speaking things that were like the truth" (XIX.203), is in many ways the prototype of the Greek poet.[8]

While the differences between the *Odyssey* and the *Classic of Poetry* are obvious, similarities must also be noted. Both works, for instance, are responses to the political turmoil of their respective eras. The *Classic of Poetry* is a collection of verses produced during the first four or five centuries of the Zhou dynasty, which conquered the Shang in 1045 BCE. Like two other classics, the *Classic of Historical Documents* and the *Classic of Changes*, it celebrates the ascendancy of the Zhou and looks back upon the early years of that ascendancy as a period when the Zhou founders possessed the charismatic virtue of those who have freshly acquired "Heaven's Charge" (*tian ming*):

> It is the Charge of Heaven
> So majestic and enduring!
> Alas, how great in glory,
> The purity of King Wen's power![9]
> (Mao 267)

> He seized victory, King Wu,
> None could match his splendor.
> Great in glory, Cheng and Kang,
> God on High raised them up!
> (Mao 274)

The Zhou rulers and those who served them gave shape to a somewhat inchoate past by claiming that their conquest was a repetition of the pattern of the Xia and the Shang dynasties. These previous two dynasties, the Zhou founders maintained, had also come to power with Heaven's Charge but had declined and fallen when their virtue weakened and the Charge passed to another. The creation of this vision of the past is one of the *Classic of Poetry*'s projects:

> King Wen said, "Oh!
> Oh! you Yin and Shang.
> People have a saying,
> 'When a tree is toppled and felled,

> Although the branches and leaves remain unharmed,
> The trunk must first have been uprooted.'
> A mirror for the Yin is not far off,
> It is in the age of the Lords of Xia."
>
> (Mao 250)

If the Yin, an alternative designation for the second half of the Shang dynasty, want to know why they have been supplanted, this poet says, they should simply look at the precedent of the Xia, the dynasty that they themselves overthrew and replaced many centuries before. And elsewhere, we hear:

> The sons and grandsons of Shang
> Were more than could be counted.
> But after God on High commanded,
> To Zhou they did submit.
> To Zhou they did submit –
> But Heaven's Charge is not forever!
>
> (Mao 235)

The implication of this political theory, so vividly expressed in the lines of the *Classic of Poetry*, is that Zhou power will also decline. And, of course, it did. In 771 BCE, a group of Chinese rebels and their non-Chinese allies attacked and overwhelmed the Zhou capital near modern-day Xi'an and drove the ruling household to the east, where they eventually settled near modern-day Luoyang. Thereafter, the Zhou court was only a figurehead government, and the small subordinate states established under the early Zhou leaders became independent and struggled with one another, in the absence of a strong central power, to enhance their own political position and prospects for survival. The *Classic of Poetry* was collected during this period of disunity, and many poems, particularly those from the "Airs" section (Mao 1 to Mao 160), which are organized according to their place of origin, reflect the period when the Charge had slipped away and "ritual" (*li*) was in decline. Confucius, Laozi, and the other great classical Chinese philosophers are a product of this age. Some scholars now look back and call the long period of disunity a "golden age" when a "hundred schools" of philosophy flourished and Chinese literature was born. But to the Chinese of that period, it was an age of danger and despair. Almost all the questions that spurred the rise of Chinese philosophy were troubled ones: "Where has the proper *dao* gone?" "How can society be stabilized again?" "How can one live out one's life in peace and security in an age of constant strife?" "How can the empire become one again?"

The *Classic of Poetry* is our primary textual record of these centuries of transition from the heroics of the early Zhou rulers (Kings Wen, Wu, Cheng, and Kang) to the disarray and troubled voices that were to follow. Our vision of this era, and the political shape of the age that preceded it, particularly the Shang dynasty, results in great measure from reading the *Classic of Poetry*. In this sense, it creates a consciousness of the past shaped around the notion of Heaven's Charge and it expresses a nostalgia for that age when sage-like kings ruled the state with "great glory."

The Homeric poems, too, create a consciousness of a glorious past and, hence, of a discrete cultural identity. The epics were sung for a Hellenic society once firmly based on the Greek mainland, but now dispersed and having its active center on the coast of Asia Minor. The events narrated in the poem refer to this once-great culture with its center of power on the Greek mainland in Mycenae. The *Iliad* and *Odyssey* are attempts by a poet or poets of Hellenic society of the eighth or perhaps early seventh century BCE both to re-create the glorious history of the Mycenean Age (*c.* 1550–1100 BCE) and to try to understand why Mycenean civilization collapsed. Homer attributes the collapse in part to the behavior of its heroes, such as Achilles and Agamemnon, who at crucial moments are guided by their passions rather than by reason. In the *Odyssey*, with emphasis upon the paradigmatic case of Ithaka, Homer describes the disastrous effects of the Trojan War on the cities that the rulers were forced to leave in order to fight for Hellas.

There are remarkable parallels between the genesis of the Homeric poems and the *Classic of Poetry*, on the one hand, and the construction of Chinese and Greek civilization, on the other. The poet of the *Odyssey* has a consciousness of a Hellenic civilization that can perhaps be traced to King Minos in Crete and which was succeeded by a glorious but flawed Mycenean Age. The Greek poet sees himself as both inheritor and critic of the by now distant Mycenean period. The authors of the *Classic of Poetry* 235 and 255, in a similar manner, see themselves as reflecting back on the origins of Chinese civilization in the Xia Dynasty, continuing in the Shang, and then being passed on to the Zhou. The Homeric revival (*c.* 900–700) was preceded by its Minoan (2600–1400)[10] and Mycenean (1400–1120) ancestors. The Zhou was, analogously, preceded by the Xia (*c.* 2000–1500) and the Shang (*c.* 1500–1045).

The rulers of ancient China must, as we have discussed, earn Heaven's Charge. The Xia yielded power to the Shang. But the Shang, according to *Classic of Poetry* 255, came to manifest many of the same sorry traits that Homer finds blameworthy in the suitors, who represent the decay Mycenean civilization experienced in the wake of the Trojan War, as many Greek rulers made their long and arduous journeys back to their homes, which were often in complete disarray. King Wen is in some ways a parallel figure to Odysseus, especially if we understand that the Chinese character *wen*, used as the king's posthumous name, literally means "culture." Odysseus, likewise, is a most cultivated man. King Wen's disdainful description of the people of the Shang sounds remarkably like Odysseus' view of the suitors: the Shang possess "an arrogant spirit" (Mao 255); they "exalt violence"; they do not "hold fast to what is seemly and fitting"; their lack of character is revealed in King Wen's description of the men of Shang as behaving and sounding "like grasshoppers, like cicadas, / Like frizzling water, like boiling soup." The Shang have forfeited Heaven's Charge by failing "to follow the old ways." The Shang, according to King Wen, are repeating history, modeling themselves after the rulers of the Xia, who likewise forfeited Heaven's Charge, a theme we have seen in *Classic of Poetry* 235 above.

The Chinese poets' analyses of the reasons for social disorder in the declining days of the Shang, then, in many ways parallel Homer's critique of Mycenean Greece as embodied in the suitors. The suitors flout the tradition of human decency established by Odysseus, who was a firm though gentle ruler, and in this sense the suitors, in the words of the *Classic of Poetry*, "do not follow the old ways."

1 Poetry and the experience of participation

The Chinese and the Greek literary and cultural traditions begin with poetry. Also common to both traditions is the fact that philosophy follows upon the heels of the poetic tradition and is nurtured by it.[11] What is the significance of the fact that both cultural traditions begin with poetry? Would it make a difference if both, or one, began with discursive prose? It does make a difference, for the earliest poetry tends to articulate a sense of participation in a cosmos that is experienced as full of gods (as in the Greek case, with Homer) or as closely attuned to the world of nature and of a family that extends beyond death through the pervasive institution of ancestor worship (as in the Chinese case, with the *Classic of Poetry*). Out of this primal experience of oneness, articulated in the compact form of poetry, intentionality gradually becomes more clearly differentiated, especially in philosophy.[12]

There are positive and negative aspects to this differentiation. On the positive side, along with a heightened awareness of the individual, intentional consciousness comes a sense of personal ethical responsibility, such as we find expressed in the *Analects* of Confucius. On the negative side, the differentiation of the intentional consciousness, and the exuberance that accompanied its discovery, could create the illusion that such acts of intentionality were not in fact occurring within a comprehensive structure of reality of which the intentional consciousness was and is itself a part. The danger, in other words, was that the libidinous desire for *knowledge* would overcome the patient pursuit of *wisdom*. While the earliest poetry tends to be a more compact and philosophy a more differentiated form of expression, this does not mean that there are not varying degrees of compactness and differentiation articulated in poetry, on the one hand, and in philosophy, on the other. While the differentiations are often registered with more analytic precision in philosophy, they are present in poetry as well. In this chapter, we will be looking at the drama of the articulation of intentionality – of Laozi's *you yu* ("having an intention") in relation to the experience of participation in the early poetry of China and of Greece.

2 Participation in family and in society

China

The earliest Chinese poetry describes an age when Heaven's Charge still rested securely in the ruling household of Zhou and also a later age when central power had declined and feudatories, originally established by the Zhou kings, had become independent states and struggled with one another for economic well-being and political prestige. Sometime in those years of decline and struggle, an anonymous poet from the northern state of Wei, a relatively small and vulnerable state, composed and sang the following lines:

> I climb a grassy hill
> And look back toward my father.
> My father says, "Oh, my son is on service.
> Day and night he does not stop.
> I hope that he takes care,
> Might come back and not stay there!"

> I climb a barren hill
> And look back toward my mother.
> My mother says, "Oh, my youngest is on service.
> Day and night he does not sleep.
> I hope that he takes care,
> Might come back and not forget us."

I climb a ridge,
And look back toward my older brother.
My older brother says, "Oh, my younger brother is on service.
Day and night he labors.
I hope that he takes care,
Might come back and not die."

(Mao 110)

The universal emotion of homesickness, the major theme of this poem, is expressed time after time in early Chinese poetry. In the poem above, a young man is away from home on government service. From the tone of danger that pervades the poem, we might presume that he is part of some military expedition, which would not have been unusual in a state that led a precarious existence and was, in fact, annihilated in 660 BCE. The narrator expresses his homesickness in a curiously indirect fashion. He does not simply say that he misses his father, mother, and older brother and that he hopes one day soon to return from his lonely journey. Instead, he thinks of his family expressing their concern for him. He constructs himself and his emotion through the imagined, imploring words of others. One might argue that a more direct confession of homesickness would be unmanly, that a "real man" in ancient China would hardly admit to such weak sentiments as homesickness. But elsewhere in early Chinese poetry, as we shall see, there is little reluctance to speak quite openly of missing family and home. The narrator sings in this indirect fashion not so much out of an individualistic wish to preserve his own dignity in the face of a very keen loneliness, but because he sees himself, above all, as part of a family and fashions his identity around that unit. He is concerned about the feelings of his father, mother, and brother because their imagined feelings are his own. His very identity is constructed as a reflection of his concern for them and for the continuity of the family which he and his siblings guarantee.[13] Such concern is one aspect of *xiao*, that traditional Chinese virtue that sounds so quaint and foreign in its usual English translation of "filial piety."

We cannot read such poetic sentiments without thinking forward several hundred years to two Confucian sayings that were to shape the way subsequent Asian readers were to understand and interpret expressions of filial piety in early Chinese literature. The first is found in *Analects* and is attributed to Confucius (551–479 BCE) himself: "While parents are alive, one does not travel far from home. And if one does travel, he must have a fixed destination" (4.19). The second appears in a somewhat later text, the *Classic of Filial Piety* (*Xiao jing*): "The trunk, limbs, hair, and skin come from one's parents. So one should not harm these."[14] Thus, staying at home and protecting his body, which is an extension of his parents' bodies, is a primary duty of the filial son. Certainly no journey could be less predictable and more dangerous than a military expedition. Moreover, a journey of this type takes one far away and makes it impossible to fulfill even the minimal duty of nourishing and serving one's parents.

In another poem from the same general time period as the poem above, a narrator on military service complains:

> Minister of War, truly unwise!
> Why roll us into sorrow?
> Our mothers lack food.
>
> (Mao 185)

This theme recurs throughout the *Classic of Poetry*. Public duty can sometimes force the filial son to become "unfilial" as he travels "far from home." On such occasions, he worries that the agricultural labor he carries out is being neglected and that his parents might not have anyone on whom they can rely for support:

> Flap, flap the bustards' wings
> As they settle on the bushy oak.
> The king's affairs are not finished,
> And we cannot plant our millet.
> On what shall our parents rely?
> Oh, distant, blue Heaven,
> When shall we make an end?
>
> (Mao 121)

Consider, also, the three concluding stanzas of another poem from the collection:

> The *zhui* doves(?) flutter about.
> Now they fly up, now they come down
> And gather on the bushy oak.
> The king's work must be done –
> No leisure to nourish father.
>
> The *zhui* doves flutter about.
> Now they fly up, now they perch
> And gather on the bushy willows.
> The king's work must be done –
> No leisure to nourish mother.
>
> I yoke four black and white steeds.
> Now they gallop, now they run,
> How could I not long to go home?
> That is why I make this song,
> To announce my wish to nourish mother.
>
> (Mao 162)

The poem appears to be suggesting that humans, like doves, are part of the natural order, but that martial and civic duty subvert this natural order when it prevents men from attending to their filial obligation to feed their parents. In this last poem, it is of particular interest that the poet expresses concern about his mother twice and his father only once.

Anxiety about providing nourishment for parents, throughout much early Chinese literature, tends to center upon one's mother. Perhaps the most famous example of this theme appears in the most often read story from *Zuo Commentary* (*Zuo zhuan*), a historical text probably written in the last decades of the fourth century BCE that was later enshrined as a Confucian classic. In this story, a filial son, Kaoshu of Ying, inspires the repentance of a less filial son, the Duke of the state of Zheng, by putting food aside for his own mother:

> Kaoshu of Ying gave a present to the Duke. The Duke gave him food. As he was eating, Kaoshu put aside the meat. When the Duke asked him about this, Kaoshu said, "I, the small man, have a mother who always tastes my food. But she has never tasted your gruel. I request to have it sent to her." (Duke Yin, yr. 3)[15]

Later stories of filial piety carried this theme to such an extreme that filial sons and daughters actually cut off pieces of their own flesh to nourish a sick or hungry parent. These extreme expressions of anxiety over mothers who "lack food" are an extension of the notion that the individual body belongs to the body of the family. Just as the mother gives a portion of her body, her milk, to assure the continuation of the family line, so a filial child even gives his own flesh, if necessary, to assure the well-being of a parent.

The filial child in the *Classic of Poetry* is concerned not just about providing nourishment for the immediate family but also about supplying the needs of deceased ancestors. Ancestor worship is the earliest and most enduring of Chinese religious practices. It is attested on the oracle bones, the earliest written texts from ancient China, and fills the pages of the *Classic of Poetry*:

> Oh! Glorious ancestors!
> Great are their blessings.
> Gifts that know no limit
> Reach to your place here.
> We brought them clear wine,
> And they will grant success.
> We also have mixed gruel,
> Full of flavor and fit to soothe.
> (Mao 302)

The practice of ancestor worship is based upon the belief that the family reaches across the barrier of death and that deceased ancestors, at least those of recent generations, are capable of either blessing or cursing living descendants. Moreover, deceased ancestors, it was believed, depended upon their descendants for food, since the dead could not nourish themselves.[16] The particular ancestors one must worship belong to one's own family lineage. Confucius sets these limits quite clearly when he says that "To offer sacrifice to the spirit of an ancestor not one's own is obsequious" (*Analects* 2.24). This institution of ancestor worship has had a profound influence upon Chinese civilization. Benjamin Schwartz, for example, argues that ancestor worship is responsible for "the relative paucity of myth ... in the 'high cultural' religion of China," the highly permeable boundary in Chinese religion between the world of the human and the divine, the dominance of what he calls "the biological metaphor" in Chinese thought, and a number of other critical features of Chinese culture.[17]

A filial son must make sure that a family has sufficient food not just to nourish its living members but also to honor and secure the assistance of the glorious fathers and mothers of the past. The family, as a unit that extends through time as well as space, defines the parameters of both social and religious responsibility. To be estranged from the family is to be lost indeed.

The Chinese state, however, often exists in tension with the family and must develop strategies to tap the prestige of the family in order to enhance state political power. The tension between family and state appears here and there throughout the *Classic of Poetry* and is seen particularly in poems of military service:

> Let us go home, let us go home,
> The year is already late.
> But the king's work expands,
> And we have no time to rest.
> (Mao 167)

In both early and modern China, the state repeatedly attempts to strengthen its own power by appropriating the language of the family and re-creating the state as a super family. Thus, a ruler becomes the "parent of the people"; state ideology promotes political loyalty as a logical extension of filial piety, and the imperial lineage is portrayed as a super-lineage in which all other lineages have some stake. One of the earliest Confucian disciples, Youzi, becomes a spokesman for the connection between piety to one's parents and loyalty to the state when he says, "There has never yet been a case of a filial and brotherly man who was inclined to rebel against superiors" (*Analects* 1.2).

It is tempting to argue that there is no individual in ancient China, that one's total identity is with the family unit and, to the extent that the state's super-family strategy is successful, with the state. This would be much in harmony with the view that the very notion of the individual is a fairly recent one. However, early Chinese poetry not only portrays tension between loyalty to family and loyalty to state but also reflects a tension between loyalty to family and individual desire. This latter type of tension often arises in expressions of romantic feeling. In these cases, the individual in love identifies powerfully with an emotion that can, and often does, tug against the boundaries of the family. The female narrator of the following poem, a poem composed in the state of Zheng in perhaps the seventh century BCE, is in just such an emotional state:

> Oh, Zhongzi!
> Do not cross into our village;
> Do not break the willows we planted.
> How could I care about them?
> But I fear my parents.
> Zhongzi I would embrace,
> But my parents' words
> Also would I fear.
>
> Oh, Zhongzi!
> Do not cross over our wall;
> Do not break the mulberries we planted.
> How could I care about them?
> But I fear my brothers.
> Zhongzi I would embrace,
> But my brothers' words
> Also would I fear.
>
> Oh, Zhongzi!
> Do not cross over our garden;
> Do not break the sandalwood we planted.
> How could I care about them?
> But I fear the people's many words.
> Zhongzi I would embrace,
> But the people's many words
> Also would I fear.
>
> (Mao 76)

A young woman narrator here both invites and rejects her lover. Her desire to embrace Zhongzi is balanced in each stanza by fear of the judgments of her family and the gossip of her fellow villagers. This tension between individual desire and the fear of others' censure unfolds in a highly artistic fashion: as Zhongzi draws closer, penetrating village, then wall, then garden, the circle of the narrator's concern widens from parents, to brothers, to "the people" in general. That is, as Zhongzi moves inward, the narrator's concern spreads ever outward and leads the reader to suspect that her concern, as it broadens, is becoming more diffuse and is about to disappear in the embrace of the man she "would embrace," the final "penetration" accomplished.

It is important to note that the narrator's fear, as she contemplates a tryst with Zhongzi, is based not upon some notion of morality or divine judgment but entirely upon what others in her social circle might think. Ancient China has been described as a "shame culture' – that is, a culture where concern about the opinion of others restrains behavior more than guilt-producing notions such as divine law or abstract principle.[18] Whether or not one can make a firm distinction between guilt and shame cultures, what is quite clear – as suggested by this poem and by many other pieces of early Chinese literature – is that this is a culture that harbors considerable anxiety about reputation. You are what others think you are.

Still, the world of the *Classic of Poetry* is filled with voices tugging against social constraint. Many of those voices of discontent or struggle, as in the example above, are female. In the patriarchal and patrilocal society of Zhou China, women marry out of their natal family, leaving the security of their own parents and brothers for a lifetime of participation in the family of their husbands:

> The cloth-plant spreads
> At the edge of the river.
> Forever far from my brothers,
> I call another "father."
> But he whom I call "father"
> Pays no heed to me.

> The cloth-plant spreads
> On the high bank of the river.
> Forever far from my brothers,
> I call another "mother."
> But she whom I call "mother"
> Cares nothing for me.

> The cloth-plant spreads
> Along the margins of the river.
> Forever far from my brothers,
> I call others "kin."
> But they whom I call "kin"
> Do not hear my words.

> (Mao 71)

Despite the presence of voices in the *Classic of Poetry*, particularly female voices, straining against the boundaries of social convention, the individual's embeddedness in family, tradition, and society remains primary and this experience profoundly shaped expressions of individual desire and individual valor. Odysseus is a hero because of martial prowess, resourceful deeds performed during long years of travel, and the wisdom that he finally brings back to his kingdom. While one can compare Odysseus to much later Chinese heroes, as Lisa Raphals has done, there is nothing in the *Classic of Poetry* that resembles the heroic journey and great individual valor of this Greek hero.[19] There are heroes, to be sure, in the texts of ancient China, but they differ markedly from Odysseus.

One of these heroes of the *Classic of Poetry* is Houji, the founder of the Zhou dynastic line, who is memorialized in a fairly long ode (Mao 245). This particular ode, in contrast to so many others, rises above the mundane world, at least temporarily, and stands somewhere between the worlds of myth and of legend. Houji's mother becomes pregnant when she "treads upon the print of god's big toe." Her child, Houji, is born as easily "as a lamb" "with no tearing nor splitting" and then miraculously overcomes a series of threats against his life. If our model of the hero is derived from our experience of the Homeric poems, we might expect to hear of some martial act or some epic journey in which the hero defies social norms or political constraints.[20] But the life of this Chinese hero takes a quite different turn:

> Truly far, truly grand,
> His voice was full and strong.
> And then he began to crawl,
> Could stride, could stand firm,
> To seek food for his mouth.
> He planted large beans;
> The beans hung down like streamers.
> His rows of grain were thick in sprouts,
> So hemp and wheat covered the ground,
> And gourd stems spread about.
>
> And so Houji's husbandry
> Had a way to aid the growth.
> He cleared the thick grass,
> And planted yellow grain.
> It was even, it was dense,
> It was heavy, it was tall,
> It flowered, it set ears,
> It was firm, it was good,
> It ripened, it hung down.
> Then it was he made his home in Tai.

As C. H. Wang has noticed, "there is no poem in the corpus of the

Classic of Poetry that permits the reader to witness the clash of arms."[21] Houji's heroism exists not in warfare but in his great "husbandry," his contribution as a sort of agricultural scientist to the society in which he lived. And this results not just in food for the living, but for the dead as well:

> Houji began the sacrifices.
> We hope with no flaw nor regret
> They have continued until this day.

However much his conception, birth, and childhood might point toward a transcendentally heroic status, Houji plunges into the mundane world, a world of large beans, paddy lines, hemp, wheat, and young gourds. It is his full participation in this very material world of agriculture that wins him esteem and that makes of him a hero of the *Classic of Poetry*. Odysseus too is eventually reintegrated into family and political life, but the emphasis in the *Odyssey* is equally upon the long years of journey and lonely struggle. In early China, one always remains a part of the larger social fabric, however much the desire for asserting the differentiation of intentionality might tear at that fabric. Participation in this social fabric, in the end, dominates.

Greece

Family and social embeddedness are important in the contemporaneous Hellenic experiences as well, but freedom from societal convention is often seen as exhilarating rather than as dangerously imprudent. The peculiar beauty of *Classic of Poetry* 76 is the result of how delicately the poem is balanced between the desire of the young woman for her lover Zhongzi, on the one hand, and her fears of what people will say, on the other. The imagined tryst is strongly felt, but the gestures toward self-assertion are timid and muted, especially when they are seen in contrast to a roughly contemporary Greek poem, Sappho 16 (the poetess was born *c.* 620 BCE). The poem, like virtually all of Sappho's lyrics, exists in fragments, but enough of it remains to give us a clear idea of the whole:

> There are those who say that a band of cavalry, others that a band of
> infantry,
> still others that a fleet of ships is the most beautiful thing
> on the black earth. But I say
> It is what one loves.
>
> It is perfectly easy to make this truth intelligible
> to everyone. For she who far surpassed

all humankind in beauty – I mean Helen – forsaking
    her most noble husband,

Set sail and came to Troy.
Neither did her child nor her dear parents
Enter her thoughts, but [love?], with her nimble and seductive steps,
gave her her marching orders.

And now she has made Anaktoria, who is not here,
enter my thoughts.
I would rather see her lovely walk
and her brilliantly animated face
than Lydian chariots and foot soldiers
    with their bulky arms.

In the world of Homer, as in the Chinese *Classic of Poetry*, you are largely what others think of you. This is how individual identity is experienced. A contemporary reader who is not aware of this fact would find the quarrel between Achilles and Agamemnon in the *Iliad* merely silly and, therefore, perhaps incomprehensible. We are not dealing there so much with petty egos as we are with two heroes whose worth (*timê*) is determined by the prizes they possess. If those heroes are stripped of their war prizes, their status, and thus their self-worth, is immeasurably lowered. In the *Odyssey*, as we shall argue, we are moving toward the articulation of a more modern sense of individual responsibility, but even that poem lives much of the time within the parameters of a shame culture.

The young woman who is the speaker of *Classic of Poetry* 76 is deeply fearful of what people will say (*ren zhi duo yan*). Sappho, too, considers what people say (*phais'*, 2). Convention would have it, and particularly epic convention, that the fairest things on earth are hosts of cavalry and infantry. But that is not what Sappho thinks. She thinks erotic passion is far more beautiful, despite what people think other people think. Why? Because Sappho herself deeply experiences such passion. This is not, the poet suggests, just a question of subjective preference. You can look at the epics themselves, those supposed vessels of conventional opinion and outlook, and clearly (*pangchy*, 5) see the truth of this claim. For did not Helen begin the Trojan War because she was so smitten by love that she left husband, child, and parents? Passion moves the world, not convention. Because Sappho feels erotic passion for the absent Anaktoria, about whom she muses now, that loved one is far more beautiful to the poet than are images of the kind of conventional military glory with which her poem began. The authority of truth is derived from the power of individually experienced *erôs*.[22]

Intentionality and personal responsibility

In the *Iliad*, Homer tells the story of how Achilles must eventually assume ethical responsibility for causing the death of his greatest friend, Patroclus. It is pointless, Homer suggests, for Achilles to blame forces outside of himself for the destruction that his withdrawal from the fighting has caused his countrymen. The tragic choice Achilles makes, in Book XVIII, is to reenter the fighting and ward off destruction from his fellow Greeks, even if this means that he must meet his own death. The *Odyssey* deepens Homer's articulation of men and women as intentional agents of their own destiny. People are responsible for their own actions. They must choose and act, and not continually blame the gods for their misfortunes. This note is programatically struck by Zeus himself in the theodicy with which the *Odyssey* begins. Why, Zeus asks (I.32ff.), are mortals always blaming us gods for the evils that befall them?[23] The positive side of seeing yourself as an intentional agent is that you will assume responsibility for your actions. Such acts of intentionality are not in conflict with one's participation in the divine cosmos. Indeed, they will bring one closer to the divine, especially since they are powerfully represented by the poet as sanctioned by Zeus, the father of gods and humans.

Problems arise, however, when acts of intentionality shade into self-assertion and the participatory dimension is ruptured. Homer is particularly interested in analyzing this process. Indeed, as we have suggested, the *Odyssey* can be read as Homer's articulation, within a mythic context, of the nature of the intentional consciousness. The poet is concerned to stress both the irreversible advantages of the emergence of intentionality, sometimes referred to as the "metic" intelligence (*mêtis*),[24] as well as some of its less positive consequences. The eclipsing of the participatory consciousness is strikingly, if subtly, portrayed by Homer in one of the strangest scenes of the poem, Odysseus' testing of his father Laertes near the poem's conclusion.

Fathers: Odysseus' testing of Laertes

We have discussed the importance of the individual's participation in family to ancient Chinese culture, an importance that finds its paradigmatic articulation in the Confucian virtue of *xiao* (filial piety). It would be wrong to say that we do not find this trait of *xiao* exhibited in Homer's *Odyssey*. The first four books of the poem – the Telemachy – amply record Telemachus' desire to find and even to emulate his father. That very act of emulation, however, stands in contrast to the Confucian dictum that the child stay close to home. In the Greek case, filial piety means traveling in order to emulate, and show yourself worthy of, the paternal model. As Athena says to Zeus, Telemachus must embark upon his mini-odyssey so that the boy can earn "noble fame" (*kleos esthlon*, I.95) in the eyes of others.

One of the most remarkable expressions of at least one Homeric version of *xiao* appears in the recognition scene between Odysseus and his father, Laertes.[25] Odysseus has not seen his father in twenty years. The suitors have by this time all been killed. There is the possibility of the outbreak of minor insurrections on the island, but victory has largely been secured. Odysseus seeks out his father and finds him busily and desperately working in his orchard, thoroughly dispirited by his conviction that injustice will prevail and that his glorious son will never return to right that injustice. How does Odysseus, the long-lost son, greet his aged and chronically grief-stricken father whom he has not seen in twenty years? Let us look at the text (XXIV.205–348):

> When they [Odysseus, Telemachus, the swineherd Eumaios and the
>   cowherd Philoetius] came down from the city, they swiftly arrived
> at the beautifully cultivated country dwelling of Laertes,
> a place Laertes himself acquired and over which he had toiled mightily.
> His [Laertes'] farmhouse was there, and all around it
> were the huts of the bondservants who worked to please their master –
> in these huts they would eat, sit down, and sleep.
> There was an old Sicilian woman
> who assiduously cared for the old man on his homestead outside the city.
> There Odysseus spoke to his servants and his son:
> "Go inside the well-built house,
> at once sacrifice the best of the pigs for our meal.
> I shall put our father to the test [*peirêsomai*] and see
> if he will know me and recognize me with his eyes,
> or if he will fail to recognize me because I have been gone for so long."

Odysseus is an inveterate tester and experimenter, and it appears that the urge to test and experiment, to objectify his experience, has temporarily eclipsed the filial bond he should naturally share with his father. Why, precisely, does he want to test Laertes?[26] He appears to want to do so, at least in part, out of a sense of emotionally disengaged curiosity: will he recognize me, he wonders, after I have been gone for so many years? Homer contrasts Odysseus' distancing of his own filial emotions with Laertes' assiduous caring for his garden and his country estate. And the poet contrasts it, as well, with the attitude of Odysseus' servants, who despite their subordinate status nonetheless attentively care for the old man's needs: the bondservants accomplish the things that Laertes cares about and holds dear (*phila*, 210); and the old

Sicilian slave woman looks after his every need (*endukeôs komeesken*, 212).

Others will care for Laertes. "I," however, "shall test [*peirêsomai*] our father," Odysseus announces. Homer continues:

> He spoke and gave his arms to his serving men [Eumaios and Philoetius].
> They went quickly into the house, but Odysseus
> approached the fruit-filled orchard searching [*peirêtizôn*] for his father.
> As he walked down to the long rows of trees, he did not find Dolios
> nor any of Dolios' servants or his sons. They
> had gone to gather stones to build a wall around the garden
> and the old man was leading the way.
> He found his father in the well-tended garden
> digging and loosening the soil around a tree. He wore
> a dirty tunic that was patched and unseemly, and around his shins
> he had tied leggings that were sewn together and which protected him
>   from scratches,
> and he wore gloves on his hands because of the thorns. On his head
> he wore a goatskin cap – this attire served only to increase his suffering
>   [*penthos aexôn*].
> When godlike, much-suffering Odysseus saw him
> afflicted with old age, weighed down with such great suffering,
> as he stood there beneath the tall pear tree, he wept.
> Then he pondered in his mind and heart
> whether to kiss and embrace his father
> and to tell him everything – how he had come and returned to his
>   fatherland,
> or if he should first question him about everything and test him.
> Upon consideration, it seemed more advantageous to him
> first to have his father tested with cutting words [*kertomiois epeesin*].
>
> (219–40)

Odysseus' decision to test his father, which he had just announced to Telemachus, Eumaios, and Philoetius, is itself now seriously tested by the sad reality of seeing his father alone in the orchard. The scene is meant to arouse deep pathos both in Odysseus and in the audience. Everything about Laertes announces how grief-stricken he is: the fact that he is alone; that his assiduous gardening appears to serve as a distraction from his cares about his lost son; his filthy and ignoble attire. In the course of the poem, Odysseus – by nature a prudent hero – has had to learn the virtues of even greater prudence and self-control. Here, in the orchard of Laertes, he must draw on what he has learned from all those lessons if he is to resist his strong and natural inclination immediately to embrace his father.

But why must he resist that temptation here? He cannot realistically suspect his father's character, and besides, with the suitors now killed, even in the unlikely event that his father were found to be disloyal, there would be virtually no opposition for the old man to join. There is, perhaps, one understandable reason for his prudence. The last half of the poem is filled with recognition scenes. In the first half of the *Odyssey*, Odysseus is largely tested by others. In this second half, he tests – usually intentionally, sometimes not – those around him. One of the unintentional testing scenes is the famously pathetic passage (XVII.290–327) in which the disguised Odysseus, along with Eumaios, approaches his palace and discovers his aged dog Argos lying, neglected, on a pile of dung. Odysseus may be in disguise, but his faithful dog recognizes him, and the recognition is too powerful and sudden for the poor creature. As soon as the dog recognizes his beloved master after so many years, he dies.[27] There are strong similarities between the two recognition scenes. The decrepit physical appearance of both Argos and Laertes evokes pity in Odysseus and in the audience. Both scenes are introduced with an identical formulaic phrase (*hôs hoi men toiauta pros allêlous agoreuon* ["Thus they were saying this like this to each other"], XVII.290; XXIV.205) that occurs only seven other times in the poem. The situational and linguistic similarities thus suggest that these scenes are linked. Perhaps Homer is juxtaposing these scenes in order to make the point that a sudden recognition of Odysseus by the aged Laertes might prove as fatal to the frail father as it had to the loyal hound. A gradual recognition would be a gentler and therefore perhaps more effective means of achieving his desired end.

Let us return to the central Odyssean theme of testing and being tested. There is another scene to which this one is both thematically and linguistically linked. As mentioned above, in the course of the poem the already prudent Odysseus must learn to be even more self-controlled and hence even more the master of his emotions. In Homer, characters often sow the seeds of their own misfortunes, as Zeus proclaims at the beginning of the *Odyssey*. As the *Odyssey* commences, we learn that the hero is being relentlessly pursued by Poseidon. Why? If Zeus' view that humans often, "through their own acts of folly, have sorrows beyond what is ordained" (I.34) is correct, we should perhaps seek to find a cause for Odysseus' persecution by Poseidon. Odysseus had indeed committed an act of folly that provoked Poseidon's wrath. Poseidon is harassing Odysseus because the hero pridefully revealed his identity to the Cyclops, Polyphemos, after he had blinded him so that he could remove his men and himself from the cave without being noticed. The trick worked. When asked by the Cyclops his name, Odysseus had answered that it was "Nobody" (*Outis*).[28] And so, when Odysseus was in the process of blinding him, Polyphemos shouted to his fellows that

"Nobody is killing me" (IX.408). The other Cyclopes, not by nature particularly intelligent and living long before they could have heard Abbott and Costello's routine about "Who's on first?," believed there was nothing to be concerned about, since "nobody" was harming their companion.

Odysseus escapes with his life, but many of his men, who became meals for Polyphemos, were not so lucky. Angered at the outrageous treatment he and his men received from Polyphemos, Odysseus, from his departing ship, calls out to the Cyclops and taunts him "with jeers" (*kertomioisi*, IX.474). After this first "jeer" (475–9), Polyphemos in response hurls a peak of a mountain at his ship that barely misses its intended target. Odysseus taunts him a second time, and his men try to restrain their leader. But it does not work. Odysseus hurls insults again at Polyphemos, and this third time he less than prudently reveals his true identity: the person who blinded you, the hero shouts, was none other than "Odysseus, destroyer of cities, ... the son of Laertes, and who has his home in Ithaka" (505–6). Polyphemos then proclaims that *his* father is Poseidon. This doesn't impress Odysseus, and he taunts him yet a fourth time. Polyphemos then prays to his powerful father and begs him to pursue Odysseus and inflict troubles on him and on his household. The prayers are granted. If Zeus is correct in programmatically stating that mortals receive the fates that they deserve from the gods, then we can conclude that Odysseus here has demonstrated a pride that he must tame in the course of the poem.

The scenes in the Cyclops' cave, which paint a picture of a small Odysseus dwarfed by the huge and monstrous Polyphemos surrounded by his rams and cheese, create the atmosphere of a fairy tale. If we allow the poem's symbolism to work on us, we might feel that Odysseus is there presented as a little boy. When he returns to Ithaka, he comes in disguise as an old man. He has thus, symbolically, spanned the gamut from youth to old age in the course of the poem, and by the time he returns – if he is to be a true hero – he should have learned to temper his emotions. Since it was his announcing of his identity as Laertes' son that provoked the ire of Poseidon, it is perhaps not surprising that, by the end of the poem, he is being very careful about revealing that identity again. His shouting at Polyphemos "with jeers" (*kertomioisi*, IX.474) has a verbal parallel in the passage we are scrutinizing in Book XXIV, for Odysseus here decides to have his father tested through Odysseus' own "cutting [or 'jeering'] words" (*kertomiois epeesin*, 240).

Let us attend to the "cutting words" that Odysseus addresses to his father.

Having decided to carry out his test, at once divine Odysseus approached
   him.
Head down to the ground, he was digging around a plant.
Standing beside him, his famous son spoke:
"Old sir, you do not lack the skills required for tending to an orchard.
Everything here is well cared for in every way.
Not a plant, fig tree, or grapevine; not an olive tree,
pear tree, or bed of leeks goes uncared for in your garden.
But let me tell you this, and do not be angered by it:
You yourself are not cared for at all, but – on top of grievous old age –
You are badly dried up and are wearing unseemly clothes.
No lord, through sloth, fails to care for you.
There is nothing slavish about you, judging from the appearance
Of your face and stature. You seem kingly.
You look like someone who, after he has bathed and eaten,
would sleep in a soft bed, as is only fitting for elders.
But come now, and tell me this and recount it to me accurately:
Whose slave are you? Whose orchard are you tending?
And truly tell me, so that I can know for sure,
if this country we have come to is really Ithaka,
as that man told me while I was on my way here;
he was not a very sensible man, since he could not bear
to speak or to listen to what I had to say when I asked him
about my friend – whether he is still alive
or has died and is in the house of Hades.
I will tell you this, and take heed and listen to what I say.
I once befriended a man who had come
to my dear native land; and never has any other mortal
coming as a guest from a foreign land been as pleasant.
He claimed to be an Ithakan and he said
that his father was Laertes, son of Arkesios.
I led him to my house and I was a generous host,
attending to his every need, even though my house was already filled with
   guests.
And I gave him gifts of friendship, as one ought:
seven talents of gold that had been fashioned into jewelry,
a mixing bowl made of pure silver and adorned with patterns of flowers,
twelve simple cloaks, as many blankets,
twelve beautiful linen cloaks and as many woolen tunics.
And I gave him, besides, four lovely women of his choice,
flawlessly skilled in handicrafts.

A rhetorician is one who understands and can manipulate the emotions,
and Odysseus is the supreme rhetorician. He has told Telemachus,
Eumaios, and Philoetius that he wished to test Laertes, to determine
whether or not he will recognize his famous son. Perhaps when the three

left, they were persuaded of the sense of this design; or perhaps they left simply scratching their heads. In any event, his rhetoric here seems to be designed to coax Laertes out of his justifiable but nevertheless profound and destructive state of alienation and isolation precipitated by his son's long absence and probable demise. Laertes has taken Voltaire's advice and responded to the vicissitudes of life by tending his own garden, obsessively so. A sudden revelation of identity, as we have suggested on analogy to the recognition scene with Odysseus' dog Argos, might prove fatal; or it might be met with utter disbelief, since Laertes has persuaded himself that Odysseus will never return and has structured his entire psychological existence around that fact. The disguised stranger must therefore attempt to bring up the subject of Odysseus gradually.

First, he tries teasingly to restore Laertes' self-esteem: it is ironic, he suggests, that the person who so assiduously cares for his own garden is himself so unkempt and gives the appearance of being so uncared for. But beneath this appearance, the disguised stranger suggests, is surely a person who is truly kingly. He then mentions a person he had just allegedly met who did not want to hear anything about the stranger's old friend, Odysseus. This person was not very sane (*antiphrôn*, 261) and surely – the implication to Laertes is – you would not be so foolish as not to want to talk and learn about Odysseus. The stranger then goes into details about what a wonderful guest Odysseus was and how well he treated him and the particular gifts he had given him. He has now penetrated Laertes' protective shield:

Then, letting fall a tear, his father answered him:
"Friend, you have indeed come to the land which you asked about,
but arrogant and wicked are the men who rule her now.
Fruitless were those guestgifts you bestowed in such abundance,
for if you had met him, still living, among the people in Ithaka,
he would certainly have reciprocated and, with splendid
    hospitality, sent you away with gifts –
for that is just and proper, once the process of gift exchange has begun.
But come now, tell me this, and answer me with accuracy:
how many years has it been since you hosted
that unhappy stranger, my ill-starred son (if he ever existed)
whom – far from his loved ones and fatherland –
either fish have eaten in the sea or on dry land
has been prey for wild beasts and birds?
For his mother and father – we who nurtured him –
did not have the opportunity to wrap his body up in a shroud
and weep for him. Nor did his richly dowered wife, wise Penelope,
mourn her husband on his funeral bier, as is fitting,
closing his eyes; for the dead are owed this.

In being challenged to respond to the alleged stranger's references to Odysseus, Laertes is given the chance to express, and therefore to vent, some of his grief over the fate of his lost son. He is no longer simply repressing its overwhelming grip over his total being. Laertes is coming out of his closed circle of private suffering and is able to recognize the otherness of the supposed visitor to Ithaka, and he treats him appropriately:

> "Who are you? Where are you from and who are your parents?
> Where, may I ask, is anchored your swift ship that brought you
> and your godlike companions here? Or did you come as a passenger
> on a foreign ship with those who, having brought you to shore, have now
>   departed?"
> In response, quick-witted Odysseus replied:
> "I will tell you everything with the utmost accuracy.
> I come from Alybas [Wanderville?], where I live in a famous house.
> I am the son of Apheidas [Unsparing?], who is the child of Polypemon
>   [Much Suffering?].
> My own name is Eperitos [Struggleman?]. A god
> drove me here, against my will, from Sikania.
> My ship is anchored in the country, away from the city.
> But as for Odysseus, this is now the fifth year
> since he sailed off and left my fatherland.
> Ill-fated, that man was. But the bird-signs were favorable at his going,
> for they passed on the right. Rejoicing in this, I sent him off,
> and he, as he departed, rejoiced. Our hearts were hopeful
> that we would mingle again in friendship and give each other shining
>   gifts."

Odysseus has indeed broken through Laertes' defensive shield. The old man is coming out of his state of self-absorbed alienation and is able to ask suitable questions of the alleged stranger posing as a guest in a foreign land. Odysseus says he will reply truthfully, then immediately launches into a lie. The lie, however, has a level of truth to it. Odysseus, it appears, wants to suggest that he is, in fact, Laertes' returning son, but he wants to do so by subtle and tactful indirection. The names he gives are fabrications, but their etymologies, admittedly difficult to verify with accuracy, appear to hint at the truth: the stranger comes from Wanderville; his father, the son of Lord Suffering, is Unsparing (in his generosity towards others?); and the man from Wanderville is named Struggleman. The hints are there, then, that Odysseus hopes will awaken and alert Laertes to the truth of his son's return.

We now come, however, to a curious detail. The alleged stranger then says that it has been five years since he befriended Odysseus. That is a very long time, and it does not serve to encourage the old man about the chances for Odysseus' safe return.[29] Who knows what terrible things could have befallen Struggleman, the grandson of Much Suffering, in those five years? Why didn't the stranger say it had been only a few weeks since he had seen Odysseus? Perhaps so short a time would have seemed too coincidental and therefore lacked verisimilitude, but surely several months would have sufficed as a credible detail. Could it be that Odysseus' love of fabricating a good story and his indulgence in the explorer's thrill in investigating reality – in this case, the reality of the human emotion of a father's grief over a long-lost son – has gotten the better of his humanity and his filial affection? This is perhaps an example of that same curiosity that initiated Odysseus' persecution by Poseidon. At the beginning of his travels back from Troy, Odysseus had put his men at fatal risk because of his curiosity about Polyphemos. He was lured to the Cyclops' den simply because he ached to "see" the remarkable Polyphemos for himself (*ophr' auton te idiomi*, "so that I could see him"; IX.229).[30]

Struggleman is indeed, as the alleged stranger painfully acknowledges, "ill-fated" (*dysmoros*, 311). Immediately following the appearance of that adjective, Homer, in a phrase introduced by two adversative particles (*ê te*), tries to soften the blow by suggesting that the omens were favorable at Odysseus' departure from Wanderville five years earlier, but it is all too much for the old man:

> Thus he spoke. And a black cloud of grief enveloped Laertes.
> Grasping sooty dust with both his hands,
> he poured it over his gray head, ceaselessly grieving.
>
> (315–17)

If part of Odysseus' strategy in this encounter with Laertes was to spare his father the perhaps fatal shock of a sudden, joyful recognition, at this moment he has failed dismally. For he is now faced with the possibility that his father, as had his mother (as she recounted to her son in Book XI), will perish from sorrow rather than joy. Laertes' reaction is described in words that could not possibly be more powerful indicators of the depth of his grief. For these are the very words that Homer uses in the *Iliad* to describe the reaction of Achilles – the most powerfully emotional of any Greek hero – when he is brought the news of Patroclus' death.

In the recent Oxford commentary (1992) on the *Odyssey*, Alfred Heubeck asserts: "There can be no doubt ... that the use of these lines from the *Iliad* [XVIII.22–4] is intentional" (III.396). But what, precisely, was Homer's intention in recalling those Iliadic lines here? The death of Patroclus is the *peripeteia* (i.e. the turning point) of that poem, for it is Patroclus' death that brings Achilles back into the fighting and that allows the plot of the poem to be brought to its conclusion. At the beginning of *Iliad* XVI, Patroclus had come to Achilles in tears and begged him to reenter the battle. The Trojans are about to burn the entire Greek fleet, but Achilles still will not yield. If you will not enter the battle yourself, Patroclus says to Achilles, at least let me borrow your armor. Achilles will not enter the battle himself, but he allows Patroclus to borrow his armor and to fight in his place.

The plan works. Almost. Patroclus does beat the fire from the Greek ships and repulse the Trojans, but in the process, after killing many of the enemy in battle, Patroclus is in turn killed by Hector. Achilles' withdrawal has now resulted in the death of his greatest friend and it is Achilles' experience of Patroclus' death that brings him back into the fighting. In his obsessive anger, Achilles had become numb to the slaughter of his comrades. Only the death of someone as close to him as Patroclus could allow him to break out of the closed circle of his merely private suffering.

When Achilles gets the news of Patroclus' death, he is distraught. Achilles laments the death of Patroclus to his mother, the sea nymph Thetis, and he realizes now that he must reenter the battle and avenge Patroclus' death by killing Hector, even if this means that, as Thetis reminds him, he himself must die, since it has been decreed that Achilles' death must follow soon after Hector's. Achilles' anger was originally justified, but then turned into a private obsession. He became virtually dazed to the slaughter that was going on around him until Patroclus was killed wearing his (Achilles') armor. By Achilles experiencing the loss of his greatest friend, death now becomes a reality for him – a reality in the sense, first, that he now understands what his fellow Greeks have suffered in his absence; and second, that, just as his troubles deepened when he tried to bend reality to fit his own construction of it, so now he has learned to accept his own limitations, specifically to accept his fate – his *moira* – which is to play the role of the great warrior he is and to assume that public responsibility even if this results in his death.

The great grief experienced by Achilles when he is brought the news of Patroclus' death, then, is all the greater because he himself feels responsible for his beloved friend's tragic death. And hence the words Homer uses to describe Achilles' grief ("Thus he spoke. And a black cloud of grief enveloped him. / Grasping sooty dust in both hands, / he poured it over his head." [*Il.* XVIII.22–4]), and which the poet employs once again (*Od.* XXIV.315–17) in the scene we are scrutinizing in *Odyssey* XXIV, carry with them that same sense of tragedy deepened by the burden of personal responsibility for the catastrophe. Odysseus sees the devastating results – narrated by Homer in those famously tragic,

Iliadic words – which his own fabrications have elicited from his father, and his coolly objective detachment is shattered:

> His heart was stirred, and now there shot
> a stinging force through his nostrils as he looked upon his dear father.
>
> (318–19)

Odysseus had earlier in our passage pondered "in his mind and heart" whether he should at once "kiss and embrace his father" (235–6) or test him. Odysseus' heart is now so suddenly stung by experiencing the grieving that his test has provoked that his mind is bypassed altogether and he pursues the course he had earlier rejected: he "kissed" (320) Laertes and, having rushed towards him, was "embracing" (320) him. He then, at long last, reveals his identity to his father:

> I am the very one, father, about whom you are inquiring.
> I have returned, after twenty years, to my fatherland.
> Cease your mournful lamentations and your tears.
>
> (321–3)

Mothers: Antikleia and Odysseus in the underworld

In the *Odyssey* (XI.84–224) we have a passage that might be seen as a companion-piece to the scene just discussed. Upon his visit to Hades, a journey he must undertake if he is to find his way back home, Odysseus encounters his mother, Antikleia. She is the second shade he meets. Kirkê had warned Odysseus that he must not let any of the shades approach him and talk to him until he had first questioned Teiresias and gotten what information he could from him. Menelaos' battle with Proteus (IV.365–570), in which the Spartan chief must face his own mini-underworld, has prepared us for this perilous quest; that was an instance of a hero's having to overcome multiplicity and the entanglements of the natural world in order to find his way through to intentional action. The prudent Odysseus remembers Kirkê's advice here, although he feels overpowering emotion at seeing his mother for the first time in many years and in discovering that she has died since he left for Troy. He resists yielding to this emotion, painfully turning from his mother in order to consult with Teiresias. From the famous blind seer the prudent Odysseus learns that he has not been prudent enough. He must learn to restrain the desire (*son thymon erukakeein*, 105) that he had not sufficiently restrained in the past. Teiresias here refers to Odysseus' blinding of the Cyclops and the resulting anger of Poseidon, thus strongly suggesting that this episode exemplified Odysseus' lack of perfect restraint.

Odysseus here restrains his natural inclination to speak with his mother by choosing to listen to Teiresias first. Then Odysseus has his mother drink the blood that allows the shades to speak. In a recognition scene that anticipates the many recognition scenes in the second half of the poem, including the recognition scene between Odysseus and Laertes that we have just discussed, Homer says that Antikleia at once "recognized" (*egnô*, 153) her son. She asks how he could possibly have made it alive to these infernal regions and whether he has yet returned to Ithaka. He answers her questions, and then asks a pressing question of his own:

> What manner of remorseless death subdued you?
> Was it a lingering sickness, or did arrow-pouring Artemis,
> coming up to you with her painless shafts, slay you?
>
> (171–3)

He then asks a series of questions about how his father, son, and wife have been faring in his absence. She answers his queries about Penelope, Telemachus, and Laertes first, saving the explanation of her own sorry demise for last. Laertes, she tells Odysseus, anticipating the recognition scene we have just discussed, is miserably attired and during the harvest time spends his nights sleeping on beds of leaves in his orchard, longing for his son's return (*son noston potheôn*, 196), even as he suffers the usual afflictions of old age. "And thus it was that I was destroyed and met my fate." She continues:

> Not in my home did the sharp-shooting arrow-pourer,
> coming up to me with her painless shafts, slay me,
> nor did some lingering sickness fell me, the kind of sickness which,
> after miserably wasting you away, strips the life from your limbs.
> No, shining Odysseus, it was my longing for you, for your wise counsel
>   [*ta te medea*]
> and your gentle ways, that took the sweet life from me.
>
> (198–203)

Is there a gentle hint of irony in the formulaic repetition (*iocheira | hois aganois beleesin epoichomenê katepephnen* ("the arrow-pourer, coming up to me with her painless shafts, slew [me]", 172–3; 198–9), by the still-grieving shade of Antikleia, of her son's ignorant words? As W. B. Stanford remarks in his commentary, "There is much *Pathos* and perhaps a touch of bitterness in Antikleia's repetition of her son's cool words [198–9] in 172–173."[31] No, Odysseus, she tells him, it was not, as you say, Artemis or some lingering disease that killed me: it was my longing for you. This comes as something of a shock to Odysseus. He seems not to have envisioned the possibility that his mother's death might have come about as the result of her sorrow for her son's seemingly endless absence. Unlike the soldier in *Classic of Poetry* 110 ("I climb a grassy hill / And look back toward my father. / My father says ..."), which we discussed earlier, Odysseus has not allowed himself to imagine the depth of the grief experienced by his mother and father in his absence. Homer beautifully portrays Odysseus' strong feeling for his mother, but he also stresses that it is just this kind of strong, instinctual familial feeling the hero must overcome if he is to take responsible, intentional action.[32]

Odysseus certainly is not unfeeling. His own mother remembers him for, along with his cleverness, his great gentleness of spirit (*sê t'agonophrosynê*, 203), a trait shared by that most gentle and Confucian of all Homeric heroes, Hector, whose lamented corpse Helen addresses in the *Iliad* (XXIV.772) with precisely the same phrase (*sê t'agonophrosynê*), occurring at precisely the same initial position of the poetic line. Homer's Odysseus, most assuredly, is not yet the icy and untrustworthy opportunist he was to become in Greek literature, such as we see, for example, in the *Philoctetes* of Sophocles in the fifth century BCE.

Nor is he yet the Ulysses that would come to represent, for the Virgil of the *Aeneid*, the unscrupulous metic intelligence of the Greeks. Virgil grants the metic brilliance of the Greeks, but his analysis suggests that such a notion of intelligence was, from an ethical perspective, deeply flawed. Homer implicitly criticized the Trojans for their sentimentality, such as in the scene on the ramparts in *Iliad* III (161–5) in which he portrays Priam as fatally and uncritically captivated by Helen's beauty. In his depiction of the fall of Troy in the deeply moving second book of the *Aeneid*, Virgil shows that he fundamentally agrees with Homer's analysis of Troy's soft-heartedness and its fatal consequences. What was a fault to Homer, however, becomes, in Virgil's conception of the Trojans (the Romans-to-be), that indispensable trait of *pietas* that would profoundly distinguish the compassionate Romans from their wily Greek predecessors. Indeed, as Virgil sees it, it was precisely compassion that undid the Trojans, from whom the Romans – in the Virgilian construction – descended. Homer's two central heroes are Achilles, the greatest of Greek warriors, in the *Iliad*; and Odysseus, the embodiment of metic intelligence *par excellence*, in the *Odyssey*. The Roman Virgil, in Confucian fashion, would champion the hero who was a family man, taking the figure of the Trojan Hector – who is not a Greek – as his paradigm.

The Homeric tension between familial obligation, on the one hand, and responsible intentional action, on the other, is hardly what we find in the *Classic of Poetry*. The problem in the latter, as we have seen, exists in two tensions, the first between the conflicting obligations to the

47

family and to the state, and the second a tension between individual desire and duty to the family. At the center of both of these tensions is the family, the unit of primary and fundamental identity in China. Participation in the family in China is so complete, as we have seen, that the individual's body is regarded, in a very real sense, as a part or a member of the body of the family. But such participation in the corporate body of the family is not always easy. Individual desire can pull one away from that center, though always with the fear of exposure and shame, as can obligation to the state, though always in this case with regret and concern for the well-being of the family left behind. Little room is left in this Chinese model for the heroism and adventure of an Odysseus. And certainly reintegration into the family, from which one is hardly ever emotionally detached in the first place, does not come through the intentionalist testing and the cool withdrawal of natural sympathy shown by our Greek hero. But the latter has been on a journey of trial and discovery and can now return to assume his place in society with a wisdom that he has won through hardship and adventure. In China, by way of contrast, wisdom is gained close to home and not on the frontier's lonely hills.

3 Participation in the natural world

At times in Homer, then, it appears that the assertion of intentionality demands an eclipsing of one's experience of participation in a greater whole, as we argued in our analysis of the recognition scene between Odysseus and Laertes – the greater whole, in that case, consisting of the family. This very scene in the *Odyssey* suggests the existence of another pattern which we would now like to explore. Homer paints a decidedly unheroic portrait of Laertes in this passage. He is an old man dressed in dirty rags, and when Odysseus first sees him he is digging around a tree (*listreuonta phuton*, 227). It is, in part, Laertes' association with his own garden – with agriculture and the earth – that suggests his profound alienation from his former, and proper, status as king and warrior. Laertes' horticultural skills hardly make him, for Homer, the hero that Houji so clearly is in the *Classic of Poetry*.

The geographer Yi-Fu Tuan has described "topophilia" as "the affective bond between people and place or setting."[33] This sense of topophilia, we shall be suggesting, is more pronounced in the *Classic of Poetry* than in the *Odyssey,* where, as Jeffrey M. Hurwit has argued, "that nature is best that mortals exploit."[34] Hurwit mentions Odysseus' admiring a deserted island (*Odyssey* IX.116–41) from a purely utilitarian perspective: its beauty in the eyes of Odysseus, Hurwit remarks, "lies in its untapped potential for exploitation."[35] The

Odyssey, we have been arguing, articulates those moments when the intentionalist consciousness emerges out of the experience of participation in the cosmic whole. We have discussed this experience of participation in relation to the family. We wish now to focus on the experience of participation in the natural world.

Nature and nature imagery in the *Classic of Poetry*

Every reader of the *Classic of Poetry* notices immediately the strong presence of the natural world in almost every poem, particularly those poems of the "Airs" and "Lesser Odes" (*xiao ya*), which constitute the first two-thirds of the book (Mao 1–234). It is not always transparently clear, however, why a particular nature image has been juxtaposed with a particular human emotion or action. Nor is it easy to discern what kind of philosophy of nature underlies this ancient Chinese text. Here we must consider briefly several of the most subtle and controversial problems in the study of early Chinese culture.

Twenty-five years ago, Frederick Mote wrote a small book, *Intellectual Foundations of China*, that has remained the strongest and most succinct summary of an array of issues pertinent to the study of early China. One of his most important and controversial claims is the following:

> The basic point which outsiders have found so hard to detect is that the Chinese, among all peoples ancient and recent, primitive and modern, are apparently unique in having no creation myth; that is, they have regarded the world and man as uncreated, as constituting the central features of a spontaneously self-generating cosmos having no creator, god, ultimate cause or will external to itself.[36]

Subsequent research has challenged Mote's claim that the ancient Chinese had no creation myth. Although texts with such accounts are relatively late, the persistence of certain motifs and patterns in early Chinese thought and literature may point toward the existence of myths that were not transmitted to later generations. Still, the second half of Mote's assertion, that the Chinese believe in a "spontaneously self-generating cosmos" with "no ultimate cause or will external to itself," can, as yet, hardly be challenged. In discussing Mote's insight, Tu Wei-ming has recently emphasized that "[t]he real issue is not the presence or absence of creation myths, but the underlying assumption of the cosmos: whether it is continuous or discontinuous with its creator."[37]

In discontinuous creation, which finds a classic expression in the Hebrew Bible, God stands outside his creation and shapes it very much as a sculptor molds clay or a carpenter frames a house. One may argue that there is some aesthetic continuity between such creators and their creation, but they remain distinct from the world they fashion. In contrast, continuous creation unfolds from within. The powers that move and transform the cosmos, in this conception, are implicit within it from the beginning. One recent study argues that the recurrence of certain images and symbols in early Chinese philosophy, particularly Daoism, points toward a notion of a primal chaos (Chinese *hundun*), represented as an egg or as a gourd, from which the world of "the ten thousand things" (*wan wu*) came forth.[38] But in such a cosmogony, creation is a transformation of preexisting stuff rather than a birth of something entirely new. One late, rather abstract, but fairly typical Chinese account of beginnings describes a "shapeless, dark expanse ... a vacant space" that spontaneously produces "the Dao," then "Breath," then *yin* and *yang*; and then, from the interplay of these latter essences, all other creation comes forth.[39]

The important point is that in discontinuous creation it becomes quite normal to regard the elements of creation not only as discontinuous with God but as discontinuous with one another. That is, creation is not the result of some natural evolution or unfolding but results from a conscious act of objectification. It is the result, to return to terms we have introduced earlier, of actions that are fully intentional. In the Hebrew tradition, God creates the world very much as an object quite apart from himself, and the man he creates "in the image of God" is in turn instructed to "have dominion over the fish of the sea, and over the fowl of the air, and over every living thing that moveth upon the earth" (Genesis 1:28). Man proceeds to name the animals in a highly intentional fashion and then presides over them. In the case of continuous creation all things are typically seen as interrelated, as full participants in a cosmic whole which they share with one another. In Chinese cosmology "the world of man and the world of nature constitute one great indivisible unity. Man is not the supremely important creature he seems to be in the western world; he is but a part, though a vital part, of the universe as a whole."[40]

Early Chinese Daoism expresses this essential unity of all creation through the notion of the *dao*, and Mencius and other Chinese thinkers speak of a "psychophysical stuff" or a "breath," *qi*, that suffuses all things. Later historians of philosophy have spoken of a Chinese worldview in which "the ten thousand things" are seen as a part of a pattern. Joseph Needham describes this as a "philosophy of organism" and says that all things, in this manner of thinking, "were thus parts in existential dependence upon the whole world-organism."[41]

It is possible to argue that all of these notions of the *dao*, *qi*, organism, and even the creation mythology we have alluded to above are only attested in Chinese texts very much *after* the time of the *Classic of Poetry* and are thus hardly relevant to the pre-Confucian and pre-Daoist period under discussion here. Certainly the *Classic of Poetry*, it is true, contains no story of creation. Like the first comprehensive Chinese history, *The Records of the Historian (Shi ji)*, the poems describe a world that begins with legendary cultural heroes and not with cosmogony. And no lyric in the *Classic of Poetry* presents, in any overt fashion, a philosophy of man and nature as "one great indivisible unity."[42] Still, we believe it is possible to discern in the *Classic of Poetry* a world not at all far removed from what we have described above, a world where there is no sharp break between the realm of humans and that of nature. Indeed, the peculiar power of much of this poetry derives, in large measure, from the intimate way humanity is represented as participating in, and responding to, the natural world.

The selections in the *Classic of Poetry* are set, for the most part, in the countryside, where the majority of Chinese lived then and still live now. Survival depended upon a keen awareness of every aspect of both the seasons and the physical environment. As Fei Xiaotong, the eminent Chinese sociologist of the countryside, has argued, this is not a world of "abstract general principles" but is a place where "knowledge" is "acquired from familiarity."[43] Such knowledge tends to be specific and relevant to immediate human needs. Indeed, the heroes of the *Classic of Poetry*, as we have noted in our discussion of Houji, provide very concrete social and mundanely material benefits to the people. Houji "planted large beans" (Mao 245); Liu the Duke "tied up dried meat and grain / In knapsacks, in bags" (Mao 250); Danfu the Duke "drew the boundaries of big plots and little" (Mao 257); and King Wen "felled the trees" and "cleared the bush" (Mao 270).

Nature imagery abounds in the *Classic of Poetry*, and these images are usually highly specific. Confucius advocated study of the *Classic of Poetry* because, among other reasons, "one would become a great deal more familiar with the names of birds, beasts, plants, and trees" (*Analects* 17.8). Certainly to a modern reader one of the biggest difficulties in reading the poems in this collection is in gaining the necessary familiarity with the huge array of flora and fauna referred to in the anthology. The feeling for nature most often expressed in the *Classic of Poetry* is experienced as intimately related to human concerns rather than as sublime and distantly "other." Nature is depicted as highly particular and intimate. There are many more references to a specific grass, plant, or bird, for example, than to a lofty peak or a mighty river. Indeed, "high hills" and "desert wilds" often connote the frontier, a place where nature becomes unfamiliar and hence threatening.

The presence of such intimate details in so many of the lyrics from the *Classic of Poetry* might make the work appear, from a classically Western perspective, as lacking in the kind of elevation that is traditionally associated with the highest style. In Greek philosophical thought, it is often observed that that which can be known or rendered with exactitude and experienced by the senses will inspire less wonder than that which is more difficult to know or render with exactitude. This principle becomes the epistemological basis of the ancient characters or levels of style and their corresponding literary genres. As in Plato's and Aristotle's formulations about the objects of knowledge and their representation, so with regard to the classical levels of style there is an inverse relation between the degree of verisimilar accuracy or of intimacy that should be expected in any representation, on the one hand, and the achievement of stylistic elevation, on the other. The high style is appropriate to the genres of tragedy and epic.[44] It is elevated above the concerns of the everyday and it is meant to evoke, through the grandeur of its language and of its subject matter, the emotion of wonder. The low style – the style appropriate to comedy, the epigram, the epistle, and satire – depicts everyday, "realistic" details.

Indeed, there is an antagonistic relation in ancient Western literature between elevation and the kind of mundane realism that we find in the *Classic of Poetry*, and this antagonism is discussed again and again by ancient critics such as Aristotle, Longinus, and Quintilian. In his famous comparison between the *Iliad* and the *Odyssey* in the *Peri hypsous* ("On Elevation," *c.* first century BCE), the great literary critic Longinus praises the consistent sublimity of the *Iliad* but says that "in the *Odyssey* one likens Homer to the setting sun; the grandeur remains without the intensity" (IX.10).[45] Why is the *Odyssey* less sublime than the *Iliad*? Because, in part, it depicts intimate, everyday details; it is more "realistic" and hence more like comedy. As Longinus concludes his comparison between the Greek epics, he says that great authors, with the decline of their emotional power (*pathos*), give way to realistic character-study (*êthos*). And he then says that "the realistic description of Odysseus' household forms a kind of comedy of manners" (IX.15).[46] Aristotle anticipates these remarks when he says, in the *Poetics* (1459b14), that the *Iliad* may be characterized as "pathetic" (*pathetikē*) and the *Odyssey* as "ethical" (*êthikē*). Aristotle's and Longinus' association of the *Iliad* with *pathos* and of the *Odyssey* with *êthos* is, as D. A. Russell has suggested, fundamentally a distinction between the kind of work which is intensely elevated and the kind of work which is "more realistic, nearer to everyday life" and "milder in emotional tone."[47]

The antagonism between the appropriateness of representing that which is elevated and that which is more intimate and particularized is present in all classicizing periods in the West. In the Western Middle Ages, however, when the classical levels of style are not so rigorously separated, the sublime and the everyday may be found in the same literary work, as they are in Dante's *Divine Comedy* and in the plays of Shakespeare, whose methods of literary representation owe much to the later Middle Ages. This is the profound insight of Erich Auerbach and is the central theme of *Mimesis*.[48] The tragedies of Racine and Shakespeare both inhabit what Sir Joshua Reynolds refers to as "the higher provinces of art."[49] But Shakespeare, unlike the neoclassical Racine but like the medieval Dante, can in his tragedies deal as well with "whatever is familiar, or in any way reminds us of what we see and hear every day."[50] In the course of the Renaissance, when what Auerbach refers to as "the Christian-figural scheme" began to lose its hold, "antique models ... and antique theory reappeared, unclouded."[51]

If even the heroic *Odyssey*, from the perspective of classical Western theories of how best to elevate style, is perceived as lacking in the requisite elevation when compared with the *Iliad*, then many of the poems of the ancient Chinese *Classic of Poetry* would no doubt appear to such eyes as even further removed from Iliadic heights. There is indeed a relationship between the stylistic elevation of the Western epic tradition and its attendant heroic vision. Perhaps there is a relationship, as well, between the nobility of the elevated style, which necessitates bold departures from idiomatic usage, and the emergence of an intentional consciousness which experiences itself as individuated from the primary experience of participation in a cosmic whole. Chinese literature does not begin with a long, unified, and glorious epic and a corresponding heroic vision. Nor are the most moving poems in the *Classic of Poetry* particularly elevated. On the contrary, the poems often lament the consequences of the epic struggles of those in power, as we have discussed, for the families and loved ones that the soldiers have left behind. And they do so in brief lyrics, consisting of basically four-syllable lines of rhymed verse that would have struck an ancient Greek audience, accustomed to the unrhymed and comparatively very long dactylic hexameter line, as decidedly unelevated and unheroic. Yet what these ancient Chinese poems preserve, particularly in regard to their representation of the natural world, is a profound sense of the individual's necessary participation in the cosmic whole. It is precisely this experience of participation in the natural world that a hero like Odysseus must overcome, as we have been arguing, if he is to achieve heroic status in the *Odyssey*.

Despite the abundance of nature imagery, the *Classic of Poetry* does not contain "nature poetry," if we mean by this poetry that describes nature for its own sake. The main focus of the poets' attention is the human world, and "the key challenge for commentators," as Pauline Yu has said, is "one of relating the natural image to the human situation."[52] Traditional Chinese commentators usually spoke of the relationship between nature image and human situation in the *Classic of Poetry* in terms of three rhetorical devices: *fu*, *bi*, and *xing*, which Stephen Owen translates, respectively, as "exposition," "comparison," and "affective image."[53]

Perhaps the clearest and most influential explanation of these three terms is provided by the Song Dynasty philosopher and classical commentator Zhu Xi (1130–1200): "*Fu* is to expound some affair by speaking directly of it. *Bi* is to take that thing and compare it to this thing. *Xing* is to first speak of another thing in order to evoke the words one would sing."[54] *Fu*, then, is direct exposition. When the poet says, "I climb a grassy hill / And look back toward my father," he is "expounding" an action by "speaking directly of it." *Bi*, like *fu*, presents no great interpretive problem and may be equated with English "simile" or "metaphor." To refer back to Zhu Xi's explanation, one simply likens "this" to "that." In Mao 181, for example, the poet says,

> Minister of War,
> We are the king's claws and teeth,
> Why do you roll us into misery?

The speaker in this poem, presumably a soldier, likens himself and his fellows to "claws and teeth." This is a metaphor and might be labeled, in Chinese poetics, as an example of *bi*.

The most elusive (and allusive) of the three devices is *xing*, and since many of the most vivid nature images in the *Classic of Poetry* are identified by classical commentators as *xing*, it is important to consider this term at somewhat greater length. As we have seen, Zhu Xi notes that the *xing* is not a simple comparison but "evokes" or "gives rise to" (*yin qi*) the poem. Unlike the case of *bi*, the relationship between the image and what follows may not, in a poem that employs the device of *xing*, be transparent at all. Indeed, some Chinese scholars have gone so far as to say that in many such cases "there is no relationship at all."[55] To interpret several lines in a very short lyric as having "no relationship at all" to the remainder of the poem is questionable. Most scholars who take this position regard the *xing* as a vestige of some musical or performative element of the poem that is no longer fully understood. That is, the *xing* may simply set the tune, or establish a rhyme pattern, or, as Ch'en Shih-hsiang argues, engage a work unit in some collective musical performance – that is, "an ejaculation uttered when a group of people were lifting up a thing together."[56]

The earliest Chinese dictionary defines *xing* as "to begin" or "to give rise to." As a poetic device it always occurs at the beginning of a stanza, and it is invariably drawn from nature. The term *xing* first appears as the name of a poetic device in the Han dynasty, but Confucius twice uses the word in reference to the *Classic of Poetry*. In *Analects* 8.8 we find the following short injunction: "*Xing* by *Poetry* [*shi*], take your stand in the rites and be perfected by music." Here poetry seems to initiate the first of three essential stages in self-cultivation. One could translate *xing* simply as "begin" ("Begin with *Poetry*"), thus making the *Classic of Poetry* the first text recommended for study in the Confucian curriculum, a position it did indeed seem to occupy. But the term probably implies more than just "to begin." *Xing* also carries the implication of "stimulate, arouse, incite," which may derive from a causative use reflected by the Manchu translators' *yabubumbi*, "to make begin, to put into effect, to initiate."[57] Thus, we would translate the first clause of 8.8 much as did D. C. Lau: "Be stimulated by the *Poetry*."[58] Elsewhere, in *Analects* 17.8, Confucius appears to be distressed that his students are not more diligent in studying the *Classic of Poetry* and he says that the first benefit one can derive from such study is that "*Poetry* can stimulate (*xing*)." To be stimulated or stirred up is good, this passage makes clear, if one then shapes subsequent action in accord with ritual. Confucius is probably alluding here to a balance between literary culture and ritual that he articulates elsewhere: "Broaden me with literary culture, but restrain me with ritual" (*Analects* 9.11; cf. 6.27). The *Classic of Poetry*, as the great work of Chinese literary culture, broadens and stimulates, but this effect, at least in Confucianism, must always be curtailed and shaped by appropriate social forms, a topic we shall return to in Part III.

The Han commentators on the *Classic of Poetry* who identified and discussed so many of the nature images in the text assuredly had Confucius's statement firmly in mind. These images "stimulate" the poet's imagination. Indeed, it might be more proper to say that they "stimulate" the poem – that is, the poem somehow grows out of the image in an *organic* way. Part of the Chinese notion of the world as organism, mentioned above, is that correlations and connections link the cosmos in unexpected patterns of resonance, much as veins and nerves link and join together quite disparate portions of the human body. The later correspondences and categories established for the sixty-four hexagrams of the *Classic of Changes* or "the five phases" (*wu xing*) are examples of this manner of thought.[59]

As Pauline Yu has pointed out, the predominant method used by commentators to interpret the *Classic of Poetry* has been to search for some relationship of similarity between the *xing* and the main topic of the poem.[60] The suggestions of these commentators often seem far-fetched, and indeed they, like us, are often far removed from the precise correlations suggested by the details of the natural world depicted in this ancient anthology. Furthermore, the very attempt to specify categories of correlative association for the *Classic of Poetry* is an example of the intentional consciousness being applied to a world of participation. John Henderson notes that "in the historical development of cosmology in China, it seems that general ideas of 'resonances' or 'participation' preceded attempts to explain resonant effects."[61] This consciousness of participation in the physical cosmos, an experience which shapes the earliest Chinese poetry, does not rely upon rigidly systematic associations of natural scene and human sentiment. Instead, a sentiment or a situation appears to flow quite organically and spontaneously from a nature image. The *xing* effect creates the poem not as a logical, intentionalist argument that properly belongs to a different and historically later form of consciousness, but through a sense of unity that is evoked, to anticipate Daoist terminology, in the image of "the uncarved block."

We now turn to several examples of *xing* nature imagery and the interpretive problem they present, humbly cognizant of the fact that in our own analyses, no less than in those of the commentators of the past, it may well be our own intentional consciousness that is, to a large extent, determining what we find.

In the following poem, the initial *xing* image, which we have identified with italics, is repeated at the head of the subsequent two stanzas with minor, but significant, variation:

> *The wild geese go into flight;*
> *Flap, flap their wings.*
> These men go out to march,
> To toil and labor in the wilds.
> Alas for the pitiable men;
> Sad that men and women are both alone.
>
> *The wild geese go into flight,*
> *And roost in the middle of the marsh.*
> These men go out to build walls,
> And a hundred cubits all are raised.
> Although they toil and labor,
> At last they have a safe house.

The wild geese go into flight;
Sadly their calls resound.
It was these wise men
Who called us to toil and labor.
It was those foolish men
Who called us to brag and boast.

(Mao 181)

Traditional Chinese exegesis of the *Classic of Poetry*, attested from the first century of the Han dynasty (*c.* 200–100 BCE), tended to link the anonymous poems of this collection to specific historical events described in other classical texts such as the *Historical Documents of Antiquity* (*Shang shu*) and, especially, the *Zuo Commentary*. These poems were then read as a highly moralistic political commentary on those events. Whether such readings are imaginative nonsense, as some scholars have claimed, and bury the simple beauty of the poems beneath a heavy crust of ponderous exegesis, or whether they have some basis in historical fact is a topic we will leave to others.[62] No serious examination of these poems can, however, fail at least to make note of these traditional readings.

The earliest commentators connect the poem quoted above to the rebellion against the Zhou ruler King Li that occurred in 842 BCE and the succession and restoration of "the kingly way" that took place under King Xuan in 828. The great scholar Zheng Xuan (127–200), very much captivated by the traditional reading, then provides the link between the *xing* image and the description of soldiers on the march in the first stanza: "Wild geese understand *yin* and *yang* and cold and heat. The *xing* draws a comparison [between the geese and] people who know how to depart from rulers without the Proper Way and go to those who have the Proper Way."[63] In discussing the subsequent two stanzas, Zheng then traces his comparison between what "wild geese know" and what "the people know."

Zheng Xuan has provided an explicitly discursive link between the nature image and what follows, but one wonders if such a reading is necessary in order to make sense of the poem. The images of geese flying restlessly, then alighting in a marsh, and then calling out in discontent resonates quite organically with the human narrative that follows each of these images. Indeed, the peculiar beauty of this poem – as of many of the lyrics from the *Classic of Poetry* – derives from the suggestive correlations created by the poet between the nature imagery and the analogous human situation. There is no discontinuity here that requires elaborate explanation.

Elsewhere the situation is not so simple:

>*Broken fish-trap at the weir,*
>*Its fish are bream and roach.*
>As a child of Qi goes to wed,
>Her suite is like the clouds.

>*Broken fish-trap at the weir,*
>*Its fish are bream and tench.*
>As a child of Qi goes to wed,
>Her suite is like the rain.

>*Broken fish-trap at the weir,*
>*Its fish swim freely about.*
>As a child of Qi goes to wed,
>Her suite is like the stream.
>   (Mao 104)

Commentators link this poem to the marriage of the incestuous Lady Wenjiang of the state of Qi to Duke Huan of Lu (*rd.* 711–694 BCE), an event that led to the murder of the Duke.[64] This particular link is no doubt facilitated by the mysterious reference in each stanza to the marriage of "a lady of Qi." But what do fish in a broken fish-trap have to do with this event? The intrepid Zheng Xuan gives it a try: "The bream and the roach are easy to control. But the fish-trap is broken and cannot control them. The *xing* image is comparing this [the broken fish-trap] to the weakness of Duke Huan of Lu, who will not be able to withstand Wenjiang."[65]

Zheng's explanation seems forced, and later commentators have struggled to work out the various possible correspondences between the *xing* and what we know of the particular historical event. However, for those who are not persuaded that the poem is a comment on a critical moment in the history of Qi, no easy linkage can be established between the first two lines of each stanza and the second two. Perhaps connections existed in ancient China between the image of the fish finally freed from a broken trap and a woman going to be married. Bernhard Karlgren, following several earlier studies, has argued that fish in ancient China are a symbol of fertility.[66] If so, then this is a connection that is hardly transparent and requires that we possess some culture-specific information, which Karlgren has provided. But even beyond this possible connection between fish and fecundity, there does seem to be some resonance between the image and what follows: a life of containment is now at an end, and the bride and her entourage can swim like a freed swarm of fish toward a new home. Not only this, but the containment of sexuality, expected of all unwed women in early China, is about to end.

A modern Western reader, to be sure very far removed in time and

place from the *Classic of Poetry*, is repeatedly struck by the abundance
of nature imagery in these poems and the profound resonance between
human emotion and the natural scene. In the example below, even a
modern reader can feel the frustration of the female speaker left at
home, who picks cocklebur, perhaps somewhat listlessly, and then, as
the scene shifts to her absent man, such a reader can vividly experience
how the "craggy hill" of the second stanza, the "high ridge" of the third,
and the sick horses of the fourth all reflect the soldier's emotional state
of distant and mournful separation from home:

> I pick and pick the cocklebur,
> But do not fill the slanting basket.
> With a sigh for the man I love,
> I place it on the road to Zhou.
>
> "I climb that rocky hill,
> My horses are spent and stagger.
> I pour a drink from my ewer
> So as not to yearn forever.
>
> I climb that high ridge,
> My horses turn black and yellow.
> I pour a drink from my horn vase
> So as not to yearn forever.
>
> I climb that muddy slope,
> My horses founder,
> My driver sinks,
> How miserable this is!"

(Mao 3)

What is particularly remarkable about such descriptions of nature in
the poems of the Chinese *Classic of Poetry* as we have just examined is
that, on the one hand, they stand on their own as accurate accounts of
the natural world; and yet, on the other, they mirror human emotions as
well. The accuracy of the physical descriptions suggests an abiding
knowledge and respect, on the part of men and women, for the natural
world; and the ways in which such descriptions represent human
emotions create a strong sensation, even in a modern reader, of how the
poets, and the characters they are portraying, must have experienced
themselves as participants in that natural world. If they could speak to
us today, the anonymous poets of this anthology might say that the
patterns of interrelatedness and of participation in nature that we find in
their poems, and our ability to respond to those patterns, derive "not
from the orders of a superior authority external to themselves, but from
the fact that they were all parts in a hierarchy of wholes forming a
cosmic pattern."[67]

A simile from the *Odyssey* and *Classic of Poetry* 23: views of nature

There is comparatively little description of the natural world in Homer. If we are looking for such descriptions, we will most often find them in the similes.[68] It might be useful to compare the first simile in the *Odyssey* with a poem from the *Classic of Poetry*. In Book IV, Telemachus is in Sparta trying to discover, from Menelaos, anything he can about the whereabouts of his father Odysseus. He tells Menelaos how the suitors are taking advantage of Odysseus' absence, and Menelaos predicts a favorable outcome as soon as Odysseus returns. In making his prediction, he uses a simile, the first in the poem:

> Just as when a doe, having put to sleep
> her newly born and still suckling fawns in the lair of a mighty lion,
> wanders through the valleys and grassy gorges
> looking for food, and then the lion, returning to his bed,
> deals an unseemly doom [*aeikea potmon*] to both these fawns;
> so shall Odysseus deal an unseemly doom to those men.
>
> (IV.335–9)

The analogy of Odysseus to the lion is beautifully conceived, but the comparison of the suitors to the fawns seems strangely inappropriate. The suitors are vulnerable, as are the fawns, it is true, but we are certainly not pleased to see the innocent deer killed by the lion upon his return to his lair, as we might be so gratified to see the haughty suitors receive their just deserts upon the return of Odysseus. As does the poet of *Classic of Poetry* 23, Homer elsewhere in the *Odyssey* associates deer with maidenhood and female chastity.[69] Homer's example from the natural world in Book IV, however, does not quite match the human situation it is supposed to illuminate, for his audience might well feel that fawns are delicate and sympathetic creatures, quite unlike the suitors.

In this respect, the poet of *Classic of Poetry* 23 shows a greater sensitivity toward the natural world. The Chinese poet gives us a deer that more aptly corresponds to the human situation:

> Fields show dead deer.
> White reeds wrap her.
> Spring draws girl near.
> White knight clasps her.
>
> In the thick brush
> A dead deer – hush! –
> Bound in white rush.
> Jade girl was such.

"Slowly, gently, Oh!
Touch my sash not, No!
Should the dog bark, Oh!"[70]

Here there is a greater reciprocity between the human and natural worlds. The young woman is far more deerlike than the suitors. Like the suitors, she is vulnerable; but unlike the suitors, she is a delicate and sympathetic creature who – the name implies – will meet a truly unseemly fate.

We have been discussing this critical topic of the portrayal of nature in the *Classic of Poetry*. Before we leave this subject, it is worth remarking upon one crucial difference between the similes in Homer and the comparisons between the worlds of men and nature in the *Classic of Poetry*. In Homer's similes, the natural world is evoked as a way of commenting upon the human situation. In the *Classic of Poetry*, we begin with the natural world and then move to the human context. In the Homeric case, the human situation is the focus; in the Chinese, the human situation is placed in the context of the natural world.

It is now time to turn our attention to Homer and to Odysseus, who is just now becoming disenchanted with Kalypso and her alluring meadows.

Nature and nature imagery in the *Odyssey*: between meadows

As the action of the *Odyssey* begins, Odysseus is being detained by the beautiful nymph Kalypso (I.14,52ff.). He has been there, we later learn, for seven years, but now "the nymph was no longer pleasing" (*ouketi hêndene nymphê*, V.153) to him. Following Zeus' programmatic speech in Book I in which the authoritative god declares that mortals, through their own acts of folly, increase their misfortunes, we can perhaps infer, despite Athena's special pleading in the speech that follows (45–62), that Odysseus is to some degree responsible for having succumbed to Kalypso's charms. Odysseus may be longing for home now but, as that phrase in V.153 suggests ("the nymph was no longer pleasing"), clearly Odysseus had found considerable pleasure in Kalypso's company before this point.[71]

Homer mentions that Kalypso is the daughter of *oloophronos* ("death- [or destruction-] minded") Atlas (I.52), a curious epithet for the figure whose great physical strength is responsible, as Homer will go on to say, for sustaining and balancing the weight of the world. Atlas is a Titan, a member of the order of gods that preceded the Olympians. Plato, in the *Sophist*, refers to this order of pre-Olympian gods as the

61

materialist giants (246c). Homer says (I.53–4) that Atlas "knows the depths of every sea, and himself buttresses the huge columns that hold earth [*gaian*, 54] and heaven [*ouranon*, 54] together." These details are hardly as gratuitous as the Oxford commentators suggest (I.81). Atlas, with his legs grounded in the depths of the seas, holds together both the immaterial "sky" or "heaven" (*ouranon*) and the material earth in the compact experience of a single cosmic whole.[72] In order to journey home, Odysseus must leave this daughter of Atlas. He must, in other words, differentiate his own intentional consciousness from the cosmic whole of which it is a part. Were he not to do so, were he to continue to succumb to the nymph who "charms" (*thelgei*, 57) him to forget that he must journey home, then he would indeed give credence to the power of the epithet "death/destruction-minded" (52) that describes Kalypso's father and that has been working through the charms of this daughter of the Titan Atlas. Odysseus must leave the meadows that are associated with such stagnation.

Meadows, in the *Odyssey*, often threaten to lure the hero back into the cosmic whole from which his intentional consciousness wishes to differentiate itself. Odysseus must leave Kalypso. As we shall discuss in Part III, Plato and Aristotle describe the philosophical life as one of unrest and tension. The philosopher is in search of the ground of his or her existence. He must be going somewhere. Homer's symbol of the voyage, while certainly literally a voyage, deeply influenced both Plato and Aristotle. The greatest heroes, in the *Odyssey*, must be going somewhere. At the beginning of the poem, Odysseus is going nowhere. But Telemachus, in order to prove himself worthy of being Odysseus' son, goes on a dangerous odyssey of his own in search of news of his father. One of his destinations is Sparta, which Telemachus visits in order to see what he can learn from Menelaos and Helen. Sparta is lush and beautiful. Telemachus tells Menelaos that he feels tempted to stay in this paradisal setting much longer, but action calls; he must continue his voyage. Homer gives a rich description of the lush agricultural landscape of Sparta and contrasts it to rocky Ithaka, where there is no meadow (*oute ti leimôn*, 605).

Motif and variation are the narrative equivalents of the repeated words and variations that characterize the oral-formulaic style.[73] Telemachus' voyage, as we have mentioned, is the miniature *Odyssey* that begins the *Odyssey* proper, and it is perhaps therefore no coincidence that Telemachus' resistance to tarrying any longer in Sparta foreshadows Odysseus' soon-to-be-made-evident resistance to remaining any longer with the lovely nymph Kalypso. Only a couple of hundred lines later, Odysseus announces to Kalypso that he will leave. This is preceded by a passage (V.63–84) in which Homer describes, in particularly evocative language, the lush beauty of the landscape surrounding Kalypso's cave, which includes soft meadows (*leimônes*, V.72). It is from the seductive beauty of this landscape that Odysseus must separate himself if he is to return to rocky Ithaka, where there are no beautiful meadows (*oud' euleimôn*, IV.607), as Telemachus had just recently observed.

Here, then, are two meadows – one in Sparta, the other on Kalypso's island – from whose charms these two heroes, son and father, must escape if they are to continue their respective journeys. Such meadows threaten to draw the intentional consciousness back into a predifferentiated cosmic whole. But then there is the other side of the coin. In Book XII, Odysseus must resist the Siren song, which promises not a total immersion in materiality but rather complete knowledge, another end to the journeying that Homer appears to see, almost in anticipation of Plato and Aristotle, as the nature of human beings. The Sirens sing as they are seated in a meadow (*en leimôni*, XII.45) in front of the heaps of bones and shriveled skins of those who have been lured to their meadow. In the first two instances (the meadows in Sparta and on Kalypso's island), the temptation is toward stagnation, a rejection of the tension of existence through a passive return to the meadow of predifferentiated participation in the material reality of the cosmos. In the third (the Sirens' meadow), the temptation is to close off the tension by entering the meadow of immersion in the illusion of *gnôsis* – that is, the possession of absolute knowledge that will obviate the need to continue seeking wisdom. Intentionality should assume that the experience of seeking after the permanence of knowledge and wisdom, regardless of how passionate the desire to achieve such permanence, always has its locus in the concrete, physical body of the seeker. Hence, Homer depicts the dream of absolute knowledge as a willful forgetting of the bodily located consciousness that intends objects. This willful forgetting will turn the dream of absolute knowledge into a nightmare of disembodiment. Those who succumb become part of the large heap (*polus this*, XI.45) of human bones covered with shriveled skin that lies at the Sirens' feet. Even this antimaterialist extreme, however, is couched in language drawn from the natural world, as if to recall the earlier temptation of returning to the predifferentiated cosmic whole, for Homer depicts the Sirens as sitting "in a meadow" (*en leimôni*, 45). Human beings, Homer suggests, must learn to exist between these meadows representing the extremes of unconsciousness immersion in the material world, on the one hand, and of disembodied abstraction, on the other.

In Book IV of the *Odyssey*, Menelaos' description of his struggles with Proteus, the old man of the sea, has parallels with Odysseus' and

Telemachus' necessary rejection of the natural world. The threateningly beautiful trees described in the garden of Kalypso at the beginning of Book V become, by the middle of the book, the raw materials Odysseus uses to build the ship in which he tries to sail home. Nature has been tamed and controlled. Before Menelaos can return home, he is told by Proteus' daughter that he must trap her father and then get what information he can out of him. But truth will not stand still. Menelaos must be devious in order to force Proteus to reveal his secrets. Hence the trick of the sealskins, under which Menelaos hides himself in order to surprise the old man at high noon. Proteus changes shapes in order to elude Menelaos' grasp, and these shapes all mimic the natural world: a lion, serpent, leopard, great boar, fluid water, a tree with huge branches (IV.456–8). In order for Menelaos to return home, nature must be subdued.[74]

The Garden of Alkinöos (*Odyssey*, VII.112–32) is quite a contrast to the Ithaka that Odysseus describes to the Phaiakians as "rugged" (*trêcheia*, IX.27). This passage clearly recalls the grove of Kalypso (V.63–74). Hermes "marveled at" (*thêeito*, V.75) the first, Odysseus "marveled at" (*thêeito*, VII.133) the second. Once again, the natural world is associated with the temptation of stagnation, of the hero's being definitively and fatally derailed on his journey. The tone here has changed, however. This garden is less threatening than Kalypso's grove, just as Nausikäa is less threatening than Kalypso. But Nausikäa, nevertheless, represents something of a threat to Odysseus. She is a brave, beautiful, young, marriageable princess, and her father King Alkinöos even offers his daughter's hand in marriage to Odysseus (VII.313ff.). We are introduced to Nausikäa via a simile that compares her, "an unwedded virgin" (*parthenos admês*, VI.109), to the chaste Artemis, who delights in the hunt by running with boars and deer (*elaphoisi*, 104). Had Odysseus yielded to the temptation of staying in Phaiakia with Nausikäa, the result might have been as tragic for her as it was for the maiden – also compared to a deer – seduced by the knight in Mao 23 of the *Classic of Poetry*, which we discussed earlier in this chapter.

Nature and the feminine: the *Odyssey*

The *Odyssey*, we have been arguing, explores that historical moment when the intentionalist consciousness definitively and self-consciously emerges out of the experience of participation in the cosmic whole. Women are often associated with matter – that is, with this experience of participation in a cosmic whole – and in this sense the achievement of intentionality is often represented as necessitating a separation from the feminine. At the very beginning of the *Odyssey*, for example, we learn from Athena that Odysseus is being detained from his responsibility to return to Ithaka by the seductive Kalypso ("she who hides").[75]

This necessary separation has its parallel in the Telemachy. Telemachus must take charge in Ithaka by separating himself from his powerful mother Penelope and by voyaging on his own odyssey in the first four books. He begins to assert himself toward the end of Book I when he rebukes his mother for silencing the singer Phemios. Penelope says she would rather not hear his songs about the homecoming of the men from Troy because she has suffered so much through Odysseus' absence. "Your heart and spirit must be emboldened to listen.... Odysseus is not the only one who has lost the day of his homecoming in Troy," Telemachus tells his mother; "many others were also destroyed" (I.353–5). She then goes back inside the house "in amazement" (360) at her son's bold words. The action of the *Odyssey*, as we have mentioned, is structured around constantly repeating motifs that are constantly varied in a way that is analogous to how the oral style itself is so structured through pattern and variation. The paradigm in the *Odyssey* for effective and responsible action, announced by Zeus at the beginning of the poem (I.32–43), is Orestes' revenge upon Aegisthos and Klytaimnestra for murdering Agamemnon upon his return from Troy. In such post-Homeric literature as Aeschylus' *Oresteia*, and arguably in Homer as well, Orestes murders his mother in order to avenge his father – a rather emphatic act of separation from the originary female![76]

While the assertion of the intentional consciousness might be associated with separation from the female, it would certainly be wrong to infer from this that the *Odyssey* is a misogynistic work. Quite the contrary is the case, as is suggested by the fact that it has even been argued that the author of the poem was a woman.[77] Indeed, the poem seems to have been composed, in large part, to rectify the bad reputation associated with women in the aftermath of that most traumatic of *nostoi* (return voyages), the return of Agamemnon to Argos. Klytaimnestra's murder of Agamemnon haunts the *Odyssey*. In his trip to the underworld, for example, Odysseus speaks with the ghost of Agamemnon, who recounts the horrible story of his return and who concludes that "women can no longer be trusted" (*ouketi pista gynaixin*, XI.456). With his representation of the faithful Penelope as the wife who awaits her husband's return from Troy, Homer is quite consciously attempting to reverse the misogynistic consequences, for Hellenic culture, of the view toward women that Agamemnon expresses here. Nor does Homer wish to associate the feminine only, or even primarily, with nature, the earth, and domesticity. He presents his audience with a number of female characters who are models of intelligence and prudence such as Penelope, Nausikäa, and Aretê (the queen of the Phaiakians).

Nature and the feminine: the *Classic of Poetry*

We have been discussing how nature and the female are often threatening to the Homeric hero. One might compare, here, the relatively unthreatening – and, to Western eyes, perhaps for that very reason rather strange – description of a bride in the *Classic of Poetry:*

> Hands like soft sprouts,
> Skin like frozen lard,
> Neck like the tree-grub,
> Teeth like melon seeds,
> Cicada head and moth eyebrows.
>   (Mao 57)

According to the traditional commentators, who, as we have noted, try to link almost every poem to some important historical moment described in other classical texts, this piece describes the wedding of Zhuang Jiang to the Lord of Wei in 757 BCE, at approximately the very time that Homer was composing his epics. In this particular case, there is good reason to accept the traditional ascription, for the stanza just before the one quoted above provides an unusually specific identification. The series of similes, all drawn from the natural world, are surely meant to describe an enticing and much-admired woman (as well as highlighting for the Western reader how culture-bound descriptions of beauty can be!). This imagery, had we found it in the *Odyssey*, would almost certainly be taken for a danger sign. One can imagine that such imagery might be associated with Kalypso or Kirkê, but hardly with Penelope, who is the Homeric figure corresponding most closely in rank and importance to Zhuang Jiang.

In a later Chinese text, such as the *Zuo Commentary*, written in the fourth century BCE and very much influenced by the teachings of Confucius, a description of a woman's physical beauty is almost always a prelude to disaster. In fact, beautiful women, throughout much of Chinese literary history, are portrayed as seductresses who would, Kalypso-like, derail men from attending to their more important public and familial duties. Such an attitude arises, at least in part, from a later Confucian emphasis upon female subservience to male ambition and achievement. But the *Classic of Poetry* perhaps "reflects an age when relations between the sexes were somewhat healthier, with a more natural air."[78] This is not to say that the *Classic of Poetry* presents a world where men and women are equal. If China ever was a matriarchal society, as has been repeatedly argued but never conclusively proven, by the early Zhou it had become predominantly male-centered and patriarchal. The different status of a male child and a female child is clearly demonstrated in these famous lines from Mao 189:

> And so, he bears a son.
> Then he lays him on a bed,
> Then clothes him in robes,
> Then gives him jade tablets as toys.
> The child cries out loudly.
> In red apron so splendid,
> A kingly lord of house and clan.
>
> And so, he bears a daughter.
> Then he lays her on the ground,
> Then clothes her in wrappers,
> Then gives her loom-whorls as toys.
> Nothing wrong but nothing dignified.
> Her only duty wine and food,
> And giving no worry to parents.

For the male child, then, there is a hope for status and leadership; for the female child, the highest imaginable hope is that she might "give no worry to parents." Despite occupying a subordinate status in early Zhou society, however, women play a major role in a vast number of poems in the *Classic of Poetry*.[79] And what is particularly noteworthy, they are given a voice. There is no way to prove, conclusively, that the female voice that speaks so frequently in these poems is a genuine one. Later Chinese male poets often spoke *vocibus feminarum*, and this may be the case in the *Classic of Poetry* as well.[80] But the female voice here in the *Classic of Poetry* does indeed seem sufficiently authentic that even male-centered critics, such as those in the Mao commentarial tradition, have ascribed many of these poems to women.

Let us now look at two poems which most commentators believe to be spoken by a female voice. These poems clearly suggest that the *Classic of Poetry* is an extremely rich, and as yet a largely unexplored, trove of material for the study of women in ancient Chinese society:

> Adrift, that cypress boat
> In the middle of that river.
> With two tufts dangling down over his brow,
> Truly he would be my spouse.
> "Till death," he swore, "no other."
> Oh, mother! Oh, Heaven!
> What an untrue man!

Adrift, that cypress boat
By the side of that river.
With two tufts dangling down over his brow.
Truly he would be my mate.
"Till death," he swore, "no wrong."
Oh, mother! Oh, Heaven!
What an untrue man!

(Mao 45)

The kudzu grows and covers the thorns,
The creepers spread out to the wilds.
My handsome one has left this place.
With whom would I be? Alone I dwell.

The kudzu grows and covers the brambles;
The creepers spread out to the borders.
My handsome one has left this place.
With whom would I be? Alone I rest.

The horn pillow so fine!
The brocade cover so bright!
My handsome one has left this place.
With whom would I be? Alone I greet the dawn.

The days of summer –
The nights of winter –
One hundred years will pass,
And I will go to his dwelling.

The nights of winter –
The days of summer –
One hundred years will pass,
And I will go to his home.

(Mao 124)

Although the early commentators, as we have noted, acknowledge the existence of the female voice in each of these poems, they sometimes seem willfully desirous of muting, or of transmuting, the presence of this voice. It is of interest, for example, that in discussing the first of these poems, the earliest Mao commentary says that "Heaven" here "means father," an interpretation that has been surprisingly persistent in later readings and translations. In other words, what appears to be a cry to Heaven and an appeal to maternal sympathy, with no mention of father at all, is turned by the commentators in the direction of patriarchy. What is clear is that the poem concerns the unfaithfulness of a male, who is likened to an unsteady "cypress boat" in the middle of a river.

The second poem seems almost as if it is being spoken by a Chinese

Penelope. The speaker apparently is a lonely woman whose companion is far away. The earliest commentators assure us that "the husband is on military service" and claim that the poem is criticizing Duke Xian of the state of Jin, who was "fond of war" and sent many young men on prolonged military expeditions. Whatever the case, the woman in this poem, like Penelope, preserves her solitude and is willing to do so, as the last stanza indicates, until she comes "to his home," which, after one hundred years, could only be their mutual grave. This second poem returns us to our consideration of nature and the way in which nature resonates so evocatively in the *Classic of Poetry* in response to human emotion. The spreading of cloth-plant across the thorns and of bindweed across the wilds concisely and powerfully conveys the passing of time, the forlornness of the woman, the barren environment in which her husband now finds himself, and the way in which time slowly covers – but cannot erase – the experiences of pain and loneliness. The *xing* image in this poem, as in so many others in the collection, is both appropriate and delicately suggestive.

Summary and conclusion

The presence of the feminine, then, looms large in the *Classic of Poetry*, as it will in the *Dao de jing*, which we shall discuss at greater length in Part III. Laozi, who associates the feminine and nature with the experience of participation in the *dao*, was no doubt drawing upon a rich tradition of such associations, including perhaps the *Classic of Poetry* itself.

In our exegesis of the first chapter of the *Dao de jing*, we discussed Laozi's analysis of the relation of language to the structure of the human consciousness. The sage, for Laozi, must live in the tension between the nameless and the named. Naming is necessary if we are to differentiate one thing from another, if we are to manage and manipulate reality – as Odysseus so brilliantly does – as we must if we are to survive. But naming, while necessary, can also separate us from the very experiences that the naming, such as the naming of the experience of oneness with the *dao*, is attempting to describe and thus name. The experience of participation will thus be eclipsed when we forget that acts of intentionality (*you yu*) in fact occur within a larger whole.

We noted a similar figuration to Laozi's in Homer's description of the Siren song, which lures Odysseus with the deceptive promise of an experience of total participation in being that, if accepted, would in fact abolish the individual, bodily-located consciousness. While the figurations are similar, the emphases are different. In the Chinese case, Laozi seems more concerned with reminding his listeners of the experience of participation in the *dao* that will be overshadowed when they focus too exclusively on "having an intention" (*you yu*). In the Greek case, Homer seems more concerned about the threat of the obliteration of the intentional consciousness if we seek an experience of total participation that promises to remove the need for further seeking. In the third chapter we will discuss how Plato, in a philosophical context analogous to Laozi's, will reformulate the issue by means of a figurative language whose emphases are much closer to Laozi's.

Both the *Classic of Poetry* and the *Odyssey*, we have been arguing, enact the drama of the differentiation of "having an intention" (*you yu*) from the primal experience of oneness or participation to which Laozi will attempt to recall his listeners by suggesting that they "have no intention" (*wu yu*). The sense of participation, in the *Classic of Poetry* and the *Odyssey*, takes several forms: participation in the physical cosmos, in family, and in society. While Homer and the authors of the *Classic of Poetry* both describe the emergence of intentionality, the Chinese poets worry more than does Homer about the dangers involved in eclipsing the experience of participation.

In Part II we shall explore the tension between participation and intentionality in two great historians, Sima Qian and Thucydides. Sima Qian, we shall argue, wishes above all to present himself as someone who fully participates in the grand design of the dynastic history of China. His presentation is often undone, however, by the persistent recurrence of the very intentionality that he consistently attempts to repress. Thucydides wishes, in the most objective manner reminiscent of Odysseus' testing of Laertes, to analyze the disorder of his age of warring Greek city-states of the fifth century BCE. The Greek historian's analysis, we shall suggest, is often skewed by his forgetting of the way in which he himself is in fact complicitous in the very intentionalism that he sees as the cause of the catastrophe he is analyzing. Let us now turn to Thucydides and Sima Qian.

Notes

1. That some poems may have been reworked well after this date is indicated by the phonological studies of William H. Baxter III, "Zhou and Han Phonology in the *Shijing*," in William G. Boltz and Michael Shapiro (eds), *Studies in the Historical Phonology of Asian Languages* (Amsterdam: John Benjamin, 1991), pp. 1–34.

2. Even this claim, so frequently voiced in the secondary scholarship about China, must now be qualified. See E. Bruce Brooks and A. Taeko Brooks, *The Original Analects: Sayings of Confucius and His Successors* (New York: Columbia University Press, 1998), p. 255.

3. From the "Canon of Shu" section of the *Classic of Historical Documents*. The translation is that of Stephen Owen, *Readings in Chinese Literary Thought* (Cambridge, MA: Harvard University Press, 1992), p. 26.

4. This comes from the "Great Preface" to the *Classic of Poetry*, which almost certainly reached its present form in the second or first century BCE. See the text and a somewhat different translation in Owen's *Readings in Chinese Literary Thought*, p. 40. For a further excellent study of this early definition of *shi* and its implications for Chinese poetics, see Steven Van Zoeren's *Poetry and Personality: Reading, Exegesis, and Hermeneutics in Traditional China* (Stanford, CA: Stanford University Press, 1991), pp. 52–79.

5. For a somewhat different translation, with full context, see Owen, *Readings in Chinese Literary Thought*, p. 243.

6. On the relation of Aristotle to Homer, see Steven Shankman, *In Search of the Classic: The Greco-Roman Tradition, Homer to Valéry and Beyond* (University Park: Pennsylvania State University Press, 1994), pp. 63–76.

7. Odysseus himself, just as he is about to launch into a falsehood, repeats the first of these Iliadic lines in *Odyssey* XIV.156.

8. Homer's wording (*iske pseudea polla legôn etumoisin homoia*) is close to Hesiod (*Theogony*, l.27), to whom the Muses reveal that "we know how to speak falsehoods that are like the truth" (*idmen pseudea polla legein etumoisin homoia*). Haun Saussy, in "Writing in the *Odyssey*: Eurykleia, Parry, Jousse, and the Opening of a Letter from Homer," *Arethusa*, 29 (1996): 299–338, notes that "Odysseus in beggar's guise has been recognized as a type of the oral poet" (p. 331). See also, as cited by Saussy, Bernard Fenik, *Studies in the Odyssey,* Hermes Einzelschriften 30 (Wiesbaden: F. Steiner, 1974), pp. 167–71; Mina Skafte Jensen, *The Homeric Question and the Oral-Formulaic Theory,* Opuscula Gracolatina 20 (Copenhagen: Museum Tusculanum Press, 1980), pp. 51–3; Sheila Murnaghan, *Disguise and Recognition in the Odyssey* (Princeton, NJ: Princeton University Press, 1987), pp. 148–75; Gregory Nagy, *Pindar's Homer: The Lyric Possession of an Epic Poet* (Baltimore: Johns Hopkins University Press, 1990); and Pietro Pucci, *Odysseus Polytropos: Intertextual Readings in the Odyssey and the Iliad* (Ithaca, NY: Cornell University Press, 1987), pp. 157–95, 228–35.

9. For the *Classic of Poetry*, we provide all poems with the number of the poem as found in *Mao shi yinde*, Harvard–Yenching Sinological Index Series, Supplement no. 9 (Beijing: Harvard–Yenching Institute, 1934). All translations are our own unless otherwise noted. To compare the popular Waley versions, see the correspondence chart in *The Book of Songs: The Ancient Chinese Classic of Poetry*, trans. Arthur Waley (New York: Grove Press, 1960), pp. 350–5, or the new edition of this text, edited by Joseph Allen, who has restored the original Mao order (New York: Grove Press, 1996).

10. Through Odysseus' many false tales in which the hero presents himself as a Cretan (e.g. XVII.523; XIII.256ff.; XIV.192–359; XVII.415–44; XIX.172ff.), Homer is perhaps establishing Odysseus as the heir to Minoan civilization, the model for the now ailing Mycenean civilization. As Odysseus fibs to Penelope, he (disguised as a beggar) comes from Crete, where you can find the city Knossos, "the great city where Minos, / a close friend of great Zeus, ruled for periods of nine years. / He was the father of my father" (XIX.178–80). "Odysseus" – who "knew how to say many false things as if they were true sayings" (XIX.203) – here clearly represents himself as the grandson of the founding father of Hellas, King Minos. Plato, who likewise looked to Minoan Crete as the divine source of Hellenic culture, alludes to this Odyssean passage in his late work, *The Laws* (624).

11. The term "philosophy," we realize, is a Greek coinage. Since "philosophy" means "the love of wisdom," however, it is as applicable to the writings of the Chinese sages as it is to the Greek philosophers. We will discuss this terminological issue at greater length in Part III.

12. The terms "compact" and "differentiated" are drawn from Eric Voegelin, who uses them throughout his work. History, for Voegelin, is constituted precisely by our human awareness of a transition from compact to more differentiated experiences of reality. See *Order and History*, 5 vols (Baton Rouge: Louisiana State University Press, 1956–87). Such transitions, however, are never final. Our experiences of reality, for Voegelin, are simultaneously compact and differentiated. In his useful glossary of terms from Voegelin's thought, Eugene Webb defines "differentiated" as "Voegelin's term for consciousness in which the distinguishable features of a previously 'compact' field of experience are noticed as distinct" (*Eric Voegelin: Philosopher of History* [Seattle: University of Washington Press, 1981], p. 279). "Compact" is glossed by Webb as "Voegelin's term for experience having distinguishable features yet to be noticed as distinct" (*ibid.*).

13. Hall and Ames, in a discussion much more general than our own but relevant to the topic here, note that in early China one is "self-conscious, not in the sense of being able to isolate and objectify one's essential self, but in the sense of being aware of oneself as a locus of observation by others" (*Thinking from the Han*, p. 26).

14. *Xiao jing*, *Shisan jing zhushu* edition, 8: 1.3a.

15. *Chunqiu Zuo zhuan zhu*, ed. Yang Bojun, 4 vols (revised edition, Beijing: Zhonghua shuju, 1990), pp. 14–15.

16. David Keightley notes that this differentiates the Chinese dead and the dead of Greece. See "Death and the Birth of Civilizations: Ancestors, Arts, and Culture in Early China and Early Greece," unpublished paper, p. 11. (Available from David Keightley, Department of History, University of California, Berkeley.)

17. See Benjamin Schwartz, *The World of Thought in Ancient China*, pp. 20–8.

18. Wolfram Eberhard, while acknowledging the importance of shame, particularly among the elite, finds plenty of room in traditional China for guilt. See his *Guilt and Sin in Traditional China* (Berkeley: University of California Press, 1967).

19. In *Knowing Words*, she compares the *Odyssey* to the sixteenth-century Chinese novel *Journey to the West*, and she also finds a parallel to Odysseus' "metic" intelligence in Zhu Geliang, the "kingmaker" of the fifteenth-century Chinese novel *Romance of the Three Kingdoms*.

20. We have in mind here Lord Raglan's still useful summary of the life of the hero. See *The Hero* (1936; rpt., New York: New American Library, 1979), pp. 173–85.

21. *From Ritual to Allegory: Seven Essays on Early Chinese Poetry* (Hong Kong: Chinese University Press, 1988), p. 62.

22. See Eric Voegelin, *Order and History*, vol. 2: *The World of the Polis* (Baton Rouge: Louisiana State University Press, 1957), pp. 201–2. Our translation is based on the text printed in the first volume of *Greek Lyric*, ed. David A. Campbell (Cambridge, MA: Harvard University Press, 1982), pp. 66–7.

23. For a classic study of the development of the concept of moral responsibility in early Greek thought, see Arthur W. H. Adkins, *Merit and Responsibility: A Study in Greek Values* (Oxford: Clarendon Press, 1960). Chapters 2 and 3 concern Homer.

24. On the importance of the "metic intelligence" (i.e. *métis*) in Greek thought, see particularly Marcel Detienne and Jean-Pierre Vernant, *Cunning and Intelligence in Greek Culture and Society*, trans. Janet Lloyd (Chicago: University of Chicago Press, 1991). On the ambivalent nature of Odysseus' intelligence and its relevance to the definition of modernity, see Max Horkheimer and Theodor W. Adorno, *Dialectic of Enlightenment*, trans. John Cumming (New York: Continuum Books, 1996). See also Peter Rose, *Sons of the Gods, Children of the Earth: Ideology and Literary Form in Ancient Greece* (Ithaca, NY: Cornell University Press, 1992).

25. On the importance of recognition scenes in Greek epic, see Gregory Nagy, *Greek Mythology and Poetics* (Ithaca, NY: Cornell University Press, 1989), pp. 202–22.

26. In his commentary, W. B. Stanford says that "deceptions" give Odysseus "an intrinsic pleasure, and he rather selfishly does not spare" his father "now." See *The Odyssey of Homer, with General and Grammatical Introduction, Commentary, and Indexes*, 2 vols (London: Macmillan, 1965), vol. 2, p. 420. Others who see this test as a purely gratuitous instance of compulsive behavior are U. von Wilamowitz-Moellendorff, *Die Heimkehr des Odysseus* (Berlin: Weidmann, 1927), p. 82; P. Von der Mühll, "Odyssee," *Paulys Realencyclopädie der Classischen Altertumswissenschaft*, ed. G. Wissowa, W. Kroll, and K. Mittelhaus, Supplementband vii (Stuttgart: Alfred Druckenmuller, 1940), p. 766; Renata von Scheliha, *Patroklos: Gedanken über Homers Dichtung und Gestalten* (Basle: B. Schwabe, 1943), pp. 19–20; and G. S. Kirk, who refers to Odysseus' testing of Laertes as a "bizarre plan" in *The Songs of Homer* (Cambridge: Cambridge University Press, 1962), p. 250. See also Friedrich Focke, *Die Odyssee* (Stuttgart: W. Kohlhammer, 1943), p. 378; Johannes T. Kakridis, *Homer Revisited* (Lund: C. W. K. Gleerup, 1971), pp. 160–1; A. Thornton, *People and Themes in Homer's Odyssey* (Dunedin: University of Otago Press, 1970), pp. 115–19; and Richard Rutherford, *Greece and Rome: New Surveys in the Classics, No. 26* (Oxford: Oxford University Press, 1996), p. 76 ("The way in which Odysseus tests and plays games with his wretched father has outraged many critics, but it should not surprise those who recognize that the hero is not simply a paragon of gentlemanly virtues. . . . It is consistent with both his character and the thematic tendencies of the poem that he should choose the more devious and potentially more painful option").

27. As recognized in the scholia. See N. J. Richardson,"Recognition Scenes in the *Odyssey*," in F. Cairns (ed.), *Papers of the Liverpool Seminar*, vol. 4 (1983): 227–8.

28. The pun implied by Odysseus, the embodiment of *métis* (which means "cunning," but also "not anyone"), by naming himself *Outis* after performing an act of exemplary metic intelligence was not lost on Homer. See Stephen V. Tracy, *The Story of the Odyssey* (Princeton, NJ: Princeton University Press, 1990), p. 61, who cites *Odyssey* IX.414.

29. As P. V. Jones remarks, "Five years is long enough; but if the omens were good when Odysseus left the stranger's house, the time-lapse becomes even more ominous" (*Homer's Odyssey: A Companion to the Translation of Richmond Lattimore* [Carbondale: Southern Illinois University Press, 1988], p. 222).

30. On Odysseus' dangerous curiosity in this episode, see Giacomo Bona, *Studi sull' Odissea* (Turin: Giappichelli, 1966), p. 82 n. 39, p. 102, and Herbert Eisenberger, *Studien zur Odyssee* (Wiesbaden: F. Steiner, 1973), p. 135.

31. *The Odyssey of Homer*, Vol. 2, p. 388.

32. In the case of Telemachus, who must assert his own identity as a hero who is at least to some degree worthy of his famous father, deep filial affection for his remarkable

mother Penelope seems virtually absent. Homer does not appear to be critical of the rather cool and impatient attitude of Telemachus toward Penelope, but perhaps this simply reveals the genius of a poet who, with an exquisite and timeless sense of verisimilitude, is portraying the need of an adolescent boy to break away from an extraordinary mother.

33. *Topophilia: A Study of Environmental Perception, Attitudes, and Values* (Englewood Cliffs, NJ: Prentice-Hall, 1974).

34. "The Representation of Nature in Early Greek Art," in Diana Buitron-Olivier (ed.), *New Perspectives in Early Greek Art* (Washington, DC: National Gallery of Art, 1991), p. 56. On this passage, see also Bernard Knox's "Introduction" to Robert Fagles's translation of the *Odyssey* (New York: Viking/Penguin, 1996), pp. 27–8. Knox sees this passage as "a clear reminiscence of Greek voyages of exploration in the West" (p. 27).

35. *Ibid.*

36. New York: Alfred A. Knopf, 1971, pp. 17–18.

37. *Confucian Thought: Selfhood as Creative Transformation* (Albany: State University of New York Press, 1985), p. 35.

38. See N. J. Girardot, *Myth and Meaning in Early Taoism* (Berkeley: University of California Press, 1983).

39. The account summarized here is found in *Huainanzi*, ch. 3, a text from the second century BCE, and is translated in Anne Birrell, *Chinese Mythology: An Introduction* (Baltimore: Johns Hopkins Press, 1993), p. 32.

40. Derk Bodde, "Dominant Ideas in the Formation of Chinese Culture" *Essays on Chinese Civilization*, ed. Charles Le Blanc and Dorothy Borei (Princeton, NJ: Princeton University Press, 1981), p. 133.

41. *Science and Civilisation in China* (Cambridge: Cambridge University Press, 1956), 2: p. 281.

42. The opening lines of one poem, Mao 237, might allude to primal gourds from which people come forth:

> The young gourds spread and spread.
> The people after they were first brought into being
> From the River Tu went to the Ch'i.

43. *From the Soil: The Foundation of Chinese Society*, trans. Gary G. Hamilton and Wang Zheng (Berkeley: University of California Press, 1992), p. 43.

44. For our awareness of the significance of the ancient epistemological principle that there is an inverse relation between, on the one hand, the degree of accuracy to be expected in any representation and, on the other, the degree of elevation or the importance of the subject matter, we are indebted to Wesley Trimpi, *Muses of One Mind: The Literary Analysis of Experience and Its Continuity* (Princeton; NJ: Princeton University Press, 1983), pp. 97–102. See these pages for Trimpi's citation of the relevant Platonic and Aristotelian passages.

45. *"Longinus" on the Sublime,* trans. W. Hamilton Fyfe (Loeb Classical Library, 1927; rpt., London: Heinemann, 1965), p. 153.

46. *Ibid.*, p. 155.

47. D. A. Russell, *"Longinus" on the Sublime* (Oxford: Clarendon Press, 1964), p. 99.

48. The ancient antagonism between realism and elevation is resolved in medieval literature, Auerbach suggests, because "the story of Christ, with its ruthless mixture of everyday reality and the highest and most sublime tragedy ... had conquered the classical rule of styles" (*Mimesis: The Representation of Reality in Western Literature*, trans. Willard Trask [Princeton, NJ: Princeton University Press, 1953], p. 409). Auerbach makes the same point in the essay "*Sermo Humilis,*" in *Literary Language and Its Public in Late Latin Antiquity and in the Middle Ages* (Princeton, NJ: Princeton University Press, 1965), pp. 25–66, where he explains that those subjects which would, from the point of view of antique literary theory, be considered as appropriate for treatment only in the low style, become matters of ultimate importance for the Christian.

49. *Discourses on Art*, edited by Robert W. Wark (London: Collier, 1969), p. 207. This remark, from the famous artist's thirteenth *Discourse*, was delivered on December 11, 1786.

50. *Ibid.*

51. *Mimesis*, p. 279.

52. Pauline Yu, *The Reading of Imagery in the Chinese Poetic Tradition* (Princeton, NJ: Princeton University Press, 1987), p. 45. Wai-lim Yip has noted that true landscape poetry develops in China during the Six Dynasties period and that in earlier poetry, such as the *Shi jing*, "Landscape plays only a secondary or subordinate position; it has not become the main object for aesthetic contemplation." Interestingly, he says that this is true of landscape in Homer too. See *Diffusion of Differences: Dialogues between Chinese and Western Poetics* (Berkeley: University of California Press, 1993), p. 101.

53. *Readings in Chinese Literary Thought*, p. 45.

54. *Shi jing jizhu* (Hong Kong: Guangzhi, n.d.), I.1.

55. See, for example, Gu Jiegang,"Qi xing," *Shi jing yanjiu lunji*, ed. Lin Qingzhang (Taipei: Xuesheng, 1983), pp. 63–9. In making this assumption, Gu is following earlier Chinese critics such as Zheng Qiao (1104–62).

56. This is Ch'en's reconstruction of the original meaning of *xing*. He goes on to outline what he thinks are the communal origins of *Shi jing* poetry in "The *Shih-ching*: Its Generic Significance," *Studies in Chinese Literary Genres*, ed. Cyril Birch (Berkeley: University of California Press, 1974), pp. 8–41. Pauline Yu summarizes the arguments of those who claim that there is "no empirical basis for the image at all." See *The Reading of Imagery*, p. 62.

57. The Manchu translation of the term as it appears in *Analects* 8.8. See *Sse-schu, Schu-king, Schi-king*, in *Mandschuischer Uebersetzung* (1864, Leipzig; rpt., Neudeln Liechtenstein: Kraus Reprints Ltd., 1966), p. 32.

58. *Confucius: The Analects* (New York: Penguin, 1979), p. 93.

59. On this topic, see the excellent work of John B. Henderson, *The Development and Decline of Chinese Cosmology* (New York: Columbia University Press, 1984), pp. 1–58, and A. C. Graham, *Yin–Yang and the Nature of Correlative Thinking* (Singapore: Institute of East Asian Philosophies, 1986).

60. *The Reading of Imagery*, p. 65.

61. *The Development and Decline of Chinese Cosmology*, p. 27.

62. A topic explored most thoroughly and subtly in Haun Saussy's *The Problem of a Chinese Aesthetic* (Stanford, CA: Stanford University Press, 1993).

63. *Mao shi Zheng jian*, SBBY edition, 10.1.

64. On this episode, see *Zuo zhuan*, Duke Huan 18, translated by Burton Watson in *The Tso Chuan: Selections from China's Oldest Narrative History* (New York: Columbia University Press, 1989), p. 17.

65. *Mao shi Zheng jian*, SBBY edition, 5.6.

66. Bernhard Karlgren, "The Book of Odes: Kuo Feng and Siao Ya," *Bulletin of the Museum of Far Eastern Antiquities*, 16 (1964): 204.

67. Joseph Needham, "Human Law and the Laws of Nature," in *The Grand Titration: Science and Society in East and West* (London: George Allen & Unwin, 1969), p. 328.

68. See Carrol Moulton, *Similes in the Homeric Poems* (Göttingen: Vandenhoeck & Ruprecht, 1977).

69. See, for example, the simile in VI.104 describing our first view of Nausikäa, a simile hauntingly imitated by Virgil in *Aen.* I.498–504.

70. This translation is not quite literal, since we have tried to simulate, in this instance, the rhyme scheme and syllable count of the Chinese. When attempting such fidelities in translation, it is usually not possible to be faithful, as well, to the literal meaning of the original.

71. See Jenny Strauss Clay, *The Wrath of Athena: Gods and Men in the Odyssey* (Princeton, NJ: Princeton University Press, 1983).

72. This Hellenic cosmic whole that combines "heaven" (*ouranos*) or "sky" and "earth" (*gaia*) has its parallel in the compact ancient Chinese description of the universe as *tian di* ("heaven and earth"), as in *Dao de jing* 1.5.

73. See Mark W. Edwards, "Homer and Oral Tradition: The Formula, Part I," *Oral Tradition*, 1 (1986): 171–230; "Homer and Oral Tradition: The Formula, Part II," *Oral Tradition*, 3 (1988): 11–60; "Homer and Oral Tradition: The Type-Scene," *Oral Tradition*, 7 (1992): 284–330; and Richard P. Martin, *The Language of Homer: Speech and Performance in the Iliad* (Ithaca, NY: Cornell University Press, 1989). For an exploration of the possible relevance of such Homeric oral formulaic theories to the *Classic of Poetry*, see C. H. Wang, *The Bell and the Drum: Shih Ching as Formulaic Poetry in an Oral Tradition* (Berkeley: University of California Press, 1974).

74. Do we have here a parallel to the Exodus story? V. Bérard, in *Did Homer Live?* (trans. B. Rhys [London: J. M. Dent, 1931], pp. 82ff.), argues that the name Proteus is a Greek version of the Egyptian "Prouiti" which was a title of the Pharaohs. See Stanford's commentary, vol. 1, p. 279. The Exodus story in the Hebrew Bible describes the transition in men's and women's experience of the divine from the pantheistic vision of the cosmological empires of the Near East (e.g. Egypt) to the Israelite conception of the unseen God whose reality and presence transcends the physical cosmos. Helen, earlier in the Book, had described Egypt as a "fertile land" (p. 229), hence perhaps emphasizing, as in Exodus, the association of Egypt with the material world of the cosmos.

75. On the etymological significance of the name Kalypso, see Alfred Heubeck, *Kadmos* 4 (1965): 143.

76. Homer says that Orestes buries his mother (III.309ff.), but it is not clear that Homer

thinks it was his hand that actually did the killing. Stephanie West, in the Oxford commentary, asserts that "it would be far-fetched to suppose that Orestes' matricide is a post-Homeric development" (Alfred Heubeck, Stephanie West, and J. B. Hainsworth (eds), *A Commentary on Homer's Odyssey,* Vol. 1 [Oxford: Oxford University Press, 1988], p. 181). For the correspondences between the two return stories of Agamemnon and Odysseus, see Samuel H. Basset, "The Second Necyia," *Classical Journal,* 13 (1918): 521–6; E. F. D'Arms and K. K. Hulley, "The Oresteia Story of the *Odyssey,*" *Transactions of the American Philological Association,* 77 (1946): 207–13; and Albin Lesky, "Die Schuld der Klytaimnestra," *Wiener Studien,* 80 (1967): 5–21.

77. See Samuel Butler, *The Authoress of the Odyssey* (London, 1922; rpt., Chicago: University of Chicago Press, 1967).

78. Liu Dalin, *Zhongguo gudai xing wenhua* [The Sexual Culture of Ancient China] (Yinchuan: Liaoning chubanshe, 1993), p. 134.

79. Xie Jinqing's workmanlike examination of this issue as it appears in the *feng* section of the *Classic of Poetry* lists 85 of the 160 poems as "concerning the woman question." See *Shi jing zhi nuxing de yanjiu* [A Study of Women in *Classic of Poetry*] (Shanghai: Shangwu, 1933), pp. 85–95.

80. As early as the third century BCE, the poet Qu Yuan (who was a man) frequently impersonates the female voice.

PART II

Before and after philosophy: Thucydides and Sima Qian

The Chinese *Classic of Poetry* and the Homeric poems were composed at roughly the same time. Philosophy too flowers at about the same moment in both Greece and China. Parts I and III of this study, then, treat works from the Chinese and Greek sides that are contemporaneous. Part II, however, breaks with this pattern of comparing works from China and Greece that were composed contemporaneously. What difference does this make?

For us, it makes quite a difference, for the philosophical differentiations decisively expressed, with varying degrees of analytical precision, by Confucius, Laozi, Zhuangzi, Plato, and Aristotle virtually created a before and after that might be said to constitute history. Although largely ignored in their own day, Confucius and Plato created history in the sense that their insights into the nature of the "gentleman" (*junzi*), on the Chinese side, and the "philosopher" (*philosophos*, "lover of wisdom"), on the Greek, initiated a form of existence on a fuller and more differentiated level of humanity. These parallel differentiations constituted history in the sense that they were recognized as such by later thinkers, such as Sima Qian in the case of China, who could not retreat to less-differentiated forms of existence once he had ingested the transforming power of Confucian thought.[1] Philosophy, then, creates history, understood not as a miscellaneous series of pragmatic events such as battles or dynastic successions, but as the unfolding of a meaningful "pattern," in T. S. Eliot's phrase, of "timeless moments."[2] History consists of a pattern created by the experience of timeless moments in which, as Laozi might put it,

79

human beings express in language their experience of participation in the *dao*.[3]

We have been speaking of history as a pattern of timeless moments, as the articulation, by concrete individuals, of their experience of participation in the *dao*. "History," in the sense of *meaningful temporal existence*, is thus experienced as possessing meaning specifically in reference to a person's relative successes and failures in living in attunement with the *dao*. Classical Chinese literature is filled with allusions to historical events and personages. It is for this reason that the work of Laozi stands out as conspicuously lacking in such historical allusions. The *Dao de jing* seems almost to exist outside of history. Laozi's work can be said to contain a philosophy of history, however, if we understand history, as we have discussed above, as "meaningful temporal existence." Our temporal existence, according to Laozi, is shaped by our experience of participation in the *dao*.[4]

Let us sum up our reflections on how philosophy creates history. In the wake of the "philosophical" differentations experienced and then articulated by Plato, Confucius, and Laozi, "history" is discovered as meaningful temporal existence, the meaning of which consists precisely in the degree to which temporal existence, as it runs its course in time and society, manages to find attunement with the "timeless patterns" of the ideas or forms (of the good or of justice, for example), in the case of Plato, or with the *dao*, in the case of Confucius and Laozi. And these philosophical discoveries are precisely the events that – through revealing this to be the case – divide history into a "before" and an "after."

There is, of course, another, more conventional understanding of history as an accurate account of the events of the past. Thucydides and Sima Qian are historians in this more conventional sense of the word. We cannot begin to compare their efforts as historians without noting that Thucydides writes *before* Plato; Sima Qian composes his work *after* Confucius and Laozi. Thucydides, in other words, writes *before* Platonic philosophy and Sima Qian *after* the speculations of the great Chinese sages such as Confucius.[5] There is a world of difference between a prephilosophical (as in the case of Thucydides) and a postphilosophical (as in the case of Sima Qian) view of history. In the case of Thucydides, we have an instance of historical writing that appears at times to be edging towards, but never quite achieving, an articulation of the historian's participation in a level of being that transcends the merely pragmatic succession of bloody battles and self-interested maneuverings.[6] Sima Qian's great work *Records of the Historian*, on the other hand, is deeply informed by the ethical tradition of the sages, and particularly by Confucius, who had attempted to articulate, and thus to participate in, the nature of the *dao*, as he understood it. Although Sima Qian's relationship to the man whom he calls "the ultimate sage" and, more particularly, the Confucianism of his own day is a complicated one, the Chinese historian cannot ignore the formulations of the esteemed thinker who preceded him. "Philosophy," Whitehead has remarked, "never reverts to its old position after the shock of a great philosopher."[7] Nor can the writing of history, in Greece and in China, be quite the same after Plato and Confucius.

1 History and tradition

Sima Qian and his predecessors

Sima Qian (145–*c*. 86 BCE) is sometimes called "the father of Chinese history" and put alongside Herodotus (490–*c*. 425 BCE) and Thucydides (*c*. 450–399 BCE), who are assigned a comparable position in the West. Sima Qian, to be sure, does establish a form for presenting history that profoundly influences all subsequent historiography in China, but he is a son as much as a father, who inherits and honors a long and rich tradition of historical writing. In fact, his immense 130-chapter *Records of the Historian* (*Shi ji*) is best seen as a grand synthesis of both the content and forms of the historical records that preceded him.

The Chinese tradition of historiography is a venerable one. The earliest examples of writing in China, the oracle-bone inscriptions from the last centuries of the Shang era (*c*. 1250–1045 BCE), are historical records. These inscriptions, carved upon tortoise shells and the scapula bones of cattle, of which there are more than fifty thousand published examples,[8] are records of the attempts of priests to ascertain the disposition of spirits toward the problems and plans of the Shang Kings. For our purposes here, the important point is that the inscriptions were carved *after* the divination itself was complete and were then stored in vast caches that we might justifiably label historical archives. While we do not know precisely why such records were maintained, the practice of inscribing and storing these bones and shells does seem to indicate a desire to keep records in a form that allows later consultation. In other words, these texts preserve a memory.

Certainly, many bronze inscriptions from the first centuries of the Zhou dynasty are an effort to transmit a recollection of some significant historical event. For example, one of the richest of these inscriptions, found on a bronze water basin unearthed in 1975, presents an adulatory description of the earliest Zhou kings. Edward Shaughnessy, a distinguished authority on early Chinese inscriptional texts, dates this vessel to "shortly before 900 B.C." and describes it as "probably the first conscious attempt in China to write history."[9] This bronze vessel, and most others as well, were cast by royal families for use in the ceremonies performed in ancestral shrines, and the inscriptions were "intended not for the caster's contemporaries but rather for his descendants."[10] In other words, the inscriptions preserved for a powerful family a memory on metal of a distinguished ancestor's accomplishments, as well as a wish, expressed in most of the inscriptions quite formulaically, that descendants might continue forever to use the vessel in honoring their ancestors.

Arguing from these examples, we can say that the tradition of Chinese historiography appears a full millennium before Sima Qian. The bone and bronze inscriptions, moreover, show two characteristics that typify much early Chinese historical writing: first, they are linked to royal courts and are produced as official acts, some might even say "bureaucratic acts";[11] second, there is a ceremonial context – one could even say a "sacred context" – to these inscriptional records.

During the Zhou dynasty, historical writing proliferates. The first scholar to attempt a classification of these writings was Liu Xiang (77–6 BCE), whose scheme is preserved in Ban Gu's (32–92 CE) *Han History*. The latter explains that Zhou historical texts can be divided into two broad categories, those that "record words" (*ji yan*) and those that "record events" (*ji shi*).[12] Certain chapters of the *Classic of Historical Documents*, which probably date from the first centuries of the Zhou dynasty, are examples of "those that record words" and purport to be transcriptions of important speeches or announcements. No doubt these particular texts were produced by Zhou officials eager to glorify the royal family and to awe current and potential enemies into compliance. *Spring and Autumn Annals*, a work from the state of Lu traditionally attributed to Confucius, is the purest example of Liu's second category. This text is composed entirely of short notices of important events that took place in Lu and its neighboring states between 722 and 481 BCE. We know from a contemporary witness that *Spring and Autumn Annals* is only one of many such records maintained by the various feudal states.[13] In fact, the preservation of a state's annals must have been an official expression of political sovereignty.[14]

Eventually these two forms, those that "record words" and those that "record events," converged. For example, the highly influential *Zuo Commentary*, which was probably written in the late fourth century BCE as a history of the Spring and Autumn period, alternates between fast-paced descriptions of events and lengthy quotations of speeches and dialogues. The historian intrudes into this text as a self-conscious presence relatively rarely and then in quite clearly marked passages, a feature that gives *Zuo Commentary* a tone of self-evident authority.

We have already noted the ceremonial or sacred context of early Chinese inscriptional records. Such a tone also pervades early Chinese historical writing and is extremely important for understanding Sima Qian's enthusiasm for compiling his comprehensive record of the past. The early Chinese *shi*, which we might translate "scribe" or, with some liberality, "historian," was a government functionary who had a variety of official duties. We shall refrain from engaging in the long-standing controversy concerning what etymological and graphic analysis might tell us about the original function of this official,[15] but by the Spring and Autumn period, one eminent Chinese authority has identified six basic tasks of the *shi*: to offer prayers, manage divination, regulate the calendar, explain calamities, read out government commands and appointments, and regulate clan genealogies. Several of these tasks required careful attention to record-keeping, so that soon scribes were identified with the task of making permanent records of the movements and the words of kings and dukes.[16]

True to their origins in ceremonial activities, a religious aura surrounded the early Chinese scribes and granted them considerable power. As historians, they were expected to keep records accurately and not to hide the faults of their superiors. Originally, these records might have been as much a declaration for the attention of spirits as for the attention of later human beings. Note, for example, the following passage from *Zuo Commentary*, in which Yanzi, an influential minister from the state of Qi, puts scribes alongside priests and declares their sacred responsibility:

> When the priests and scribes are setting forth the truth, they are to speak of errors. If they cover offenses and list [only] what is praiseworthy, they are distorting and deceiving. ... Therefore, the ghosts and spirits will not accept the offerings of that state and will bring calamity to it. And the priests and scribes will share in this calamity. (Zhao 20 [522 BCE])

Inaccurate historical records, particularly those that hide the misdeeds of the ruler, bring the displeasure of spirits and therefore have the power to disrupt the government. However, under the influence of Confucius and his followers, who were much more concerned about serving humankind than serving ghosts and spirits (see *Analects* 11.12), Chinese historical scholarship gradually became more secular and humanistic. One of the first steps in this process of secularization was to argue that the actions and attitudes of spirits are entirely dependent upon human beings. An important passage in *Zuo Commentary* asserts that spirits "act by relying upon human beings" (Zhuang 32 [661 BCE]), and a lost passage from the *Book of Documents*, quoted by the philosopher Mencius (*c.* 372–289 BCE), declares that "Heaven sees with the eyes of its people. Heaven hears with the ears of its people" (*Mencius* 5A.5).

If anything, this gradual secularization of historiography enhanced the status of history. Confucius himself purportedly said that "The True Gentleman detests the fact that he might die and his name be forgotten" (*Analects* 15.20). In a culture that places much more emphasis upon this world than on the other, to be remembered became the major means to immortality. In *Zuo Commentary*, a minister from the state of Jin asks a counterpart from the state of Lu about the meaning of an ancient phrase "to die and not decay." The Lu minister explains that one should try to establish virtue, meritorious service, and wise words: "And if it be that for a long time these are not forgotten, then this is what we call 'not to decay'" (Xiang 24 [549 BCE]). The historian determines who will be remembered and for what reasons. To use the traditional Chinese expressions that are still popular today, he determines who will "hand down a fragrance for one hundred generations" (*liu fang bai shi*) and who will "leave a stench for ten thousand years" (*yi chou wan nian*).

History in traditional China can almost be considered the secular religion of the educated class and occupies a position that can hardly be overemphasized. Part of the reason for this is that Confucius himself, the most esteemed of all Chinese, is regarded as a historian who reedited the Lu state annals and thereby produced *Spring and Autumn Annals*. These *Annals* are extremely terse and appear to do little more than list major events in China between 722 and 481 BCE from the somewhat limited perspective of the state of Lu, a small state located on the Shandong Peninsula. However, later Confucian commentators attempted to demonstrate that their Master had actually used *Annals* to pass extremely subtle and trenchant judgments on his contemporaries and the important persons of the two centuries preceding him. Confucius's historical work was, from this point of view, a work of "subtle words that carry vast meaning."[17] Thus, *Spring and Autumn Annals*, the commentators argued, was not only an extremely accurate historical record but also, properly read, an unequaled work of moral and political philosophy. Such a reading, we might add, required great cleverness and considerable imagination.

The precise relationship between Confucius and *Spring and Autumn Annals*, and the question of whether the latter does indeed contain subtle judgments, remain controversial issues.[18] What cannot be disputed is that Confucius was intensely interested in history and in preserving the traditions of the past. He describes himself as one who "transmits and does not create" (*Analects* 7.1), a passage we shall come back to presently, and he once bemoaned the fact that "for such a long time" he had not dreamed of the Duke of Zhou, a hero of the past who was, in the Confucian view, *the* great transmitter of culture (*Analects* 7.5) and, in that sense, a great historian. Certainly, the early Confucian curriculum emphasized mastery of the history, poetry, and ritual of the past, so that it is with good reason that one modern scholar has said that "to Confucius the learning that constitutes knowledge essentially comes from history."[19] Moreover, Confucius was interested not just in the past but in the nature and form of historical records. He decried the fact that documentation for the Xia and Shang periods was inadequate (*Analects* 3.9), and seemed to have advocated a type of conservative historical writing that left out whatever was doubtful or speculative (*Analects* 2.18, 15.26).

We have noted already that Sima Qian, the "father of Chinese history," differs from Thucydides in that he comes *after* rather than before the major philosophers of his tradition (Confucius, Laozi, Zhuangzi, etc.) and is greatly influenced by their teachings. Furthermore, between the time of Confucius and that of Sima Qian there occurred an event that shook the world of scholarship and threatened for a time to dethrone the lofty status of history and tradition, the very foundation of Confucian learning. That event, which continued to cast a very dark shadow over Sima Qian's age, was the military unification of China under the First Qin Emperor (259–210 BCE, *c*. 221–210), and the Emperor's famous attempt to erase, or at least control, the past through an order issued in 213 BCE to burn some books and maintain others only in the imperial library where they would be accessible to the few officials who had secured permission to consult them.

The Qin Emperor's infamous policy did not, as some have implied, emerge *ex nihilo* but was the culmination of an attack upon the relevance of history and tradition that had been gaining ground for some time. It was in part a response to the intense political and philosophical competition that characterized the last century of the Warring States period. Many people, including philosophers, bemoaned the narrowness of vision that resulted from the pre-Qin organization of the kingdom into separate, competing states. For example, in the early third century BCE, a certain Gongsun Chou, a man of Qi, asked Mencius if he could replicate the successes of Guan Zhong and Yanzi, two famous ministers of the state of Qi who had lived several centuries earlier. Mencius responded as follows: "Truly you are a man of Qi, for you only know of Guan Zhong and Yanzi." Mencius then goes on to speak of Kings Wen and Wu and the Duke of Zhou, leaders who represent a Chinese unity rather than a particular state (*Mencius* 2A:1).

The implication is clear: some larger, ancient tradition had been lost, or at least was being ignored, in favor of local traditions that derived from fairly recent times.

Whether or not Mencius' concerns about the narrowness of local traditions and the growing neglect of a more general history are justified, it is certain that a number of philosophical trends in the late Zhou period were indeed hostile to the keeping of accurate historical records, or, at least, did not regard history as central to their concerns. The so-called "Mohists," who "filled the empire" during the last century of the Zhou,[20] made abundant use of historical texts in their earliest writings. But as time passed, they seem gradually to have placed more emphasis upon the importance of carefully formulated, logical argumentation than upon historical precedent. For their part, early Daoists might have made use of history, often in a humorous or ironic way, but history, for them, did not determine "what is so of itself" and hence was not a model for correct action. Laozi's *Dao de jing*, for example, makes no specific references to model kings of the past or to specific historical precedents.

The most direct attack upon history comes from a group of thinkers who were later labeled "*fa jia*," a term scholars have usually translated as "legalists."[21] The earliest legalist treatise, the *Book of Lord Shang* (*Shang jun shu*), which is attributed to the Qin state minister Shang Yang (d. 338 BCE), challenges the stability and reliability of the past as a guide to contemporary action by asking, "Since the teachings of previous generations differ, what antiquity are you going to imitate?" (ch. 1). The later legalist Hanfeizi (280?–233?) argues that the virtues of humaneness and duty were "useful in antiquity but are not useful today" and concludes that "when the times change, then political affairs change" (ch. 19). The past, for Hanfeizi, provides no guide for proper political action, which comes only from understanding current circumstances. Thus, A. C. Graham aptly describes the skepticism regarding the relevance of history widespread in the late Zhou as follows: "The denial that ancient authority is necessarily relevant to changing times is by this period common to Legalists, Taoists, Later Mohists, syncretists, to everyone except Confucians."[22]

The legalist minister Li Si (d. 208) was only building upon such antihistorical sentiments when he criticized "today's scholars" for "not following the contemporary but studying antiquity" and advocated the destruction of some historical records and the monopoly of others in the imperial archives so that no one would be able to "use antiquity to criticize present [policies]" (6:255).[23] What better way to destroy the power of historical precedent and the expertise of those who study tradition than to control access to books?

The Qin dynasty lived on for only seven years after the famous book-burning. Its successor, the Han dynasty (202 BCE–221 CE), arose in a time of profound tension between the move toward a centralized empire, a model now somewhat discredited by the excesses of the Qin, and the desire to return to a pre-Qin model of semi-independent states, with perhaps one of the states acting as leader of a loosely knit federation. After Liu Bang defeated Xiang Yu at Gaixia in 202 BCE and established the Han dynasty, he compromised, no doubt out of necessity, between the Qin model and the older feudal one. Approximately half of his empire consisted of ten kingdoms awarded to loyal supporters who became, in the late Zhou fashion, "kings" of those realms, and half of the empire was retained under the Emperor's direct control.[24] The subsequent struggle between the interests of the kingdoms and those of the imperial center characterized the first century of the Han era, with the balance shifting steadily in favor of the center. By the time Sima Qian served in the court of the Han Emperor Wu (*rd.* 141–87 BCE), the kingdoms had been greatly diminished in area and the power of the kings vastly reduced.

As we have noted, the Qin attempt to eradicate the power of those who would use the past to criticize present policies had been a serious blow to the Confucian custodians of the Chinese tradition. Furthermore, when the rebel Xiang Yu attacked the Qin capital of Xianyang in 206 BCE, he burned the palaces, including the Imperial Library, "with a resulting loss of literature that was possibly even greater than that caused by the earlier official burning of the books."[25] The first emperors of the Han dynasty were concerned primarily with the political struggle between kingdoms and the central government mentioned above and did little to promote the recovery of tradition. Nevertheless, as the process of imperial consolidation proceeded, Confucian influence grew and the court looked more and more to the traditions of the past to buttress and legitimate its authority.[26] A series of imperial actions during the first decades of the long reign of the Emperor Wu are particularly important to this process: in 136(?) BCE, the Emperor adopted the recommendation of the Confucian partisan Dong Zhongshu that "all not with the field of the Six Classics, or the teachings of Confucius, should be cut short and not allowed to progress further";[27] in 135, he established government academic posts (the so-called *boshi*, "erudites") for masters of the "Five Classics"; and in 124, he founded the Imperial Academy (*taixue*) with a curriculum based entirely upon the Confucian classics.[28]

Sima Qian no doubt regarded his own enterprise as a valuable part of this ongoing effort to consolidate and preserve a classical tradition, but his historical scope extended well beyond the conservative limits of the Confucian classics. In contrast to any of the historians who preceded him, Sima Qian produced a China-centered world history that reached from the earliest legendary emperor, the Yellow Emperor, down to his own time, a span of over two thousand years. The fact that he was less concerned with orthodoxy than inclusiveness has drawn criticism. For example, Ban Gu, China's next great historian, reproved his famous predecessor for straying too far from the classics and including material on such morally questionable social groups as "wandering knights" and "merchants."[29] But Sima Qian's *Records of the Historian* was a work of preservation that was intended to protect historical truth from any future attempts at repeating the Qin suppression of the past. In accomplishing this prodigious task, its author was not overly concerned with political and ideological correctness.

Although later scholars have sometimes spoken of Sima Qian as if he were the sole author of *Records of the Historian*, the project was begun by his father, Sima Tan (175?–110), and it is probably impossible to determine precisely how much of the work was completed before his father's death. Sima Qian himself regarded *Records of the Historian* as "the work of a single family" and took up his father's project as an act of filial devotion at a time when filial piety was regarded as the premier Confucian virtue. Moreover, Sima Qian attributes to his father a theory that a sage arises every five hundred years to consolidate the Chinese tradition. The first sage in this cycle was the Duke of Zhou, who served as minister and regent to the first Zhou kings. The second great sage, approximately five hundred years later, was Confucius, who supposedly edited or revised all of those texts which eventually were canonized as classics (Chinese "*jing*"). Now another such sage was due, and Sima Tan believed that his son could complete his historical project and become that sage; Sima Qian, that is, could become the new Confucius.[30]

In the concluding remarks of his postface to *Records of the Historian*, where he reflects upon his work as a historian more directly than at any other place in his vast text, Sima Qian makes it quite clear that he regards himself as someone who is gathering and preserving the past, and he outlines both the historical and the personal dimensions of his task. He begins his conclusion by establishing a link between the Han dynasty, which he serves, and the legendary Five Emperors of high antiquity and the three dynasties – the Xia, Shang, and Zhou – that followed. By his time, the Han had ruled for almost a century, and official ceremonial steps had been taken to establish the dynasty's claim to Heaven's Charge. But the Han "continuation of the task of the three dynasties," to use Sima's words, had to reach back across the disruptive period between the decline of Zhou power and the victory of the Han:

> The doctrine of the Zhou was thrown aside, and the Qin scattered and discarded the ancient texts and burned and destroyed the *Poetry* and the *Historical Documents*. Therefore, the maps and records in the metal chests and on jade tablets in the stone rooms of the Hall of Illumination were dispersed and in disarray. (130.3319)

Obviously, the sages of the past, with their stone rooms, metal storage vaults, and jade tablets, had intended to leave a permanent and accurate record, Sima Qian implies, but the chaotic years of the late Zhou and the malevolence of the First Qin Emperor had threatened the continuity that only historical records could provide. To Sima Qian, the essential crime of the Qin was a crime against the notion of a permanent and inviolate connection between the present and the past – an attempt to cut the thread of history, which is embodied in a lineage of texts.

Sima Qian goes on, in the conclusion of his postface, to trace the effort made by a number of early Han ministers to recuperate the past so that "the study of culture [*wen xue*] gained proper balance and slowly advanced, and the *Poetry* and the *Historical Documents* became more common and gradually reappeared." Then he claims that this century-long effort to recover the past had converged upon the office of the Grand Historian, which both he and his father had occupied:

> During this period of one hundred years, the lost writings and ancient affairs were completely gathered up by the Office of the Grand Historian, and the Grand Historians, like of old, followed upon one another, father and son, to occupy this office. (130.3319)

This notion of the hereditary succession of official historians, as we shall see, is important to Sima Qian. He contends that his work, like that of his father, is part of a family tradition: "The Sima family has, for generation after generation, managed the heavenly offices" (130.3319).[31] This claim that the Sima family had been traditionally occupied with the movements of heaven and the affairs of earth – that they were historians, in other words (a claim put in his father's mouth elsewhere in the postface [130.3285]) – is in fact without evidence. Insofar as we can trace the Sima lineage, the historian's ancestors were engaged much more in military than literary activities, so that one recent Chinese commentator on the postface says, charitably, "I am afraid this claim is not a fact" (130.3320).[32]

Sima Qian must justify his own preoccupation with the past by asserting a family tradition, just as he must assert a continuity with Confucius' authoritative historical work, *Spring and Autumn Annals*.

89

And so he continues, emphasizing the way in which his own work is an act of "remembering":

> It has now come down to me. Respectfully, I will remember! Respectfully, I will remember! I have drawn together the ancient traditions that had been scattered and lost, and what the deeds of the kings had brought forth. I have traced beginnings and examined endings, seen prosperity and decline, and have discussed and examined human actions and official affairs. (130.3319)

The *Records of the Historian* does indeed "draw together traditions." Scholars have identified by name more than eighty sources that are cited in Sima Qian's work, and there are undoubtedly many more sources that we cannot now trace.[33] In order to collect materials, Sima Qian traveled throughout China and conducted interviews with those who possessed some special knowledge of the past, but he was, in the main, a bookish historian whom we can imagine sitting at a table surrounded by the records of the past and attempting to consolidate their varied accounts.

Toward the conclusion of his postface, Sima Qian discusses the general organization of his history, an organization that is a synthesis of earlier forms and that contrasts sharply with Thucydides' *Peloponnesian War*, an issue we shall discuss later. What we wish to emphasize here is Sima Qian's profound concern with tradition and with the preservation of the past. In this respect, the spirit of Sima Qian's work was thoroughly Confucian. But the Han historian went well beyond the normal confines of Confucian historical interests. He did not rely exclusively on the words of the Confucian classics, and he was not content with only those accounts that had some clear didactic purpose.

We have noted before that early Chinese historical writing emerges in a sacred context and that some shadows of that context live on in later, secularized historiography. There is certainly something of the sacred power of the historian in the Sima family's ardor to keep alive the names and deeds of the past. In another place in his postface, Sima Qian's father lies dying and gives an injunction to his son that is quoted in the *Records of the Historian* as Sima Tan's final words:

> Now the Han has arisen, and all within the seas has been unified. Enlightened sovereigns, worthy rulers, loyal ministers, and officials who died for duty – I have been Grand Historian but have not discussed and made record of them. That the historical writings of the empire will be scattered is what I greatly fear. May you remember! (130.3295)

Immediately thereafter, Sima Qian promises that he "will not be remiss." And he was not remiss, despite a great personal tragedy that interrupted and almost ended his work. As a filial son who had made a promise to a father, as a follower of Confucius "the transmitter," and as a part of a self-proclaimed family tradition of historiographers, he takes upon himself the sacred tradition of remembering and preserving the past. With a reverence for his forebears, he will do all within his power to make sure that the sacred tradition of remembering will not be threatened again, as it had been by the Qin. Unlike Thucydides, to whom we now turn, Sima Qian honors and emulates the authors who had preceded him. This is, in part, a result of his writing in the wake of Confucius and other philosophers who had created his deep sense of history.

Homer, Herodotus, and Thucydides

Historical composition in Greece really begins with Homer, who attempts to understand the reasons for the decline of Mycenean civilization in the wake of the disastrous Trojan War. The Homeric epics, composed probably in the eighth century BCE, are sophisticated and brilliantly constructed literary works, but they are also attempts at writing a kind of praise-and-blame version of history. As Homer is composing the epics, the formerly powerful Hellas, with its center in Mycenae, is now rudderless, and much of what remains of the once great civilization is scattered among the islands along the Anatolian coast. The epics have a twofold purpose. They are meant to recall the past glory of Hellenic civilization and to praise its heroes. But they are also designed to criticize the excesses of their fiery but sometimes fatally self-centered protagonists, such as Agamemnon and Achilles. Both the *Iliad* and the *Odyssey* are based on history. The *Iliad* focuses on a specific episode – the wrath of Achilles – in the cataclysmic war between the Trojans and the Hellenes. The *Odyssey* tells the story of the return (*nostos*) of one particular hero, Odysseus, from Troy. But while the plots are based on history, it would be wrong to say that what motivates Homer is the attempt to convey a meticulously accurate, factual account of what actually happened. While Homer is concerned with verisimilitude, he is also a great creator of mythopoetic figurations that are clearly meant to resonate well beyond the literal, flatly historical level. His use of myth and symbol convey his understanding, in Laozi's terms, that the path that can be put into words is not the constant path. His poems are, to a large extent, mythic representations articulated by a consciousness that is aware of its participation in a cosmos that can never be reduced to the propositional object of a merely intentional consciousness, to Laozi's or Zhuangzi's "ten thousand things."

The rise of historical awareness, in the conventional sense, in Greek thought seems to carry with it this objectivizing tendency. What becomes eclipsed in this process is precisely the participationist dimension. We have seen a foreshadowing of this tendency clearly articulated by Homer in Odysseus' objectivizing treatment of his father at the conclusion of the *Odyssey*. We shall see it in Thucydides. The stubborn and often willful forgetting of this participationist dimension is the stuff of tragedy, particularly of the great age of Athenian tragedy in the fifth century BCE.

The word *historiê*, from which the English word "history" derives, appears in the first sentence of the work of Herodotus:

> This is a record of inquiry [*historiê*] by Herodotus of Halicarnassus, set forth in order that what is remembered by men may not be obliterated by the lapse of time, that great and wonderful deeds performed by Hellenes and barbarians may not become unremembered, and in particular the reason [*aitiê*] why they made war against each other.[34]

Herodotus's notion of "history" (*historiê*) thus has the same twofold intention as does Homeric epic. "History" both preserves the awe-inspiring deeds of the past and seeks, too, to understand the causes (*aitiê*) of current political turmoil, which, in the case of Herodotus, is the war between the Persians and the Greeks.

And what were the reasons for the conflict? There appear to be at least two. The first cause is attributed to man's place in the cosmos, the other derives from Herodotus's view of human nature. A contemporary thinker, the philosopher Heraclitus (fl. *c.* 500 BCE), observed that "war is the common reality of things, and strife is the way things are – everything happens according to strife and necessity" (B 80).[35] Herodotus applies this cosmological principle to human affairs. Strife is quite simply a natural occurrence. To this principle Herodotus adds the insight attributed to Croesus, the former King of Lydia, who gives the following advice to the Persian leader, Cyrus: "There is a wheel of human affairs which, turning, does not suffer the same men always to prosper" (I.207). So much for the cosmic principle. There is also, however, an ineluctable aspect of specifically *human* nature which must be taken into account. For this we must turn to the advice given by Queen Atossa to her husband King Darius at a time when Darius is experiencing something of a postcoital let-down between his imperialist conquests. While she was "in bed" (III.135) with Darius, Atossa tells the king:

> My lord, with the immense resources at your command, the fact that you are making no further conquests to increase the power of Persia must mean that you lack ambition. Surely a young man like you, who is master of great wealth, should be seen engaged in some active enterprise, to show

the Persians that they have a man to rule them. Indeed, there are two reasons for ending this inactivity: for not only will the Persians know their leader to be a man, but, if you make war, you will waste their strength and leave them no leisure to plot against you. Now is the time for action, while you are young.

Ambition is healthy and natural, even if the result is the relentless imposition of one's imperial will on helpless victims. Not only is Darius ambitious, but so is everyone else. If he is inactive, he will create a vacuum in which other naturally ambitious men will assert their own will to power and overthrow him. Restless physical energy and the drive for imperial expansion are what define human nature.

We would now like to observe two points of divergence between the historical investigations of Homer and Herodotus. Homer, while no simple-minded moralist, clearly disapproves of the manner in which heroes such as Achilles and Agamemnon allow their emotions to govern their actions. Achilles is glorious, but his failings are emblematic of a Hellenic culture in crisis. Homer remembers the past not only to enshrine it, but also to criticize it. We have spoken of this as the twofold, praise-and-blame intention of the Homeric epics. In the previous chapter we discussed, for example, how Homer, in his representation of Odysseus, both praises the hero's purely metic intelligence and criticizes its excesses. Herodotus marvels at the expansionist drive of characters such as Darius and Atossa. They are wonders of nature and by that fact alone worthy of remembrance in his history. Herodotus is interested in finding the reason (*aitiê*) for the East–West conflict of his day, but the Homeric adverse judgment on the excesses of human nature is often not highlighted in his analysis.

Another, and related, point of divergence is the treatment of myth by the two authors. Herodotus is a collector of stories and a first-rate storyteller. He enjoys telling stories for their own sake and he enjoys collecting them, but as a historian his interest in myth is to find the objectively historical truth contained in the stories. Nowhere is this more apparent than in his discussion of the story that lies at the heart of Homer's *Iliad*: the abduction by Paris of Menelaos' wife Helen and his absconding with her to Troy. There is an alternative account told to him by some Egyptian priests, Herodotus remarks, which he is more inclined to believe (III.115–21). Bad weather forced Paris and Helen to land their ship in Egypt. When the Pharaoh Proteus learned of Paris' reprehensible violation of Menelaos' hospitality, he refused to allow Paris to take Helen back with him to Troy. Hence, Helen never was in fact brought to Troy, which explains why Priam did not simply return her to the Greeks and avoid the absurdly destructive conflict. Herodotus' reasons make good sense, but in the process of attempting to discover what really happened, he betrays a rationalism that shows him to be something less than an ideal literary critic.

Herodotus says that Homer knew about this account of Helen's having been made captive in Egypt and that she never in fact reached Troy, but that "he rejected it as less suitable for epic poetry than the one he actually used." This observation about what is "suitable" (*euprepês*) for poetry is Herodotus' one concession to an awareness that the goals of the poet and those of the historian, as Aristotle would later observe, are quite different. For Aristotle, the historian depicts the particular, the poet the universal (*Poetics* 9). Herodotus does not straightforwardly criticize Homer for being a bad historian, as will Thucydides, but there is a slight, indeed almost unconscious, air of condescension in his attitude toward Homer's promulgating the allegedly wrong version of what actually happened. After discussing what he believes was Homer's knowledge of his own preferred account, the historian remarks, "But enough of Homer (*Homêros men nun ... chairetô*)." Or, as Aubrey de Sélincourt phrases it in his translation, "I must not waste any more time on Homer" (II.118).[36] Why is Homer a waste of time? Because Herodotus "cannot believe that either Priam or any other kinsman of his was mad enough to be willing to risk his own and his children's lives and the safety of the city, simply to let Paris continue to live with Helen" (120). The power of Homer's poetic imagination appears lost on Herodotus. Helen plays a central role in the *Iliad*. Her great beauty captivates the indulgent Priam and even the judicious Hector. Even the best of the Trojans are thus depicted by Homer as, to some degree, tragically culpable for the catastrophe of the war. Helen becomes, in Homer, a symbol of how human reason can, through narcissistic self-satisfaction, be thwarted and bring disaster upon a whole polity. For Herodotus, Homer's Helen is a factual error rather than a powerful poetic symbol.

Herodotus inquired about the cause of the great conflict of his day, a conflict that personally affected him. He was a native of Halicarnassus, which was virtually governed by Persia. Herodotus was therefore denied the kinds of privileges and possibilities for advancement that were enjoyed by his social equals in other Greek cities. Thucydides too was personally involved in the events about which he writes. He was born into a prominent Athenian family and was elected a military commander in 424 BCE. When a military expedition which he led failed, due to lack of sufficient arms rather than as a result of any incompetence on his part, he was banished. For the next two decades he lived in exile in northern Greece before returning to Athens several years before his death. His account of the ongoing conflict between

Athens and Sparta remained an unpublished fragment – although a very lengthy fragment – at the time of his death.

What Thucydides called his work was not a "history" but a "writing-up" or a "report" (*xyngraphê*) of the conflict between the Athenians and Spartans: "Thucydides, an Athenian, wrote up [*xynegrapse*] the conflict between the Peloponnesians and the Athenians" (I.1). When Herodotus inquired into the cause of the East–West conflict of his day, he was content to find it in a general cosmic pattern of rising and falling fortunes. It is, he believed, a natural human tendency for those in power to extend that power and dominion, and they will do so until they overstep their bounds and are checked by divinity and reproved for their actions. Thucydides was not content with such speculations upon ultimate causes. He wanted to find a *proximate* cause for the great upheaval (*kinêsis*) of his day, and in this sense his efforts paralleled contemporary medical writings. Hippocrates (fl. *c*. 420 BCE) rejected the validity of speculative hypotheses in investigating illness. Such vague hypotheses were perhaps acceptable in philosophical speculation, he believed, but they could not be scientifically verified and had no place in a well-developed and rigorous science.[37] In his "report" on the conflict between the Athenians and the Spartans, Thucydides is searching for the proximate cause of the conflict in order to make a diagnosis of the disease and to prescribe a medication that will suppress future occurrences. The truest cause (*alêthestatên prophasin*) of the war, Thucydides states, is "the growth of the Athenians to greatness [*megalous gignomenous*], which brought fear to the Lacedaimonians and forced them [*anankasai*] to war" (I.23). The cause of the conflict, then, lies in the extra-ordinary rise to power and glory of the Athenian *polis*, which provoked the Spartan reaction. The reason ultimately lies in the nature of the Athenian and Spartan characters, which Thucydides brilliantly analyzes. It is this analysis of character that provides a clear structure to the work, even though it was never completed. We shall return to the structure of Thucydides' "report," but we must attend, first, to the historian's attitude toward the past.

Compared with Sima Qian and even Herodotus, Thucydides had little interest in the past and in tradition *per se*. We have observed how important it is for Sima Qian the historian to be a filial son, a son not only of his own biological father, Sima Tan, but of his spiritual father, Confucius, as well. Indeed, Sima Qian, as we have noted, does not get around to narrating his own biography until he has paid lengthy homage to his ancestors. Thucydides begins rather differently. Indeed, the first word of the work is Thucydides' own name, which he proudly announces, followed by an adjective that reveals the name of his *polis*:

Thoukudidês Athênaios ("Thucydides, an Athenian"). "Thucydides, an Athenian," the historian continues,

> wrote up the war that the Peloponnesians and Athenians waged against each other, beginning at the moment it broke out and expecting that it would be great [*megan*] and more worthy of being written about [*axiologôtaton*] than any of the wars that had come before...For this upheaval [*kinêsis*] was the greatest [*megistê*] that had ever happened to the Hellenes, but also to a certain segment of the barbarians – one might even say it was the greatest upheaval in the history of humankind [*epi pleiston anthrôpôn*]... As to the events of the period just preceding this, and those of a still earlier date, it was impossible to get clear information on account of the lapse of time; but from evidence which, on pushing my investigation to the greatest point [*epi makrotaton skopounti*], I find I can trust, I think that they were not really great [*ou megala*] either in regard to the wars they waged or in other particulars. (I.1)

The aggressive self-assertion, indeed arrogance, of this passage is remarkable, especially if we view it in contrast to the postface of Sima Qian. The word "great" appears throughout in various forms, stressing Thucydides' conviction of the crucial importance of his own contemporary moment and his own literary endeavor. Not only is he convinced of the greatness of his own moment in history, but he argues that the impressiveness and weightiness of previous moments in history have been exaggerated. In pushing his own investigation to the greatest point (*makrotaton*), he is now persuaded that previous wars and moments of crisis in Hellenic civilization were really not all that impressive (*ou megala*). The greatness of his own analysis, Thucydides concludes, reveals the allegedly great conflicts of the past – the Trojan War, the war between the Greeks and the Persians, for example – to have been not so great after all.

Given his rather condescending attitude toward what he believes to have been the greatly exaggerated reports of the earlier conflicts in Hellenic history, Thucydides' condescending attitude toward his literary predecessors will not strike the reader as particularly surprising. Like Herodotus, Thucydides shows no interest in Homer *as poet*. Actually, the previous sentence is something of an understatement. Herodotus had only implicitly criticized Homer for indulging in fantasies rather than in accurately recording the truth. Thucydides feels no such qualms about belittling the greatest Greek poet – we had almost said the greatest poet of all time. Let us look at Thucydides' references to the great poet in the so-called "Archeology," the name given to the opening section in which he tells the story (*logos*) of the early (*archaios*) history of Hellas.

Not surprisingly, Thucydides judges Homer on the basis of how competent a historian he is rather than for his achievement as a poet. The first reference occurs in section 3 of "The Archeology." Thucydides is now proving his assertion about "the weakness of ancient times [*tôn palaiôn*]" compared to the present. The times were so weak, Thucydides asserts, that antiquity did not even possess a conception of a single entity called "the Greeks" or "the Hellenes," a word which was derived from the name of Hellen of Phthiotis, who lived in a later period. Of this fact of the "Hellenes" having originally possessed no single name, Thucydides writes, "Homer provides the best evidence" (*tekmêrioi de malista Hômeros*, I.3.3), since the poet had no one word by which to designate the force that came to Troy. Thucydides' comments are astute, but what he fails to consider in his analysis is the fact that it is metrical convenience and the desire for verbal variation that, in part, accounts for the different names by which Homer refers to the Greeks. He fails to consider, in other words, the poetic dimension of Homer's designation of the Hellenes.

Later in the "Archeology," Thucydides attempts to understand how Agamemnon was chosen to lead the Greek troops to Troy. A proof of Agamemnon's superior wealth and of the importance of his naval power, Thucydides remarks, can be found in Homer. Agamemnon brought the greatest number of ships with him to Troy, and he even had enough ships to supply some to the Arkadians, "as Homer has described [*dedêlôken*] it – provided that anybody can take seriously Homer's credentials as a weigher of evidence who offers positive proofs [*tekmêriôsai*]" (I.9.4). Much of the tone of condescension of this phrase in the Greek comes from the force of the word *tôi*, "to anybody," which in the context can be taken as meaning almost "to anyone in his right mind" – that is, to anyone other than protopositivist historians such as Thucydides. If we rely on Homer for this kind of information, Thucydides implies, we must be sure to remember that the old poet fell far short of respectable contemporary standards of weighing evidence and offering proofs, which is the meaning of the Greek verb *tekmêrioô*, a verb that Thucydides often uses to describe his own approach to giving an accurate account of the past.

In the next section of his history, Thucydides again judges Homer in terms of the poet's reliability as a historian. Thucydides is trying to estimate the number of Greek ships that sailed to Troy so that he can compare the magnitude of that enterprise to the conflict between the Spartans and Athenians. Mycenae is not, it is true, graced with the kinds of impressive buildings we see in Athens, Thucydides says. But neither is Sparta, and she is clearly a very powerful city.

It is reasonable [*eikos*], therefore, not to be incredulous or to regard

[*skôpein*] the appearance of cities rather than their power, but to believe
that expedition [to Troy] to be greater [*megistên*] than any that preceded
it, though falling below those of the present time, if here again one can
put any trust in the poetry of Homer; for though it is reasonable [*eikos*] to
suppose that he as a poet greatly embellished the truth [*epi to meizon men
poiêtên onta kosmêsai*], still it was deficient [*endeestera*] in comparison
with ours. (I.10.3–4)

In this instance, Thucydides suggests, Homer may have been a pretty
good historian. He was probably correct in his estimate of the relatively
large size of the Hellenic forces that traveled to Troy. Once again,
however, the condescension toward poets creeps in with the qualifier, "if
one can put any trust in the poetry of Homer." Poetry isn't to be
trusted. But even if Homer, as an untrustworthy poet, exaggerated the
size of the fleet, its poetically exaggerated size still pales before the
magnitude of today's fleets.

The very language of Confucius' *Analects* 7.1 ("Transmit and not
create," etc.), to which Sima Qian clearly alludes in his postface,
conveys the sage's reverence for antiquity and tradition. This passage of
Thucydides, in contrast, is agonistic in regard to the historian's
predecessor, Homer. It is agonistic in terms of both content and style.
In terms of content, Thucydides is arguing that his own history is more
accurate than Homer's proto- or pseudohistory. Even in regard to style,
Thucydides is attempting to vie with his predecessor, although he
allegedly has scorn for poets, who are naturally concerned with style.
One of the stylistic tropes of epic poets who compose in an elevated style
that willfully departs from the prosaic is called "tmesis," literally the
"cutting up" of a compound verb. So in this passage, Thucydides
criticizes Homer for his habitual adornment of the factual truth, yet he
does so by indulging in the very ornamentation that he is deriding. The
verb "excessively adorn" (*epikosmêsai*) is itself ornamentally cut up in a
poetic tmesis: ***epi** to meizon men poiêtên onta **kosmêsai*** (being a poet, he
greatly embellished [the truth]). And that sense of competition, of the
compulsive need to express his own superiority to Homer, is heightened
as he concludes the reference to Homer with a comparative. Even if
Homer did exaggerate and greatly embellish the size of the Greek fleet,
Thucydides' own age has got the old poet beat nonetheless. For the size
of the Greek forces was still sadly lacking (*endeestera*, the comparative
of *endees*) in comparison with those of modern-day Hellas.

As Simon Hornblower remarks, "Thucydides' polemic" in the
opening pages of his work "is harsh and bad-tempered."[38] Hornblower
then somewhat qualifies his critique of Thucydides' bad manners by
commenting, "but that was a usual feature of intellectual debate at this
time." Later in this chapter, when we discuss the Melian dialogue, we

shall return to the issue of the bad manners of the intellectual debaters of Thucydides' time, but let us now return to our discussion of Thucydides' attitudes toward tradition and his predecessors as expressed in the "Archeology." We have been looking at Thucydides' bad-tempered criticisms of Homer for his alleged imprecisions as a historian. The final reference to Homer in the "Archeology" is similarly bad-tempered and, to make matters worse, Thucydides now tosses his great predecessor Herodotus, as well, on the trash-heap of history.

As Thucydides approaches the concluding section of the opening of his work, he writes:

> Still, from the evidence [*tekmêriôn*] that has been given, anyone would not err [*ouch' harmatanoi*] who should hold the view that the state of affairs in antiquity was very nearly such as I have described it, not giving greater credence to the accounts, on the one hand, which the poets [*poiêtaí*] have put into song, adorning and amplifying [*epi to meizon kosmountes*] their theme, and, on the other, which the chroniclers [*logographoi*] have composed with a view rather of pleasing the ear than of telling the truth [*alêthesteron*], since their stories cannot be tested and most of them have from lapse of time won their way into the region of the fabulous [*to mythôdes*] so as to be incredible. He should regard the facts as having been made out with sufficient accuracy, on the basis of the clearest indications, considering that they have to do with early times. And so, even though men are always inclined, while they are engaged in a war, to judge the present one the greatest [*megiston*], but when it is over to regard ancient events with greater wonder, yet this war will prove, for men who judge from the actual facts [*ap' autôn tôn ergôn skopousi*], to have been much greater [*meizôn*] than any that had preceded it. ... And it may well be that the absence of the fabulous [*mythôdês*] from my narrative will seem less pleasing to the ear; but whoever shall wish to have a clear view [*to saphes skopein*] both of the events which have happened and of those events which will some day, in all human probability, happen again in the same or a similar way – for those to adjudge my history profitable will be enough for me. And, indeed, it has been composed, not as a prize essay to be heard for the moment, but as a possession for all time [*ktêma es aiei*]. (I.21–2)

This is a magnificent passage, to be rivaled in egoism in the Western tradition perhaps only by Milton in the seventeenth century and Hegel in the nineteenth. The Thucydidean passage is magnificent for its expression of reserved assurance of the author's own greatness, an assurance that borders on arrogance and that yet courts modesty as well. Thucydides modestly says that it will be enough for him if his work proves to be of help (*ôpheilma*) in the future, but he appears to have no doubt that what he has written is a "possession for all time." He shows

99

the good taste and reserve not to mention Herodotus by name. It is clear, however, that Herodotus is meant to be prominently included among the "chroniclers" (*logographoi*) whom Thucydides lumps in with the poets as examples of those who mutually indulge in myth and fancy rather than in truth. Thucydides makes sure to remark on the absence of the fabulous (*to mê mythôdes*, I.22.4) in his own history, a marked contrast, as A. W. Gomme observes, to the storytelling element "so common in Herodotos in his account of both earlier and later times."[39]

Before we move on to discuss the structure of the works of Thucydides and Sima Qian, it is worth making one more observation about the contrasts between their attitudes to tradition and the past. Simon Hornblower has noted the "harsh and bad-tempered" nature of Thucydides' polemic, in the "Archeology," against the alleged incompetence of his literary predecessors. Hornblower viewed that attitude as typical of the intellectual debate of his day. We concur with Hornblower's judgment. In fact, we might go so far as to say that Thucydides' extremely agonistic, indeed antagonistic, attitude toward his predecessors is an early instance of what Harold Bloom calls "the anxiety of influence."[40]

Thucydides and Sima Qian, we have been suggesting, perceive and portray their predecessors in very different ways. Sima Qian, in his postface to *Records of the Historian*, presents himself as someone who is working within a family tradition of historical writing, a tradition transmitted and reinforced by his father. Moreover, he describes Confucius as the "ultimate sage" and accepts the tradition that Confucius was the model historian who wrote the definitive history, *Spring and Autumn Annals*. However much Sima Qian "creates," he presents himself, just as Confucius presented himself four centuries before, as one who "transmits" the records and learning of the past. Plainly, Sima Qian sees himself as a filial son, an admirer of tradition, and a loyal follower of Confucius.

Thucydides, far from being overwhelmed by respect for the past, regards his predecessors Homer and Herodotus and their respective poetic and historiographic traditions as largely useless. His conclusions, he assures us, "will not be disturbed either by the lays of a poet [i.e. Homer] displaying the exaggeration of his craft, or by the compositions of chroniclers [e.g. Herodotus] that are attractive at truth's expense" (I.21). The accuracy of his report, unlike those of the writers who preceded him, has been "always tried by the most severe and detailed tests possible" (I.22). Thucydides breaks with the past and inaugurates a new tradition, one that attempts to adhere to an honest, objective scrutiny of facts.

2 The structures of written history

Records of the Historian

The structure of Thucydides' *The Peloponnesian War* and Sima Qian's *Records of the Historian* could hardly be more different. Except for a very short preface in which he quickly surveys the history of Hellas, Thucydides' history covers twenty-five years (435–411 BCE) and centers, for the most part, upon a single event: the protracted conflict between the Athenians and Spartans, a conflict that he had personally witnessed. Moreover, unlike the work of his forerunner, Herodotus, Thucydides' account is highly circumscribed in space, confined entirely to the boundaries of the Hellenic world. These temporal and spatial limitations enable Thucydides, with his powerful analytical skills, to examine the conflict in great detail and to present it as a single, chronological narrative.

Unlike Thucydides' history, Sima Qian's *Records of the Historian* is a comprehensive history that covers over two thousand years and deals with the entire world as the Han historian knew it. Furthermore, Sima Qian's history has a rather complex and, some would say, fragmented arrangement. The 130 chapters of *Records of the Historian* are divided into five sections:

1. "Basic Annals" (*ben ji*), twelve chapters which typically contain dated entries and describe events of major importance to the kings and emperors of the past;
2. "Tables" (*biao*), ten chapters which arrange the major events of the past on chronological tables and enable one conveniently to survey temporal relations and patterns;
3. "Treatises" (*shu*), eight chapters dealing with the history of major institutions such as ritual, music, the pitch-pipes and calendar, and the imperial *feng* and *shan* sacrifices;
4. "Hereditary Households" (*shi jia*), thirty chapters which provide information on powerful families, often enfeoffed with titles and territories, who played a significant role in the history of the past;
5. "Memoirs" (*lie zhuan*, sometimes called "Biographies"), seventy chapters concerning important persons, groups of persons, or even whole geographical regions that deserve historical notice but are not of sufficient status to be included in sections 1 or 4.[41]

It is possible, as scholars have shown, to find antecedents for each of these five sections, but this overall structure, which is to remain, with minor modifications, the structure of subsequent Chinese official dynastic history, is one of Sima Qian's great inventions. Despite his characterization of himself as one who transmits and does not create, he is indeed the creator of a new historical form. But what is particularly interesting in Sima Qian's case, and what has been too often overlooked, is the great likelihood that the organization of his text, and even the number of chapters found in each section, has special significance when viewed within a larger world of political and cosmological meaning. The order of the five sections, for instance, re-creates the political hierarchy of early Chinese society. *Records of the Historian* begins with three sections that focus attention primarily upon the imperial government and its institutions. It then goes on to a consideration of "hereditary households," which, in the words of Sima Qian, "assisted their lords and rulers like arms and legs." The final and largest section details the lives of those who "made a name for themselves" but were neither rulers nor a part of the most powerful feudal families. In other words, Sima Qian begins with the most powerful group and proceeds down to those whose political importance depends not so much upon rank as upon deeds.[42]

As we have noted above, such an organization was entirely new, but it is possible to find antecedents that may have inspired him. Chief among these is *Spring and Autumn Annals*, which Sima Qian attributes to the Master Confucius. The latter text is arranged by chronological, dated entries for important events, as viewed from the perspective of the state of Lu, that took place during the reigns of twelve Lu dukes who reigned from 722 to 481 BCE. By the time of Sima Qian, *Spring and Autumn Annals* was regarded as a "classic" (*jing* – which literally means "the warp" of woven thread) and was always read along with at least one of its three canonical commentaries, the *Zuo*, *Gongyang*, or *Guliang*. These three commentaries were called "*zhuan*," which literally means "what has been handed down" or "traditions." The commentaries filled out the context and meaning of the terse entries in *Spring and Autumn Annals* and were regarded as essential companions to this classic. The first section of Sima's work, the "Basic Annals," contains twelve chapters, an arrangement which is almost certainly modeled on the twelve dukes of Confucius's *Spring and Autumn Annals*. Moreover, the final and longest section of *Records of the Historian*, the seventy "Memoirs," is entitled in Chinese "*lie zhuan*," which literally means "Arrayed Traditions" and certainly alludes to the commentaries or "traditions" that were attached to *Spring and Autumn Annals*. That is, the last and largest section of *Records of the Historian* expands the outline provided in the "Basic Annals," much as the commentarial traditions to *Spring and Autumn Annals* contextualize and elucidate the cryptic entries in that text.

In addition to his use of such literary traditions, it is also probable that Sima Qian, who was a calendricist as well as a historian, used certain cosmological categories in the arrangement of his text. The early Han was a time when five-phase (*wu xing*) cosmology was very much in vogue, and all kinds of phenomena were being categorized in accord with a sacred scheme of "fives."[43] Furthermore, as several very early commentators have suggested, the twelve "Basic Annals" correspond not only to the twelve dukes of *Spring and Autumn Annals* but also to the twelve lunar months as well as the twelve stations of the Jupiter (*sui xing*) cycle, a cycle of the greatest importance in ancient Chinese astronomy.[44] The ten charts find a calendrical equivalent in the ten days of the traditional Chinese *xun* or week; the eight "Treatises" correspond to the eight sections of the seasons; the thirty "Hereditary Households" are the equivalent of the thirty days of "a great month," and the number seventy might be "rounded off" from the number seventy-two, which is one-fifth of a year and hence important in five-phase cosmology.[45] We would note, going even beyond this earlier speculation, that the first two sections of *Records* have twelve and ten chapters respectively, which are also the numbers of the "terrestrial branches" and "heavenly stems" that form the basis of the ancient Chinese system for noting days. These "branches" and "stems" of traditional Chinese calendrical science are lined up in a way that generates a sixty-day cycle of days with different names (the so-called "sexagenary cycle"),[46] precisely the number of chapters in the first four sections of *Records of the Historian*. Such an analysis would lead us to postulate that Sima's text has two great divisions, the first four sections forming a division that centers primarily on the central government and their "arms and legs" (the hereditary households), and the last division made up of the "Memoirs."

What all this implies is that Sima Qian did not, as some have argued, simply write one chapter after another in a random fashion until he finally ran out of material or energy.[47] He had an important overall scheme, and that scheme consisted of looking not just to the past, but to the patterns of the cosmos as well. One of his purposes for compiling his history was, in Sima Qian's own words, "to examine the interplay between heaven and man,"[48] and this interplay is reflected in the organization of his text as well as in the contents of particular episodes.[49] This was hardly Thucydides' intention; it is difficult to see where "Heaven" fits into his scheme – apart from the occasional earthquake or eclipse that flatters the Greek historian's conception of the unparalleled importance of the Athenian–Spartan conflict that is the subject of his work.

In summary, we see in the structure of *Records of the Historian* not only the intentionalism that is a part of the creation of any new historical form but a profound participationalism as well. Sima Qian organizes his grand account around the categories and numerology that were a part of the social and cosmological thought of his time. His creation of a new historical form is very much delimited and inspired by his own participation in a *dao* that extends through the political and social structures of his own time to the very structures of the cosmos in which he himself participates.

When we use Sima Qian's text as a guide to the history of ancient China, the organization discussed above presents a problem. While Thucydides' history unfolds as a single chronological narrative, Sima Qian's text is fragmented, with critical material concerning a single figure or a single episode sometimes appearing in a number of different places in the text. China's greatest scholar of historiography, Liu Zhiji (661–721), criticized Sima Qian on precisely this account: "Those who read *Records of the Historian* are made to feel that events are few but there are different accounts of those events, and that words are many and with considerable repetition. This is an annoying aspect of its composition."[50]

However, Sima Qian seems to have believed that there is no single story to be told. Instead, stories are determined by an institutional perspective or by a particular theme that is emphasized in some immediate context. Thus, we might find an event recorded in a "Basic Annals" chapter in a way that stresses the significance of the event for the imperial household. The same event might then recur in a "Hereditary Household" chapter with the focus shifted to the context of some feudal state, and then again in a "Memoir", where a particular participant's role in the event is explored in a way that characterizes his personality or social type. One can, of course, put these accounts side by side, but then contradictions or, at least, variations appear that are not always easy to resolve. Although this Rashomon-like quality of *Records of the Historian* might frustrate those of us who have come to the text fresh from Thucydides, perhaps this fragmentation of the historical text is part of a larger cultural pattern that we should explore.

Approximately twenty-five years ago, the Czechoslovakian sinologist Jaroslav Prusek published an article entitled "History and Epics in China and in the West" in which he contrasted the early Greek historians, whose narration "flows as powerful streams," particularly Thucydides' "great drama of struggle," with a Chinese historiography, typified most notably by Sima Qian, "where the author was aiming at the systematic classification of the material and not the creation of a continuous whole."[51] The Greek historian, Prusek believes, wants to formulate a certain theme or tell a certain story, which means that he must fashion a unified structure. The Chinese historian, by contrast, is

104

an arranger or transmitter who links rough material together to evoke certain impressions. What is of particular interest to our project is that Prusek links these contrary historiographic styles to the dominant literary form that preceded each. Herodotus and Thucydides, Prusek suggests, are influenced by the epic and Sima Qian by the lyric:

> In Greece historiography imitates the epic mode of expression; in China the categorization and systematization of facts by free linking of rough materials reminds one of lyric methods. Early Chinese historiography is interested in action to a very limited extent. The main attention is centered on philosophical, political and moral discussions.[52]

Prusek goes on to note that in early Greek writing attention is centered upon the individual, upon "the specific and unrepeatable," whereas in China the historian was concerned with "the general, the norm, the principle, the law." In other words, the attention of the Chinese historian was turned to a political or moral world against which his text had to be justified. We might say that Sima Qian's history comes *after* philosophy and is formulated in a time when Confucianism is gaining the ascendancy in China. *Records of the Historian* is profoundly influenced, even constrained, by the principles and norms of that school of thought.

While Prusek's argument is a powerful one that captures and explains something of the difference in these two historiographical traditions, the contrast between the two traditions may not be quite as stark as he would have it. For all the "fragmentation" of his text, Sima Qian pursues certain themes, and these do not seem always to be mere political or moral propaganda. Moreover, the individual, "the specific act," does not always disappear in his text into some larger fabric of principles and norms.

In a famous letter that Sima Qian once wrote to an acquaintance, an official by the name of Ren An, he explains that he wrote *Records of the Historian* "to examine the boundary between heaven and man, to penetrate the transformations of ancient and modern times, and to form the words of a single school."[53] One modern Chinese scholar has said that this passage is made up of "three golden phrases" which provide a key to understanding Sima Qian's history.[54] This may be overly optimistic. One should not seek in Sima Qian's "single school," if he was successful in creating such a school, an unambiguous set of principles or even a clear and intentional ideology. What our Chinese historian has provided, instead, is a set of concerns or interests, much more than historical laws or principles.

In his "golden phrases," Sima Qian declares an interest in the "transformations" of time, which he would like to "penetrate." The

Chinese word *tong*, translated here as "penetrate," implies finding that which persists and communicates through transformation as well as comprehending the transformations themselves. What provides a continuous thread in Sima Qian's complex and seemingly fragmented history and thereby takes on an importance sometimes overlooked is the imperial succession, which extends all the way from the Yellow Emperor to the Han Emperor Wu, a period of well over two thousand years. Even though the Yellow Emperor lived so long ago, and his very identity is shrouded in mystery and controversy, Sima Qian's history begins with him, and *all* subsequent rulers are linked genealogically to this great patriarch and source of political power. Thus, the "Basic Annals" and the "Tables" constitute a core of the text in that they provide a chronological, imperial framework to which all other events and figures may be linked.[55]

Much has been said, particularly in the People's Republic, about Sima Qian as a historian of the "common people." While Sima Qian's attention may have been drawn to segments of society beyond the imperial and feudal courts of ancient China, *Records of the Historian* is very much a history that takes the imperial institution as its core. Sima Qian lived in a time when Han power was being further consolidated, and although he may have harbored reservations about the policies of his contemporary Emperor, his history has played a political role in creating a notion of a unified, imperial China.[56]

The strongly political slant of Sima Qian's text should not surprise us since he was, after all, a participant in Han government. His father had served the state as "Grand Prefect Historian" and Sima Qian had succeeded to this position. *Records of the Historian*, as so many have noted, may not have been an official history in the sense of later, court-commissioned accounts, but it was very much ensconced in a world where power flowed from a single source, the state. G. E. R. Lloyd has noted this characteristic of early Chinese civilization in general: "All the Chinese debate presupposed the existing framework of monarchic government: indeed the ideals remained those of a government with total control and of a single political orthodoxy."[57] Such a framework provides the core of *Records of the Historian* and gives it a greater unity of political perspective than, certainly, Herodotus or even, perhaps, Thucydides.

If a unified political structure deriving from the Yellow Emperor is the constant that permeates the changing face of history, what does that change comprise? There are at least three different theories of historical cycles that are mentioned in *Records of the Historian*: first, a theory of five-hundred-year cycles, with a sage appearing at the end of each to summarize and transmit all that has preceded; second, a theory that three dynasties always follow one another with a predictable series of strong qualities and weaknesses, a pattern that will then be repeated by a subsequent three dynasties; and third, the standard theory of the five phases (or "five elements," as it is sometimes called) that are attached to dynasties and follow one another in a constant order. As certain Chinese scholars have noted, however, none of these theories is applied by Sima Qian with any consistency to the course of Chinese history. Instead, the historian utilizes each of these theories to deal with some specific issue and then places them aside. In other words, Sima Qian does not seem to be a devotee of any particular theory of cyclic change, however much appeal such theories might have had on an *ad hoc* basis.

Insofar as Sima Qian sets forth a notion of change in history that finds ample resonance throughout his text, it is in a comment that he attaches to a treatise on economics: "A thing flourishes and declines, a time reaches an extreme and then reverses, substance [*zhi*] alternates with refinement [*wen*]; these are the transformations of time" (30.1442). According to this yin–yang model of historical change, whenever any movement reaches its moment of greatest intensity, it readily reverts to its opposite. The extremes of his own time must have deeply disconcerted Sima Qian. *Records of the Historian* may indeed be a general history, but ultimately Sima Qian, as we might expect, appears to be much more deeply interested in understanding the most recent one hundred years or so than he is in all the history that preceded this relatively brief period of time. He is a servant of the Han, and the focus of his history is the Han. Indeed, it might not be much of an exaggeration to say that the bulk of his historical text is almost as contemporary as that of Thucydides.

Many have commented upon the way Sima Qian's history thickens as it draws near to his own time. This is seen most readily in the "Basic Annals" and "Tables," which we have argued is the backbone of the text. Half of the "Basic Annals" and six out of ten of the "Tables" deal with the hundred years before Sima Qian's birth – a very short time period compared with the two thousand years covered by the history. There is, of course, a logical explanation for this: the closer the historian draws to his own time, the more material he has. Sima Qian's preference for *modern* history, however, is stated quite plainly in one of the most interesting and perplexing passages in *Records of the Historian*. In the preface to the "Table of the Hereditary Ministers and Princes of the High Ancestor" (ch. 18), Sima Qian says the following:

If one dwells in the present age and scrutinizes the ways of antiquity, it is a means to regard oneself in a mirror, but they [that is, the present age and antiquity] will not be entirely the same. Each emperor and king has different rituals and diverse emphases but wants to use his success as a general principle. How can they be so confused? If one examines the reasons for obtaining honor and favor or the reasons for rejection and insult, there is, after all, a forest of successes and failures in one's own age. (18.878)

In this passage, Sima Qian, who has provided a definitive account of the events of Chinese high antiquity, proclaims the greater relevance of modern history, a preference that had been enunciated in somewhat different terms a century earlier by the great Confucian philosopher Xunzi.[58] Sima Qian's point here seems to be that since the times change, there is no constant formula for successful rule or successful service. There are plenty of models for both success and failure that one can find in one's own time, and one is wisest to make use of these.

As his history draws nearer to his own era, Sima Qian becomes more personally implicated. One of the reasons for this is that no previous authoritative account exists for the period extending from the Qin down to the reign of Emperor Wu. There is abundant documentation, to be sure, but this has not yet been shaped into a history, like *Zuo Commentary*, that Sima Qian can simply transmit, with minor adjustments or alterations. Of necessity, he becomes more of a creator, however much he may appear to disown that term. But beyond this, Sima Qian and his father served the Han court as scribes and astrologers and suffered considerably at the hands of their ruler. Sima Qian may see himself as a participant in a great tradition, one who simply allows the past to flow through him into the shape that is his text, but he is also writing with a purpose that is forged in the tempest of his own political and personal entanglements. He has a particularly strong personal investment in the history of his own time, at least, and that investment profoundly shapes his work.

In determining the nature of this investment and how it affected the structure of his history, we must consider the supreme trauma of Sima Qian's life: his involvement in the Li Ling affair in 99 BCE. Li Ling was a young general descended from a military family. In 99 BCE he led an army of five thousand soldiers deep into Xiongnu territory. His army was attacked by a vastly larger enemy force, and he was captured alive. Exactly what happened at the Han court in response to this defeat is not entirely clear. Sima Qian, we know, spoke out in support of Li Ling, and his support of a now disgraced general for some reason infuriated Emperor Wu. As a result, Emperor Wu turned his Grand Historian over to legal officials, who convicted him of "defaming the Emperor." He was sentenced to death. Even a sentence of this seriousness could be commuted upon payment of a sum of money, but no one came forth to redeem the condemned historian. Through some process, perhaps by reason of a plea from Sima Qian himself, the punishment was reduced one grade to castration. A man of nobility was expected to commit suicide rather than undergo such a humiliation. Sima Qian, however, submitted to castration in the notorious "silkworm hall," where such mutilating punishments took place.

Approximately six years later, when Sima Qian had already been politically rehabilitated and occupied the highest government position reserved for a eunuch, he wrote a letter to an acquaintance, Ren An, explaining the psychological and physical torment he had undergone and justifying his decision to remain alive rather than "settle the matter with his own hands by committing suicide." This "Letter to Ren An" is one of the most treasured and moving pieces in the Chinese literary canon.[59] What is important for our discussion here is to note briefly the reason Sima Qian says he rejected suicide, which was surely the action expected of him, and the connection Sima Qian asserts between personal suffering, especially mutilation, and literary power.

After detailing his unhappy experience with the law and mentioning those in the past who had faced the fear and humiliation of punishment, Sima Qian speaks of his comprehensive history of China and explains to Ren An why he decided to remain alive: "The draft version was not yet completed, so I submitted to the most extreme punishment without showing ire" (*Han shu* 62.3735). Sima Qian stayed alive because he had not completed his work, and, we remember, he had promised his father ten years earlier that he "would not be remiss" in finishing the huge history his father had passed on to him.

If castration meant that Sima Qian would lose his physical procreative power and be denied forever the son he did not yet have, it was an act that empowered his writing brush. In both the "Letter to Ren An" and the postface, Sima Qian links creative productivity to personal frustration and, in some cases, punishment and even mutilation:

> King Wen of Zhou, the Earl of the West, was in captivity at Youli and elaborated the *Classic of Changes*; Confucius was in difficult straits and wrote the *Spring and Autumn Annals of Lu*; Qu Yuan was banished, and only then composed the "Encountering Sorrow"; Zuo Qiuming lost his sight, and he wrote *Discourses of the States*; Sunzi had his feet amputated, and then his *Techniques of War* was produced; Lü Buwei was banished to Shu, from which has been preserved the *Overviews of Lü*; Hanfei was imprisoned in Qin and wrote "The Difficulties of Persuasion" and "The Sorrow of Standing Alone." The three hundred *Poems* were for the most part written as the expression of the outrage of good men and sages. All

of these men had rancor in their hearts; they could not carry through their ideas of the Way, so they gave an account of the past while thinking of those to come. (*Han shu* 62.3735, cf. *SJ* 130.3300).

Sima Qian's literary brilliance, this passage certainly implies, emerges out of his own sense of frustration and from an intense hope that "those to come" might yet appreciate him. There is, in this view, a personal tragedy behind every great work of literature.

The tragic structure of Thucydides' report

Thucydides in effect created his subject, for at the time he began writing, the Peloponnesian War did not exist as a discrete phenomenon. There was known to have been a Ten Years (or Archidamian) War (431–421) and a Decelean or Ionian War (414–404), and then there was the great and disastrous expedition to Sicily (415–413), which had a tangential relation to the conflict between Athens and Sparta. Thucydides himself, then, can be credited with having created the unit we now call "the Peloponnesian War."

While his subject was the Peloponnesian War, which he created as a single unit, that unit is not finished. The narrative breaks off rather abruptly in the middle of the year 411, some six years short of Athens' final defeat at Aegospotami in 405, marking the clear end of an era. While Thucydides did not finish his work, it does have a clear structure that we can call tragic. Thucydides' debt to Greek tragedy has been a question of scholarly debate. Colin Macleod, for example, believes that Thucydides' debt is perhaps greater to epic than to tragedy.[60] We shall argue, however, that Thucydides' history does indeed have a tragic structure, that his history is heir to the great Hellenic tragic tradition, with a flawed Athens as tragic protagonist. There are tragic elements and tragic episodes in Sima Qian's *Records of the Historian*, such as the famous deaths of Xiang Yu and of General Li, but we cannot say that Sima's work has an overall tragic structure, as does Thucydides' history. In a later section of this chapter, we shall discuss the ways in which this structure is even more tragic than the great historian himself saw.

As Simon Hornblower so often reminds us in his important book on Thucydides, Thucydides did not himself use the word "history" to describe the genre of his work. He was not aware of the fact that he was writing "history." It was Aristotle who later introduced the distinction between history and poetry in Chapter 9 of the *Poetics*. The historian's allegiance is to the particular, the poet's to the universal. The historian relates what *has* happened, the poet represents a probable instance of what *might* happen. Thucydides certainly wanted to report on what actually happened in the conflict between Athens and Sparta, but like a poet he often had to content himself with presenting a probable rather than an unquestionably accurate account. He has attempted, he tells us, to report the events with the greatest accuracy (*akribeia*), but when it comes to the speeches, he must relax his empirical standards. Thus, "the speeches are given in the language in which, as it seemed to me, the several speakers would express, on the subjects under consideration, the sentiments most befitting [*ta deonta*] the occasion, though at the same time I have adhered as closely as possible to the general sense" [*tês xympasês gnômês*, I.22]. When it comes to the speeches, in other words, the historian's quest for the certain must give way to the poet's decorum of the probable.

But not to just any poet's decorum of the probable. The magnitude of the events narrated, the flawed attractiveness of his work's central protagonist, and the certain catastrophe toward which its Athenian author knows that the events are leading all suggest the profound influence of that Athenian genre *par excellence*, tragedy. Thucydides must himself have attended tragic performances at Athens. Athenian culture was imbued with the experience of tragedy. Thucydides' history has a tragic feel and a tragic structure. Once again, it is to the pithy Aristotle that we should turn for our definitions of literary terms.[61]

In his famous formulation in Chapter 6 of the *Poetics*, Aristotle says that tragedy "is an imitation of a serious and comprehensive plot that is weighty and great." Tragedy evokes emotions such as "pity" (*eleos*) and "fear" (*phobos*) in the audience. In Chapter 9 he goes on to say that this *katharsis* of emotions such as pity and fear is best produced by events which appear to be surprising but are in fact the result of cause and effect, for then the sense of tragic wonder will be greater than if they happened simply by accident. The best kind of plot, he elaborates in the next chapter, is the complex rather than the simple one, for the complex plot involves a reversal (*peripeteia*) of the situation and a recognition (*anagnôrisis*) on the part of the protagonist of what has in fact transpired contrary to his expectations and wishes.

In Chapter 13, Aristotle says that the best plot should have as its protagonist a character who is neither totally virtuous nor villainous but rather one who is between (*metaxy*) these extremes. Why? Because what we want in tragedy is a *katharsis* of emotions such as pity and fear; we only pity those whose misfortune is to some degree unmerited, and our fears are best aroused when we witness the misfortunes of someone like ourselves. Hence, the best kind of tragic protagonist should be someone with whom the audience can identify, someone like them. The best kind of tragic protagonist is the person who is not preeminently just and

111

virtuous (*mête aretêi diapherôn kai dikaiosynêi*), on the one hand; nor does his downfall result, on the other hand, from an evil and depraved moral character. His descent into misfortune results rather from some mistake in judgment (*hamartia*). He must be someone who has a lofty reputation (*megalê doxê*) and apparent good luck (*eutychia*), somebody like Oedipus.

Or like Athens in Thucydides' work. As we shall argue in section II.4, King Oedipus can be taken as representing the rationalist mind of Athens of the fifth century BCE. Oedipus is Athens, Athens is Oedipus. If Oedipus is the tragic figure *par excellence*, then so is the Athens which he symbolizes. We shall soon return to the importance of this correspondence between Athens and Oedipus, but for now we shall simply state that the tragic protagonist of Thucydides' work is Athens itself. Now clearly Thucydides' work does not correspond in every detail to what Aristotle meant by tragedy. On the most obvious level, Thucydides' "history" is a narrative and not a drama. There is no chorus. It was not performed at the theater of Dionysus at the foot of the Akropolis. But Thucydides the Athenian was the inheritor of the great tragic tradition of his city. The style has the severity and weight of tragedy.[62] And the central plot, while containing many detailed episodes included by the historian in his attempt to be as comprehensive as possible, has the characteristics of tragedy, including tragic mistake (*hamartia*), reversal (*peripeteia*), and recognition (*anagnôrisis*).

Let us consider, first, the notion that tragedy represents the fall of a basically noble but flawed personality. We certainly have this in the Athenian character as portrayed, at the beginning of the work, by the Corinthian envoy to the Peloponnesian confederacy at Sparta. There he contrasts the characters of the war's antagonists, the Athenians and the Spartans. The Spartans are seen as slow, conservative, always tending toward procrastination. The Athenians, on the other hand,

> are addicted to innovation [*neôteropoioi*], and their designs are characterized by swiftness in conception and execution [*epinoêsai oxeis*]. ... They are daring [*tolmêtai*] beyond their power, bold beyond their judgment, and hopeful [*euelpides*] amid dangers. ... A scheme unexecuted is with them a positive loss, a successful enterprise a comparative failure. The deficiency created by the miscarriage of an undertaking is soon filled up with fresh hopes; for they alone are enabled to call a thing hoped for a thing got, by the speed with which they act upon their resolutions. Thus they toil on in trouble and danger, all the days of their lives, with little opportunity of enjoying, being ever engaged in getting: their only idea of a holiday is to do what the occasion demands, and to them laborious occupation is less a misfortune than the peace of a quiet life. To describe

their character in a word, one might truly say that they were born into the world to take no rest themselves and to give none to others. (I.70)

Here we have the *locus classicus* description of the Athenian character.

This Athenian character was, for Thucydides, best embodied in and cultivated by Perikles. In the famous funeral oration he gave in the first year of the war, Perikles, like the Corinthian envoy, praised Athenian innovation in contrast to Spartan conservatism. It was thought that the Spartans had modeled their institutions on those of Crete. The Athenians, according to Perikles, will engage in no such derivative endeavors: "Our constitution does not emulate the laws of our neighbors; we are rather a model [*paradeigma*] to some than imitators [*mimoumenoi*] of others" (II.37). The Athenians were successful so long as they followed the moderate imperial policy of Perikles (II.65). But Perikles died of the plague that Thucydides so brilliantly and vividly describes (II.48ff.), and the erratic, self-serving, and irresponsible Alcibiades rose to prominence. If Perikles represented the best of Athens, Alcibiades embodied the new Athens that would be led and ultimately destroyed by those who were motivated primarily by private ambition (*idias philotimias*) and private greed (*idia kerdê*, II.65.7). Perikles had kept the hubris of the Athenians in check by evoking in them, like a good tragedian, the emotion of fear (*to phobeisthai*, II.65.9). The Athenians were successful, according to Thucydides, so long as they followed the imperial policy of Perikles [II.65] and did not try to extend their empire beyond what was deemed necessary.

The *hamartia* or tragic mistake made by the Athenians was to follow the immoderate policy of Alcibiades and launch the disastrous expedition to far-off Sicily. The tragic nature of the blunder is conveyed by the very verb, cognate with the noun *hamartia*, that Thucydides uses to describe the blunder: the Sicilian expedition, Thucydides says, *hêmartêthê* ("erred," "was in error," "was mistaken," II.65.11) "in respect to many other things." In his commentary (1: p. 347), Hornblower translates the phrase *alla te polla ... hêmartêthê* as "led to many errors."[63]

Thucydides shows us the *hamartia* in formation, as Alcibiades seduces the Athenians into going through with the expedition. The Athenian addiction to innovation evolved, in the words of the prudent and balanced general Nikias, into "that mad passion [*dyserôtas*] to possess that which is out of reach" [VI.13]. Alcibiades, the manipulative intentionalist *par excellence*, derides the "do-nothing" [*apragmosynê*] attitude of Nikias. Stirred by the rhetoric of Alcibiades, the Athenians are almost helplessly seized "by a yearning [*pothôi*, VI.24] for far-off spectacles and sights." Thucydides himself seems almost taken in by the exotic appeal of Sicily, occupying as it did a prominent place on the Western frontier of the ancient Mediterranean world. At one point, the historian mentions the difficulty that the Athenian fleet would have in negotiating the narrow strait where Sicily is nearest the mainland. This, he says, is "the so-called [*klêstheisa*] Charybdis, where Odysseus is said to have sailed [*legetai diapleusai*, IV.24.4]." Thucydides, as we have seen, very often criticizes Homer for his inadequacies as a historian. Here the Homeric reference does not have quite the condescension of the previous allusions. It rather serves to build narrative suspense as we move toward the tragic denouement.

With a deep sense of tragic foreboding, Thucydides describes the Athenian display of splendorous pomp as the soldiers, cheered on by the Athenians and their allies who had come down (*katabantes*, VI.30.2) from the city of Athens at dawn, prepare to depart from the port of the Piraeus. As we shall discuss further in Part III below, Plato will open the *Republic* with the phrase *katebên*, an allusion to the famous *katabasis* – the voyage to the underworld – of Odysseus in Book XI of the *Odyssey*. Odysseus must face the darkness of death before he can resume his journey home. Socrates travels down from the city to the commercial and military port of Athens, the Piraeus, in order to confront and to help cure the disorder in the souls of the young who witnessed the demise of Athens through the years of the Peloponnesian Wars.

How conscious was Thucydides' evoking, in the phrase *katabantes*, of the weighty language of Homer? For now it will be sufficient to observe that the Thucydidean depiction of the procession down to the Piraeus has all the trappings of a tragic scene of the pride that precedes a fall. The size and appearance of the departing ships was simply "incredible" (*apiston*), Thucydides reports. The historian continues:

> This armament that first sailed out was by far the most costly and splendid Hellenic force that had ever been sent out by a single city up to that time.... Indeed, the expedition became not less famous for its wonderful boldness and for the splendor of its appearance than for its overwhelming strength as compared with the peoples against whom it was directed, and for the fact that it was the longest [*megistos*] passage from home hitherto attempted and undertaken with the greatest [*megistê*] hopes for the future. (VI.32)

One thinks here of Agamemnon, at the beginning of Aeschylus' play, ominously striding along the magnificent purple carpet prepared for him by his wife Klytaimnestra, who is about to murder him.

The scene for tragedy, then, is perfectly set. Thucydides presents us with a tragic protagonist, the city of Athens. Athens has an attractive, winning personality, but her very positive traits of a self-confident, innovative, and imaginative exuberance can turn sour under the wrong leadership. Athens' *hamartia* is exemplified by the decision to invade far-off Sicily, where, ironically, she will battle against a democracy very similar to her own. The great tragedy of the age has thus been set into motion. All that remains is the catastrophe itself preceded by a reversal (*peripeteia*) – a stark turning around of events – and a recognition (*anagnôrisis*).

The catastrophe comes in due course. In the nineteenth year of the war, the Athenian ships, having invaded Sicily, now charge the harbor in Syracuse in order to try to crush the enemy. A great sea battle rages and the famous Athenian navy, upon which Athens' imperial dominance of Hellas had been built, is badly beaten, throwing the Athenian troops into a panic. The Athenians, who are not known for their infantry, must now retreat by land. The Syracusan general and statesman, Hermokrates, concerned that the Athenians might now escape, sends a messenger who deceives the Athenians by warning them that the roads are guarded by the enemy. The deception succeeds. The famously wily Athenians, true children of Odysseus, are thus ironically defeated by the guile of the Syracusans.

The reversals and paradoxes continue, as Thucydides describes the thoroughly demoralized Athenian troops who are trapped by the Syracusan army:

It was a lamentable [*deinon*] scene, not merely from the single circumstance that they were retreating after having lost all their ships and, in place of their great hopes [*megalês elpidos*], they themselves in a state of peril; but also in leaving the camp there were things most grievous [*algeina*] both to sight and mind. The corpses were still unburied, and whenever a man saw one of his own friends lying dead, he was plunged into grief [*lypên*] along with fear [*meta phobou*]; and the living who were being left behind, wounded or sick, were to the living far more piteous [*lypêroteroi*] and more wretched than those who had perished. ... Their disgrace generally, and the universality of their sufferings, though to a certain extent alleviated by being borne in company, were still felt at the moment as a heavy burden, especially when one considered from what splendor and boastfulness at first to what a humiliating end they had now come. For this was by far the greatest reversal [*megiston ... diaphoran*] that had ever befallen a Hellenic army. They had come to enslave others, and were departing in fear of being enslaved themselves: they had sailed out with prayer and paeans, and now started to go back with imprecations quite the reverse of these, traveling by land instead of by sea, and trusting not in their fleet but in their heavy infantry. (VII.75)

We are, it is true, only in the nineteenth year of a twenty-seven-year war as we read this passage. As W. Robert Connor has written, "there is much more, and much worse, to come."[64] But we are, at this point, very close to the end of Book VII, with only one more book to go – and that one unfinished and, in many scholars' judgments, rather unsatisfactory in terms of narrative energy and force of presentation when compared to what has preceded it.

With this passage in Book VII, the tragic fate of Athens has been sealed. We are struck with tragic wonder as we read this passage, and this astonishment, as Aristotle will suggest, is the result of cause and effect, making it all the more terrible to accept, since Athens has dug its own grave. The passage abounds with words expressing fear (*phobou*), pity (*lypêroteroi*), and lamentation (*deinon, algeina, lypên*), in the best tragic style. We are presented with a stunning reversal (*megiston diaphoran*), a tragic *peripeteia* of an Athens whose famed navy had set out with the highest hopes and is leaving crushed and, ironically, dependent upon its far inferior infantry to cling to survival. Aristotle will remark that the best kind of reversal is accompanied by a recognition (*Poetics* 11.1452b). The reversal is all the more grievous and stunning in this great Thucydidean passage because it is accompanied by a recognition on the part of the Athenian soldiers of just how hopeless and horrific is their situation.

In the best Hellenic style, then, Thucydides' history has a clearly tragic structure. Thus, a single literary genre may be said to inform and unify the Greek historian's text. Sima Qian, as one who has profound respect for the textual traditions of the Chinese past, is certainly influenced by earlier literary forms, but the structure of his work cannot be explained in terms of any single literary model. Rather, it can almost be regarded as an anthology of both the textual forms and the narratives of the past. We can find, perhaps, a core to these diverse structures in the "Basic Annals," and we might also discern an overall cosmological model for the arrangement of the Chinese historian's text, but there is no single, unifying literary structure that embraces the 130 chapters. But there *is* tragedy, albeit on a level different from the tragedy we have so far discovered in Thucydides. It is the tragedy of Sima Qian himself, and the powerful frustration that emanates from this source to enliven so many of the individual narratives included in his text.

3   The tempest of participation: Sima Qian's portrayal of his own era

We claimed earlier that Sima Qian is more than a quiet transmitter of tradition. He is personally implicated in his record of the past in at least two ways: first, he reacts morally and emotionally to the events he "transmits," and he most likely intends these reactions to serve as a guide to how we, as sensitive readers, should also react; and second, he shapes *Records of the Historian*, especially those portions that concern his own era, around perspectives and prejudices that derive from his own experience, particularly his unfortunate involvement in the Li Ling affair. As we shall argue, Sima Qian's participation in his account of the past is so extensive that it is sometimes difficult to disentangle the historian from his history. Sima Qian both creates the past and is himself created through the narratives he presents.

Our claim that Sima Qian creates as well as transmits is supported by a closer examination of his well-known reference to the opposing terms *shu* ("to transmit") and *zuo* ("to make come forth, to create"). In the discussion with his fellow calendricist Hu Sui, which appears in the postface to his history, Sima Qian defends himself against the criticism that he is establishing a presumptuous parallel between his own work and Confucius' *Spring and Autumn Annals*. Sima Qian seems to disown any such comparison:

> What I am referring to is transmitting [*shu*] ancient matters and arranging traditions passed down through the ages. This is not what can be called "creating" [*zuo*]. For you, lord, to compare it to *Spring and Autumn Annals* is mistaken indeed! (130.3299–300)

But the apparent denial actually affirms the comparison. Sima Qian is alluding here to a famous passage found in *Analects* 7.1 and attributed to Confucius:

> The Master said, "I transmit [*shu*] and do not create [*zuo*]. I am faithful to and fond of antiquity. I presume to compare myself to Lao Peng."[65]

Sima Qian cleverly covers his tracks. While appearing to deny the comparison with Confucius, freeing himself of any accusation of hubris, he is actually affirming it. For our purposes, the critical point is that Sima Qian implies in his response to Hu Sui that Confucius, despite his denial, was in fact creative. In precisely the same words Confucius employed, Sima Qian says that he only transmits, which perhaps directs the reader's attention toward the creativity that he is too modest, or too cautious, to claim directly.[66]

A very interesting example of the way Sima Qian shapes and reacts to his account of the past is provided by his biographies of the distinguished poets Qu Yuan (340?–278?) and Jia Yi (200–168), which are both contained in chapter 84 of *Records of the Historian*. These poets are placed together in a single chapter for at least two reasons: first, both Qu Yuan's and Jia Yi's literary creativity is spawned by the slander of lesser men and by eventual estrangement from the centers of political power they wished to serve; and second, each of them confronts the issue of suicide but resolves this problem in quite different ways, thus creating a paradigm of possible responses to traducement, rejection, and exile. We have seen in our brief discussion of Sima Qian's own experience, as reflected most notably in his letter to Ren An, that for him these are issues of critical personal importance – certainly Sima Qian, too, portrays himself as someone who turned political frustration into literary creation and who also seriously considered the alternative of suicide.

The full story of Qu Yuan, as told in *Records of the Historian*, is readily accessible elsewhere and will not be detailed here.[67] What is noteworthy for us is the way Sima Qian directs the reader's response to this tragic figure, who was both a politician and a poet. At the very beginning of the account, we are told that Qu Yuan, who served King Huai (rd. 328–299) of the state of Chu, "possessed broad learning and a strong will, was intelligent at regulating disorder, and was skilled at rhetoric." In other words, the historian presents him as the ideal minister. But like almost all such virtuous figures immortalized in Sima Qian's account of the past, Qu Yuan is eventually slandered by the unworthy and estranged from his ruler: "Qu Yuan, correct in principle and honest in action, spent his loyalty and exhausted his wisdom in serving his lord, but slanderers estranged him from the ruler. This can indeed be called 'afflicted'" (84.2482).

The result of Qu Yuan's affliction is literary activity, which Sima Qian tells us twice elsewhere in his writings typically derives from political frustration.[68] "Qu Yuan's composition of 'Encountering Sorrow' ('Li Sao')," says Sima Qian of the poet's greatest work, "was no doubt born from this resentment" (84.2482). As Sima Qian's account of his heroic literary predecessor continues, he speaks to the reader again, telling us directly of the greatness we should see and admire in the life of Qu Yuan:

> His will was pure, and so he speaks of the fragrance of things. His actions were upright, and so he could die and not compromise. He distanced himself from muck and mud, sloughed off filth to float and drift beyond the dusty world ... he can compete for brilliance with even the sun and moon! (84.2482)

Such a hyperbolic encomium, not all that unusual in Sima Qian, assuredly is more high-pitched than Thucydides' typically restrained portraits. One can read Sima Qian's entire account of Qu Yuan as a stirring preface to the poet's eventual suicide. But before relating that final, frenzied act, Sima Qian pauses to make certain that we perceive the message of Qu Yuan's life:

> The rulers of men, whether stupid or wise, worthy or unworthy, all wish to seek out the loyal to act for them and to raise up the worthy to assist them. Nevertheless, the fact that fallen states and broken families follow one after the other and sage rulers have not come forth for generations is because those called "loyal" are not loyal and those called "worthy" are not worthy. (84.2485)

The problem is that worthy advisers are almost never heard, while sycophants and toadies succeed. In Sima Qian's presentation of political realities, it usually is not cream but scum that rises to the top. Qu Yuan's summary of his problem, spoken to a fisherman just before he composes his poetic suicide note and leaps into the Miluo River, is anything but a modest summary of his situation:

> The whole world is turbulent and muddy – I alone am pure!
> People all are drunk – I alone am sober!
>
> (84.2486)

Qu Yuan's extreme alienation from a world he deems unworthy leaves him room for neither moderation nor compromise. Suicide, for him, becomes a final way of expressing his sincerity of purpose and intensity of feeling.[69]

After Sima Qian has described Qu Yuan's dramatic plunge into the river, he proceeds to a biography of Jia Yi, who lived a century later. Jia Yi was introduced to Emperor Wen as a literary prodigy, served in the Han court, and also confronted the inevitable jealousy and slander of less able officials. Sima Qian, who has already established the pattern for understanding such characters in his earlier comments about Qu Yuan, does less direct moralizing in Jia Yi's biography. But we know that Jia Yi is headed for difficulty as soon as the historian speaks of his ability:

> Whenever an imperial decree went down for discussion and the various senior masters were unable to speak, Mr. Jia would provide a thorough response in their stead, which would be precisely what each one of them wished he had expressed. The various masters knew their ability did not equal his. (84.2492)

The experienced student of Sima Qian knows after reading the passage cited above that lesser talents will soon slander the youthful and capable official. Eventually Jia Yi falls into disfavor and is sent to precisely the area in southern China where Qu Yuan was exiled and committed suicide. Like all good Chinese literary travelers, Jia Yi visits the place of Qu Yuan's death and writes a poem in his predecessor's honor entitled "A Lament for Qu Yuan."[70] As he sympathizes with Qu Yuan's tragedy, he is also describing his own similarly unhappy fate:

> Alas! So pitiful, to meet an unlucky time.
> The phoenix hid while kites and owls soared aloft!
>
> (84.2493)

In the midst of Jia Yi's praise for the purity of Qu Yuan and his impassioned poetic indictment of the unfairness of his own age, the "Lament" suddenly veers in a somewhat unexpected direction. Speaking to the long-deceased Qu Yuan, Jia Yi asks:

> Might it have been confusion that brought you to this error?
> Was this not, after all, the master's mistake?
>
> (84.2494)

Perhaps, he suggests here, Qu Yuan's suicide was an extreme and unnecessary act, a topic Sima Qian will resume in his judgment at the end of the chapter. But before that conclusion, the Han historian complicates the paradigm by presenting another of Jia Yi's poems, one that was written, we are told, "for self-consolation." This is the famous "Owl Rhapsody" in which Jia Yi offers a thoroughly Daoist vision of the world. According to this rhapsody, one should not care about the inevitable ups and downs that life presents, for there is a loftier vision, as the final words of the poem announce:

> Float with the flowing stream, or rest against the isle,
> Surrender to the workings of fate, unconcerned for self,
> Let your life be like a floating, your death like a rest.
> Placid as the peaceful waters of a deep pool,
>   buoyant as an unfastened boat,
> Find no cause for complacency in life,
>   but cultivate emptiness and drift.
> The Man of Virtue is unattached; recognizing fate,
>   he does not worry.
> Be not dismayed by petty pricks and checks.
>
> (84.2500)[71]

The tragedy was that the young poet could not achieve the detachment and freedom from worry and dismay his own rhapsody recommends. Jia Yi was eventually rehabilitated and was appointed tutor to the king of the minor state of Liang. One day, his royal charge, who unfortunately had no posterity, went riding, fell from his horse and died. Sima Qian reports Jia Yi's reaction: "Jia Yi blamed himself that he had been tutor without good effect. He wept bitterly for more than a year and then died. At the time of his death, he was thirty-three" (84.2503).

The pattern established in this chapter is that there are two reactions to the estrangement that inevitably follows loyal but always unappreciated service: either one commits suicide, following Qu Yuan, or one constructs a compelling reason to live on, following Jia Yi. And if one chooses to live on, Daoism can be utilized to provide justification and comfort, for it offers a loftier vision that makes the turbulence of this world fade into insignificant ripples on the ocean of the Dao. But the Daoist vision, however much it might appeal, does not necessarily inoculate those of sensitive feeling, like Jia Yi or Sima Qian himself, against the inevitable tragedies of life.

Sima Qian closes his chapter by stepping forward, as he does at the end of almost every chapter, to offer a final judgment, which he always introduces with the words, "The Prefect Grand Historian says":

> When I read "Encountering Sorrow", "Questions Posed to Heaven", or "A Lament for Ying" [all poems attributed to Qu Yuan], I grieve at his desires. Whenever I go to Changsha and see where he plunged into the watery depths, I always weep and imagine what kind of a person he was. But when I came upon Jia Yi's lament for him, I also found it strange that someone with such talent, who could travel among the feudal lords with almost any state accepting him, could bring himself to this! When I read his "Owl Rhapsody," which regards life and death as equal and makes light of failure and success, I was stunned and at a complete loss! (84.2503–4)

Here Sima Qian reveals the full sweep of his empathy and the remarkable degree of his emotional involvement with the history he presents. He is deeply moved by Qu Yuan's resolute action and weeps each time he visits the site of the poet's suicide. But he also sympathizes with Jia Yi's criticism of Qu Yuan, for if the latter were so pure, certainly he could have found some ruler to appreciate his talents. Then, as he reads Jia Yi's high-minded Daoist rhapsody, the Han historian is stunned into total silence. Why? Perhaps because he too knows well the consolation Daoism offers – Sima Qian's father, after all, was devoted to the Daoist vision of the world – but, like Jia Yi, he cannot simply "cultivate emptiness and drift" in the face of failure and disgrace.

We cannot read this chapter without a profound sense that Sima Qian is unable to stand back from his historical record and distance himself from it as if he were composing a thoroughly objective account in the Thucydidean mold. He is rather a full participant in the storytelling, someone whose own experience appears to be shaping the accounts he presents, accounts to which he responds with considerable emotion. Indeed, crying and sighing are not unusual responses of this historian to the tales he himself tells,[72] and such reactions set him apart from the ostensibly rational and detached Thucydides, as we shall particularly note in our discussion of the Greek historian's representation of the famous dialogue between the Melians and Athenians.

We discussed earlier how Sima Qian writes his history of the Chinese past, especially the recent past, very much around issues of critical importance to him and his family. He is anything but a blank page upon which the tradition of the past is transcribed. This should not surprise us. Certainly, when Sima Qian alludes to the creativity of Confucius, he almost certainly has *Spring and Autumn Annals* in mind. There is no space here to survey Sima Qian's full description of the scholarly endeavors of Confucius, but it is certain that, like Mencius and Dong Zhongshu before him, he regards *Spring and Autumn Annals* as the Master's crowning achievement.[73] Sima Qian tells us that Confucius "took as basis the historical records" to produce a text that was filled with subtle moral and political judgments (47.1943). After the records of the state of Lu had passed through the hand of the Sage, they were so powerfully written that, as Mencius tells us, "disorderly ministers and violent sons were frightened."[74] *Spring and Autumn Annals* was essentially a modern history which began only one hundred and seventy years before the birth of Confucius, or 722 BCE, and extended down to 481, just two years before his death. Sima Qian, like the Master he believed had written *Spring and Autumn Annals*, was particularly interested in the events of his own lifetime and in the period of one hundred years or so that preceded him. Furthermore, Sima Qian, resembling Confucius as understood by Han commentators, also filled his text with judgments on the events of the past, particularly those that belonged to the modern period, which was his primary focus.

One of Sima Qian's judgments provides us with a fruitful place to begin a brief exploration of his portrayal of his own time. The third Han emperor, Liu Heng, was the fourth son of the founder of the dynasty and was granted the posthumous name Wen or "culture," which no doubt evokes a memory of the great King Wen of Zhou, one of the cultural heroes of ancient China. He ascended the throne in 180 BCE and reigned for twenty-three years before his death in 157. Sima Qian was born well after Emperor Wen's death, but his father, Sima Tan, almost certainly grew to adulthood during the years of Emperor Wen's reign. Moreover, Sima Tan's eclectic Huang-Lao Daoism was very much in accord with Emperor Wen's own basically *laissez-faire* policies and with the strong Daoist proclivities of his powerful wife, the Empress Dou, who remained alive until 135 BCE.[75] At the conclusion of "The Basic Annals of Emperor Wen the Filial" (ch. 10), "The Master Grand Historian says":

Confucius said that a generation must pass and only then can there be humaneness and that if skilled men govern a state for one hundred years, then they can overcome violence and eliminate killing. True, indeed, are these words! From the founding of the Han down through the reign of Emperor Wen was more than forty years, and virtue greatly flourished. Gradually a time was approaching to change the calendar and the color of imperial robes, and to offer the *feng* and *shan* sacrifices. But modestly he declined, and this was not completed until the present time. Alas! Was he not humane indeed? (10.437–8)

Sima Qian not only labels Emperor Wen "humane" (*ren*) here but elsewhere extols him for "practicing great virtue" (11.449). Sima Qian also notes, in the unusually affirmative judgment quoted above, that it takes a generation, which one commentator defines as a period of thirty years, before such humaneness can appear, thus excusing the first two emperors of the Han, Gaozu (rd. 202–195) and Emperor Hui (rd. 195–188), for not meriting such a lofty description.

The content of Sima Qian's "Basic Annals of Emperor Wen the Filial" does indeed portray this emperor in a highly positive fashion. Among Emperor Wen's numerous acts of virtue, he "abolished mutilating punishments" (10.428). It is noteworthy, given Sima Qian's unfortunate involvement with the law, that the historian later mentions specifically that Emperor Wen abolished castration (10.436). Even in his two-line introduction to the "Basic Annals of Emperor Wen the Filial" found in the table of contents that constitutes one part of the postface, Sima Qian singles out the abolition of mutilations as one of Wen's most important and kindly acts (130.3303). In addition, we are told that Emperor Wen rejected personal luxury, made no effort to increase the size of his palaces, and sent home beautiful women who were presented for his pleasure. Most significantly, at least for our analysis here, after Emperor Wen's death, his final testament was read in court. In this document, the humane Emperor speaks philosophically of death: "I have heard that of the ten thousand things under Heaven that sprout and grow there are none but die. Death is the order of Heaven and Earth, the natural principle of things. So how can one mourn excessively?" And then the Emperor provides instructions for an exceedingly modest funeral and burial (10.433).

Much more could be said about the good government Sima Qian attributes to Emperor Wen. Surely this emperor, if anyone, deserved to perform the highest imperial sacrifices and proclaim the legitimacy of the Han dynasty before heaven. But he modestly declined to do so. It is of great interest, in view of Emperor Wu's later obsession with the *feng* and *shan* sacrifices, that Sima Qian concludes his judgment of Emperor Wen by noting his refusal to perform these sacrifices.

There is little doubt that Sima Qian treats Emperor Wen as an opposite to the great *bête noire* of his history, the First Qin Emperor, whom the Han historian presents as a megalomaniac obsessed with power, ostentation, and violence. Furthermore, the First Qin Emperor was the last emperor to perform the *feng* and *shan* sacrifices, unworthily to be sure, and his compulsive fear of death and search for physical immortality are thoroughly documented on the pages of *Records of the Historian* and place him in stark contrast to the humane Emperor Wen, who faced death with resignation and courage.

There is nothing particularly subversive or dangerous in pointing a finger of scorn at the First Qin Emperor. This was a favorite theme of intellectuals throughout the first century of the Han.[76] What is subversive, however, is that Sima Qian's portrayal of Emperor Wen points an accusatory finger not just backward in time but forward too, toward Emperor Wu, under whom Sima Qian spent his entire official career, first as a Palace Gentleman (*lang zhong*), then as Prefect Grand Historian (*tai shi ling*), and finally, after his castration, as Director of the Eunuch Secretariat (*zhong shu ling*).

Sima Qian and Emperor Wu are inextricably linked and dominate our vision of early Han history. Sima Qian was born just four years before Emperor Wu, then seventeen years old, ascended the throne in 141 BCE. Emperor Wu reigned fifty-four years, one of the longest reigns in Chinese history, and died in 87 BCE, almost surely within a year or two of Sima Qian's death. If the historian's life was profoundly shaped by the power and anger of the Emperor, it must be said that most of what we know of the Emperor derives from the historian. Put somewhat differently, time has reversed the power relationship between these two figures, for it is difficult, if not impossible, to see Sima Qian's imperial master today without viewing him through an account that is entirely a product of the Han historian's writing brush.

By our claim that Sima Qian's portrayal of Emperor Wen is a rebuke of both the First Qin Emperor and the Emperor Wu, we are putting Emperor Wu in very bad company indeed and are suggesting that Sima Qian had the gravest misgivings about the Emperor he served. We are not the first to make this claim. A piece attributed to the historian Ban Gu and contained in the famous *Anthology of Literature* (*Wen xuan*), which was compiled by Xiao Tong (501–30), says that "Because [Sima Qian] himself fell into a mutilating punishment, he turned to subtle words to ridicule and disparage his own age."[77] Most recently, the French scholar Jean Lévi has written very provocatively on this topic, describing *Records of the Historian* as a "theater ... for a battle between these two figures, the sovereign and the historian."[78]

Evaluating Sima Qian's treatment of Emperor Wu is complicated by the fact that the Emperor's "Basic Annals" (ch. 12) is missing from *Records of the Historian* and has been replaced by a verbatim repetition of the text of chapter 28, "The Essay on the *Feng* and *Shan* Sacrifices." Much has been made of this issue. A scholar of the Eastern Han, Wei Hong, gives the following explanation: "When [Sima Qian] was writing the 'Basic Annals of the Emperor Jing,' he spoke in an extreme way of his shortcomings and the mistakes of Emperor Wu. The Emperor was angry and had the text scraped away."[79] Wei Hong goes on to suggest that several years later the Emperor used the Li Ling affair as a pretext to strike back at his disloyal historian. In other words, the Emperor's dislike for Sima Qian, in Wei Hong's view, preceded the famous conflict over Li Ling and recapitulated a rivalry, apparent in earlier Chinese texts, that had always existed between vain rulers and honest historians.[80]

Since the "Basic Annals of the Emperor Wu" is missing, some have assumed that although the story of the Emperor actually erasing the text might be an exaggeration, there may indeed have been some act of censorship that resulted in the loss of whatever might originally have been contained in those annals. In contrast, Jean Lévi seems to argue that the lacuna resulted not so much from censorship as from Sima Qian himself:

> By a diabolical cleverness of the historian, leaving blank the annals of the Han emperor, he [Sima Qian] entrusts to his readers to imagine the worst infamies, the most terrible villainies, so much so that in this emptiness is lodged the most severe, the most virulent attack that it would be possible to dream, and this is all the more so as their author could not be accused of malice or of perfidy since he has said nothing to us.[81]

There may indeed be "diabolical cleverness" in the absence of "The Annals of the Emperor Wu," but it is difficult if not impossible to prove just how this "blank" actually came about. There are several possibilities that we cannot explore here, chief among these the possibility that Sima Qian's original version was simply lost.[82] However, without divining the meaning of this textual silence, we can indeed find sufficient evidence that one of Sima Qian's major purposes as a historian was to attack Emperor Wu.[83] We will turn to several areas of conflict between the Emperor and his historian and then will summarize some of the issues involved in this conflict, as well as providing a particularly striking example of Sima Qian's emotional involvement in his history.

Throughout *Records of the Historian*, Sima Qian repeatedly manifests deep concern with the topic of death. For him, when and how one dies, and how one achieves genuine immortality, are critical questions. "Man assuredly has a single death," Sima Qian says in his letter to Ren An. "Sometimes it is as heavy as Mount Tai; and sometimes it is as light as a swan's feather. It is the way one uses it that makes a difference."[84] Elsewhere, Sima Qian speaks of the great difficulty of "managing death" (81.2451). As we have seen in our brief exploration of the biographies of Qu Yuan and Jia Yi, Sima Qian was particularly interested in the question of suicide, an option he considered in his own case and ultimately rejected. Sima Qian decided not to follow Qu Yuan but to side with Jia Yi, who apparently thought that a man of merit should be able to "find another way." Elsewhere, in one of his final judgments, Sima Qian commends the Han general Ji Bu for the same decision as his own. He begins by comparing Ji Bu's courage to Xiang Yu (see 7.336), a figure whose suicide is one of the most stirring reported in *Records of the Historian*:

> With a vital spirit like Xiang Yu, Ji Bu became famous in Chu for his courage. He himself managed armies and seized [enemy] pennants time after time. He can be called a brave gentleman. Nevertheless, when he faced mutilating punishment and became a slave, he did not die. How able he was to lower himself! He relied upon his talents, and therefore accepted insult and did not feel shame. He wished to have occasion to use [a life] that was not yet spent. Therefore, in the end he became a famous Han general. (100.2734)

In another section of *Records*, Sima Qian reports the mass suicide of Tian Heng and his five hundred loyal retainers. While he commends them for their virtue, the historian wonders why they could not have found some alternative other than death:

> Tian Heng had high honor. His retainers admired his integrity and followed Heng in death. Could they not be men of the highest virtue? I consequently have included them here. None were without skill in schemes, and yet not one was able to make a plan. How could that be? (94.2649)

What had kept Sima Qian alive in the face of his own crisis, as he makes very clear both in his postface and his "Letter to Ren An," was the desire to grant immortality to himself and to others through the power of the written word.[85] The sacred task of the Han historian, and certainly it was a task derived from the religious tradition of ancient scribe-priests, was to conquer the confines of time.

In Sima Qian's era, however, there was quite another method of pursuing immortality. The search for a "drug of not dying" (*bu si zhi yao*) and the practice of various techniques to prolong life are attested in the last centuries of the Zhou dynasty and gained great currency in the early Han.[86] Such beliefs seem to have stemmed largely from the ancient state of Qi, located along the coastal regions of the Shandong Peninsula, and came to be associated with a group of specialists known as *fang shi*, which we might translate as "Masters of Method," a name that emphasizes their advocacy not of a broad moral doctrine but of particular "technologies."[87] This group, and their beliefs and practices, first have a significant impact in China, at least as Sima Qian presents the past, in the days of the First Qin Emperor.

In the view of Sima Qian, the First Qin Emperor's crimes were numerous,[88] and chief among them was the Emperor's obsession with the pursuit of physical immortality. Two years after he unifies the empire in 221 BCE, a certain Xu Shi, a man of the state of Qi, presents a petition saying that "in the midst of the sea are three divine mountains ... and immortals live there" (6.247). In response to Xu Shi's petition, the Emperor organizes a huge naval expedition, comprising "young men and women numbering several thousand," to go into the sea in search of immortals. Later in his reign, other methods for achieving "not dying" are suggested to the Emperor, who is always a gullible audience, at least on this subject. In Sima Qian's narrative these episodes, in which the Emperor is being misled by self-serving "Masters of Methods," are invariably juxtaposed, quite ironically, with the high-minded, Confucian rhetoric that the Emperor regularly inscribes on steles erected here and there as he travels around his empire.[89]

The methods for prolonging his life all fail, and Sima Qian, as if satirizing the Emperor's misguided pursuit, gives him a particularly ignominious, even somewhat ridiculous death. As the Emperor is traveling away from the capital he grows ill. Badly frightened, he forbids any mention of the word "death." His condition worsens, and, at the age of forty-nine, he dies. In order to solidify the succession and make certain that their own power will continue undiminished, his ministers anxiously hide the fact of the Emperor's death until they have returned to the capital:

> The coffin was loaded in an insulated carriage attended by the eunuchs the Emperor formerly favored. Whenever the carriage stopped, they presented food, and the officials memorialized affairs as before. The eunuchs would then approve the memorials from within the insulated carriage.... It happened to be hot and His Highness's insulated carriage smelled. Thus there was an edict for the accompanying officials to order one *tan* of salted fish loaded on a carriage so as to disguise the smell. (6.264).[90]

To use a traditional Chinese idiom, the Emperor, through the power of the historian's writing brush, has literally "left a stench for ten thousand years" (*yi chou wan nian*). The First Qin Emperor foolishly tried to avert the death that only a historian's power can transcend. To be sure, he has won immortality, but his eternal life is to be spent in infamy in a written record that will never be erased.

The "humane" Emperor Wen, as we have seen, said that "Death is the order of Heaven and Earth, the natural principle of things." This calm acceptance of inevitability stands as a rebuke to the First Qin Emperor. Even more poignantly, however, it points toward Wen's own grandson, the Emperor Wu, who shared with the First Qin Emperor the same obsession with physical immortality.

The chapter on the *feng* and *shan* sacrifices, which is repeated as Emperor Wu's annals, includes much more than an account of the rather rare performance of these loftiest rituals. After providing a short history of these sacrifices and other imperial religious ceremonies, with particular attention to the ill-fated ascent of Mount Tai undertaken by the First Qin Emperor, the chapter becomes a catalogue of the engagement of Emperor Wu with "men of Yan and Qi" who advised him on means of meeting with spirits and immortals and gaining secrets of physical immortality. Sima Qian could hardly be more direct in expressing his disapproval of these activities, which he catalogues so thoroughly. For example, near the end of his record, the Han historian comments on Emperor Wu who had, by then, been through forty years of the broken promises and failed schemes of the Masters of Methods:

> The Son of Heaven was increasingly tired of and disgusted with the strange and tangled teachings of the Masters of Method. But he was ensnared and could not break off from them and still hoped to meet with one who had the truth. (12.485, cf. 28.1403–4)

Li Shaojun was the first of the Masters, many years earlier, to gain the devotion of the Emperor. He spoke of transforming cinnabar into gold and promised that by eating from vessels made of this gold, one could prolong life.[91] He urged the emperor to establish contact with immortals on Penglai, the legendary island supposedly located in the eastern sea, and he assured the Emperor that "if you meet immortals and perform the *feng* and *shan* sacrifices, you will not die" (28.1385). Next, a "man of Qi named Shaoweng" convinced the Emperor that "if the palaces and [imperial] robes are not decorated with images of the spirits, the spirits will not come" (28.1388). Later, the Emperor's favorite Master of Methods was named Luan Da, "who was tall and handsome, whose words were full of methods and schemes, and who dared to speak boldly and without the slightest doubt" (28.1390). As a result of his audacious plans and pronouncements, which included promises that "gold can be produced, the break in the Yellow River dikes can be blocked up, the drug of immortality can be obtained, and immortals can be made to appear" (28.1390), Luan Da gained so much wealth and official prestige that "everyone who lived along the seacoast of Yan and Qi," Sima Qian says, "waved their arms and said they had secret methods able to command spirits and immortals" (28.1391). Finally, the Emperor fell under the spell of Gongsun Qing, who, among other outlandish claims, quoted a mysterious Master Shen's teaching that "if the ruler of Han goes up and performs the *feng* sacrifice ... then he will be able to ascend to Heaven as an immortal" (28.1393).

In case we have missed the comparison of Emperor Wu with the First Qin Emperor that all this implies, Sima Qian writes that Emperor Wu "increasingly sent out boats and commanded several thousand men who had spoken of the mountains of the gods to go into the ocean to seek the Penglai immortals" (28.1397). These expeditions take place just over one hundred years after the First Qin Emperor's more famous naval expedition in search of the ever-elusive isles of the immortals. All of this, of course, reflects very badly on Emperor Wu, who, we must not forget, once stood by as Sima Qian was sentenced to death and then underwent castration. Certainly one sees, at the least, echoes of resentment, even disdain, in his long narrative of the Emperor's extreme gullibility.

Sima Qian does not live long enough to provide us with a description of Emperor Wu's death, although we cannot help but suspect that his description of the sad demise of Wu's imperial double, the First Qin Emperor, is a prediction of a similar ignominy that awaits the historian's contemporary. In fact, Sima Qian may be pointing toward the complete failure of the Masters of Methods and Emperor Wu's inevitable physical decline when he concludes his chapter with words that describe the hopelessness of the situation: "From this time on, the Masters of Methods who spoke of spirits and sacrifices became more and more numerous. Nevertheless, their [ineffective] results can be seen" (28.1404).

Sima Qian claims, as we have noted before, that he descends from a family of historians that stretches back into the earliest times. In his famous biography of Bo Yi and Shu Qi (ch. 61), which functions as a preface to his other biographies, Sima Qian confronts the fact that both Heaven and history are unjust – Heaven because it does not always reward the good and punish the evil, and history because it cannot transmit the names of those worthies who have themselves hidden their goodness.[92] But Heaven's blessing, be it for good or ill, is confined to the duration of an individual's or perhaps a family's life, whereas history's blessing remains as long as historical texts "are passed down to people and penetrate the villages and great cities," to quote Sima Qian's own words (*Han shu* 62.2735). The cult of immortality, which was gaining strength in his own age, threatened the control the historian exercised over the future. By allowing himself to be captured by this cult, Emperor Wu seemed to be more concerned about a futile search for physical immortality than he was about the nature of the only type of immortality he could achieve – textual immortality; and that immortality was in the control of his mutilated servant Sima Qian.

If the Sima family tradition was challenged, on the one side, by the Masters of Method, whom Sima Qian treats as frauds and tricksters, it was also challenged on the other side by the growing influence of another type of specialist, the "Confucian scholar," who was using narrow textual mastery and a broad capacity to flatter as a means to gain political power. Sima Qian's depiction of Confucians of his day is not as uniformly negative as his portrayal of the Masters of Methods. Sima Qian and his father, as we have discussed, hold Confucius himself in the very highest regard and consider study of those texts of the past that had come to be identified with Confucianism, specifically the Five Classics, as the foundation of genuine learning. Nor should we conclude from Sima Tan's essay "The Essentials of the Six Schools," which favors a form of eclectic Daoism that Sima Qian calls "Huang-Lao Daoism," that *Records of the Historian* has a clear and dogmatic Daoist agenda that is anti-Confucian. What does seem clear in Sima Qian's history is that the reigning Emperor, who should be promoting scholars of distinction, is singularly unable to discern and reward those who really do possess merit. The Confucians whom Emperor Wu so often favored were typified more by a capacity to flatter and dissemble than by a genuine mastery of the classics. Thus, they were not the real disciples of a Master who had emphasized "sincerity in speech" as one of the primary characteristics of the "Superior Man."

One short biography reported in Sima Qian's chapter "A Forest of Confucians" (ch. 121) illustrates the problem. Yuan Gu, introduced as a specialist on the *Classic of Poetry*, served originally in the court of Emperor Jing. In two successive episodes he appears as a harsh critic of Daoism. In the first of these, he engages in a dispute in the presence of Emperor Jing with Master Huang, who was probably the Daoist teacher of Sima Qian's father. Master Huang's position in this argument, a rather dangerous one, is that dynastic founders are nothing more than rebels and assassins who forcibly overthrow their rulers.[93] Yuan Gu, in rebuttal, argues that dynastic founders are righteous figures who inherit Heaven's Charge and thus take power legitimately. In the second episode, the Empress Dowager Dou, "who was fond of the writings of Laozi," asks Yuan Gu about Laozi's famous classic. When he replies that this text is "the sayings of a menial and nothing more,"[94] the Empress Dowager is furious and orders Yuan Gu thrown into a pigpen to fight a boar. Only the intercession of the Emperor Jing saves his life.

If the Sima historians were eager to pursue a strict Daoist agenda, we might expect Yuan Gu, as an opponent of Daoism, to be treated negatively. This, however, is not the case:

> When the current Emperor first took the throne, he again summoned Gu on account of the latter's virtue and goodness. The flattering Confucians frequently criticized and slandered Gu, saying, "Gu is old." They had him dismissed and sent home. At that time Gu was already more than ninety years old. When Gu had been summoned to court, Gongsun Hong, a man of Xie, was also summoned. When he looked sidelong at Gu, Gu said, "Master Gongsun, do your best to speak on the basis of correct learning. Do not twist learning to flatter the age." (121.3124)

Here, the Confucians at court, including the powerful Gongsun Hong, are condemned as flatterers both by the narrative voice and by Yuan Gu himself. When these Confucians meet a true scholar, one might even say a "true Confucian," who is characterized more by honest speech than mere textual mastery, all they can do is become jealous and slanderous.

Gongsun Hong, who is mentioned in this last episode, was one of the most successful Confucian scholars of his time. He took up the study of *Spring and Autumn Annals* when he was over forty and, as a result of his mastery of this text, rose from poverty to the position of Chancellor, the very highest position in the Han bureaucracy, which he held from 124 BCE until his death in 121.[95] Sima Qian, who includes a biography of Gongsun in *Records of the Historian*, is less than favorably impressed with this most successful Confucian:

> As a person, Hong was suspicious and jealous. On the outside he appeared generous, but within he was harsh. Although he would act as though he was on good terms with another, he secretly would try to get back at him for any offense. (112.2951)

An example of this famous Confucian's duplicity is provided in the following episode, which is also revealing in yet another way we will discuss presently:

> Once [Hong] made an agreement with the other high officials regarding a series of proposals. But when they came before the Emperor, he broke his agreement to comply with the Emperor's wishes. Ji An berated Hong in the court, saying, "Men of Qi are full of deceit and are without regard for

the truth. Originally you agreed with us on these proposals, but now in all cases you oppose them. You are not loyal!" (112.2950)

Flattery and double-dealing came all too easily to many of those the Emperor had promoted for their supposed scholarship. Meanwhile, officials who spoke frankly suffered. This is a pattern we have already seen in Sima Qian's portrayal of exemplary figures of the past such as Qu Yuan and Jia Yi, but in the case of such men as Yuan Gu and Gongsun Hong, there were probably personal entanglements hidden behind the narrative as well. While scholars like Gongsun Hong sometimes rose quickly in the bureaucracy, Sima Tan remained Prefect Grand Historian for the duration of his career. While he claimed such service was a family tradition, it was only a middle-rank position within the Han bureaucracy.[96] Moreover, there are indications in Sima Qian's writings that neither Sima Tan nor Sima Qian enjoyed great status at court.[97] Certainly Sima Qian's position after he underwent castration, although an indignity in certain respects, was a promotion over the position of scribe he had held before.[98]

The advancement into power under Emperor Wu of a whole new group of leaders must have galled the Simas. A form of narrow textual specialization was obviously preferred over the rather broader type of learning represented by Sima Tan's eclectic Daoism or Sima Qian's encyclopedic knowledge of the past.[99] But there were probably other factors that were even more important than this: there are indications in *Records of the Historian* that the Simas might also have been troubled by a decline in hereditary-based officialdom and by the rise of Qi and Lu power at court as opposed to that represented by their own home area, which was centered upon the old states of Qin and Jin.[100]

Sima Qian's attitude on the proper balance between heredity and worthiness in holding office seems complex. Obviously it was important to his father and himself to assert a family tradition, however questionable that purported tradition might be. He does seem, on occasion, to point to the family tradition of certain individuals as being a key to their achievements, and he also seems to regard those who too quickly "burst upon the scene," with little in their family tradition to point toward such success, as problematic. For example, Han Xin and Lu Wan were two generals who fought for Han against Xiang Yu. Both eventually got into trouble with their master, the future first emperor of the Han dynasty, and deserted to the Xiongnu. Sima Qian concludes their biographies by noting that "Han Xin and Lu Wan were not from lineages that had piled up virtue and accumulated goodness but, seizing upon a sudden change in the balance of power, they used deceit and power to win merit" (93.2642).

The success of Han Xin and Lu Wan was not based upon any family tradition and was therefore flimsy and easily subverted. Elsewhere, Sima Qian attributes the sterling demeanor of a particular person to the existence of a family tradition (96.2865).

Sima Qian not only appears anxious to establish himself as a "blue-blood" with a family tradition of office-holding, but also traces his genealogy well back into the Warring States region of Qin. The one of his ancestors we can identify with confidence was, in fact, a general in Qin before the empire was unified.[101] Qian Mu, the great modern Chinese historian, has persuasively argued that there was a rivalry during the Qin dynasty and early Han years between the eastern cultural center of Qi and Lu and a more legalist and military cultural tradition of the west.[102] It is of great interest that Sima Qian repeatedly identifies both the rising Confucians, like Gongsun Hong himself, and the influential Masters of Methods, as easterners (from the old areas of Qi, Lu, and Yan). As we have seen above, Sima Qian quotes Ji An, a man who is identified in *Records of the Historian* as a Huang-Lao Daoist and a westerner, describing "the men of Qi" as "full of deceit and ... without regard for truth."[103] Certainly in the "Treatise on the *Feng* and *Shan* Sacrifices," Sima Qian almost makes it appear as if every man of Qi was a swindler who was scheming to use absurd promises and superstitions in order to gain influence with the Emperor.

We conclude this examination of the way Sima Qian shapes his history around his own experience and emotional reactions with a brief excursion into one of his most stirring and admired biographies, that of General Li (ch. 109). Sima Qian begins this biography by providing us with two critical characteristics of the great general: first, he was, like Sima Qian himself, a man from the old region of Qin – in other words, he was a westerner; and second, he came from a family of generals, and the art of archery, in which the general excelled, "had been handed down in the family for generations" (109.2867). Sima Qian then informs us that General Li was not born in the right age: while the General was serving the humane Emperor Wen, the latter noted his amazing courage and said, "What a pity that you have not met the right time! Had you but lived in the time of Emperor Gao, how would even a kingdom of ten thousand households have been unworthy of you!" (109.2867). To be born out of one's proper time is a common theme in *Records of the Historian*. This was precisely Qu Yuan's problem, as it was Confucius', too. That Sima Qian identified with the theme is clear. Apart from *Records of the Historian* and "The Letter to Ren An," Sima Qian's most important extant work is a rhapsody (*fu*) entitled "A Lament for Gentlemen Who Do Not Meet [the Right Time]," and this work speaks of precisely the problem that recurs so frequently in his history:

> In truth his endowment is adequate, but his time is out of joint.
> Endlessly he toils up to the very verge of death.
> Though possessed of [pleasing] form, he goes unnoticed,
> While capable, he cannot demonstrate his ability.[104]

Only the historian can rescue those, like General Li, who are born out of their time, for he can bring them, through the power of the text, to the attention of the readership of other eras when they might gain the appreciation they deserve.

The reader knows from the fact that General Li "has not met" his "right time" that he is a man of worth and that his path through life will be a hard one. Sima Qian often regards history as constructed from the strengths and weaknesses of human beings, and he is intensely interested in the human personality. Thus, shortly after Sima Qian introduces General Li, the historian describes the personality of this particular character. As elsewhere, he does this in two ways: first, he tells us directly; and second, he reports a short incident that provides a critical key to understanding the person under consideration. The direct description of General Li is as follows:

> Guang was upright. Whenever he received a reward, he would divide it with his troops. He shared food and drink with his soldiers. To the end of Guang's life, though he made two thousand piculs[105] for more than forty years, his family had no excess wealth. To his death he said nothing about his family's financial affairs ... Guang stuttered and said little. When he was together with his men, he would draw on the ground to indicate troop formations ... When Guang was leading his troops and supplies had run out, if they came upon a river and his soldiers had not finished drinking, he would not go near the river; and if his soldiers had not finished eating, Guang would not taste his food. He was generous and kind, and his soldiers, because of this, loved to serve him. (109.2872)

Li Guang, as he is portrayed here, is the exact antithesis of so many of those who rose to power during the lifetime of Sima Qian. Confucians and Masters of Method typically gained influence through the power and appeal of words; they knew how to persuade and, as so often in Sima Qian's accounts, cared little about subordinates and cared much about the emperor. Flattery was one of their dominant features. But General Li, despite his modesty, kind-heartedness, and reticence, was not without faults. In fact, Sima Qian, like the Greek tragedians, seems most interested in those characters who possess genuine nobility but still have weaknesses and make mistakes. Thus, he relates in General Li's biography the following revealing incident:

Guang went out hunting. He saw a rock in the grass and, thinking it was a tiger, shot an arrow at it. The arrow struck the rock, embedding the arrowhead in it. When he saw that it was a rock, he shot at it time after time, but to the very end he was unable to embed it in the stone again. (109.2871–2)

In this story, after Li Guang shoots his arrow, he discovers that he is mistaken. The rock is not the tiger he imagined. Ironically, as soon as he realizes his mistake, he cannot repeat his previous feat. Sima Qian seems to be telling us that the General's most impressive accomplishments often involve some element of miscalculation. General Li, for all his nobility as a fighter, is indeed prone to mistakes. The Xiongnu feared Li more than any other Chinese general, and certainly he had won spectacular victories over China's enemies. The most noteworthy of these victories, especially as told by Sima Qian, fully demonstrates the General's amazing courage. However, Li's mistakes are also amply documented in his biography. On a personal level, he was "occasionally wounded by beasts" because of his habit of waiting until the last possible moment before shooting an arrow (109.2872). On the professional level, to quote the Emperor's rather generous opinion, "he repeatedly got himself into unusual circumstances" (109.2874).

In 119 BC, when General Li was already an old man, he was given one final opportunity to win military glory and overcome the bad fortune that had plagued his career. He was appointed as a subordinate under Wei Qing in a major offensive against the Xiongnu. This was something of an indignity. Wei Qing was a man with no family tradition of military leadership who had come to power because his sister was a royal concubine. Moreover, Sima Qian says that Wei Qing had "used amiability and compliance to ingratiate himself with the Emperor" (111.2939), qualities we would not associate with the inarticulate but experienced General Li.[106]

Unfortunately, General Li's pattern of misfortune continues. He loses his way and fails to meet up with Wei Qing's army at the appointed time. This provokes the dramatic conclusion of his biography:

The General-in-chief sent his Chief Clerk to reprimand strongly Guang's commandery and order that they respond to charges. Guang said, "My colonels are faultless. It is I who got lost. I will myself respond."

Then he went to the commandery and said to his officers, "Since I bound up my hair as a youth, I have fought more than seventy great and small battles with the Xiongnu. Now, by good fortune, I followed the

135

> General-in-chief and went forth to engage the Xiongnu chieftain. But the General-in-chief shifted my division and had me travel by a roundabout way. And so I got lost. How could this not be Heaven! Moreover, I am more than sixty years old, and am completely unwilling to face petty officials!" With that he took out his knife and slit his own throat.

Here Sima Qian returns to one of his favorite themes: choosing the correct time to die. Li Guang was not a young man who could think of another solution or hope to take his loyal service to another state. He had reached the end, and he entrusted his reputation to history. Sima Qian frequently tells us how his contemporaries reacted to an event as a guide to how we readers should react. Here, quite unusually, he tells us twice, once immediately after General Li's death and once in his final judgment:

> All the soldiers and officials of Guang's army, the entire army, cried. And when the common people heard, both those who knew and those did not know Guang, whether old or young, all wept for him! (109.2876)

> On the day Guang died, all in the empire, whether they knew or did not know him, were filled with grief! (109.2878)

Sima Qian is one of those who did personally know General Li, as he tells us in his judgment, and he assuredly was moved emotionally by the ill-fated but courageous general's final act. And just as Sima Qian is involved emotionally in his history, he wants us to be as well. We too should weep and be "filled with grief" as we read the historian's account.

But there are probably other reasons, as well, that Sima Qian is engaged with this biography. General Li was the grandfather of Li Ling, the commander Sima Qian defended before Emperor Wu in the famous case that led to the historian's mutilation. The family tradition of generalship, despite Li Guang's death, continued, as did the family tradition of misfortune. Sima Qian's courageous defense of Li Ling may well also have been a defense of a family military tradition he admired. Moreover, General Li, like Xiang Yu and so many other characters of nobility Sima Qian honored, knew when it was the proper time to die. They would die, to be sure, but their actions would be immortalized by the historian, who took it as his mission to record the names of "enlightened lords, worthy rulers, loyal officials and gentlemen who died for duty" (130.3295).

The purpose of this excursion into a few aspects of Sima Qian's portrayal of his own age has been to indicate several ways in which he shapes his history around his own personal and political experience. This should not surprise us. The same could, of course, be said about

Thucydides or any other historian, no matter how much they might assume a pose of rationality or objectivity. The interesting issue is the degree to which Sima Qian is aware of his complicity in the stories he is remembering and of his self-conscious shaping of his historical materials that will enable them to speak to his later readers in telling ways. Sima Qian is never an intentionalist who stands back and attempts to objectify his materials. His interaction, indeed his personal entanglement, with his history is complex and profound.

4 Thucydides' tragic quest for objectivity and the historian's irrepressible "I"

Thucydides is a great analyst of the *kinêsis*, the upheaval, that shook the age in which he lived. He searched for the cause of the catastrophe, and he found it in the increasingly self-interested, increasingly greedy and opportunistic nature of the Athenian character. He stops short, however, of criticizing the essential nature of the Athenian character in its paradigmatic, Periklean embodiment. The true cause of the war, he states at the beginning of the work, was "the greatness of the Athenians" (I.23). But it was not this greatness itself that was responsible for the catastrophe. The pursuit of "greatness" is not the issue for Thucydides. It is rather "the fear" that this greatness engendered in the Spartans that was responsible for the conflict. It was the Spartans' defensive reaction to Athenian greatness that caused the conflict.

We have shown how Thucydides considered the Sicilian expedition a tragic mistake, a *hamartia* in the classic Aristotelian sense. Let us return to that Thucydidean passage briefly here. The expedition, the historian argued, *hêmartêthê*, "was in error." The error, however, was for Thucydides not so much an error of judgment (*gnômês hamartêma*, II.65.11) in regard to the enemy they were attacking as it was an error of management of those at home who were consumed with quarreling among themselves and who, as a result, did not properly assist the troops that had been sent. There is more than a hint here that the Sicilian expedition was not such a bad idea. It was just bungled. We have here no critique of Athenian imperialism *per se*.

As we have mentioned, Thucydides attributes the cause of the war to Athens' rise to greatness (*megaloi*). That greatness, in the course of the conflict, turned to megalomania and paranoia, and Thucydides records this process. Yet Thucydides is himself hardly free of the very pride that is the subject of his analysis.[107] We have discussed Thucydides' prideful bad manners in the "Archeology," and we paid special attention to the historian's condescending attitude toward Homer. The hero of Thucydides' history is Athens and the person who most gloriously embodied the Athenian spirit, for Thucydides, was Perikles. Perikles died in the plague which ravaged Athens in 430 BCE, and Thucydides himself was afflicted by it, although he recovered. If Athens' leaders had continued in the Periklean vein, Thucydides believed, or if Perikles himself had not been tragically struck down by the plague, Athens might never have met disaster and been defeated in the conflict. But the Athenians chose, instead, to be led by the charismatic but vain, undisciplined, and ultimately traitorous Alcibiades, who passionately urged the Athenians to undertake the fateful Sicilian expedition.

Perikles, then, was Thucydides' ideal Athenian leader; he was Athens at her best incarnate. Even the laudable Perikles, however, demonstrates some of the same pridefulness that we observed in the Thucydides of the "Archeology." Let us return to the remarkable passage from the famous funeral oration delivered by Perikles in the first year of the war (431 BCE). Not only did Thucydides esteem Perikles, but the Athenians themselves did. The custom for such eulogies was to choose men of known ability who were considered preeminent in intelligence (*gnômê*, II.34.6). Perikles' intelligence is remarkably similar to the intelligence of Thucydides. In winding down his speech, Perikles remarks that the great monuments Athens has constructed are proof enough of his city's greatness. We are therefore marveled at today, and we shall be objects of astonishment for future ages as well, Perikles declares. And then comes the following remarkable statement:

> We shall not need the praises of Homer or of any other panegyrist whose poetry may please for the moment but whose presentation of the facts will be discredited by the truth. No, we have forced every sea and land to be the highway of our daring, and everywhere, whether for evil or for good [*kakôn te k'agathôn*], we have left imperishable monuments behind us. Such is the Athens for which these men fought. (II.41.4–5)

As Jowett observed in a footnote to his translation, and as Hornblower also remarks in his commentary, these Periklean comments about Homer echo Thucydides' own bad-tempered words in the "Archeology."[108] And there is an echo, as well, of the contrast between Homer's momentarily pleasing but finally allegedly superficial poetry and the factually solid and clear-sighted history of Thucydides. The echoes are unmistakable. What is less clear, however, is the point of the echoes. There is a pridefulness in Perikles' speech that is troubling and portentous. Perikles announces, with great self-satisfaction, the remarkable Athenian achievement of presently compelling (*katanankasantes*) every sea and every land to obey her power and daring (*tolmê*). If readers were to confront this speech on its own merits, they might well conclude that Thucydides is surely revealing, however subtly, the pride that preceded Athens' fall. The echoes of Thucydides' own aggressive "Archeology," however, may strike a reader oddly, since these echoes would tend to reflect poorly on this most self-aware historian's degree of true self-awareness.

In other words, in his representation of Perikles' funeral oration, Thucydides appears to be subtly criticizing Perikles' pride.[109] We must also note here, in drawing an analogy between the pride of Perikles and the pride of Thucydides, Hornblower's comment upon how often Perikles uses the word "great" in reference to Athens in his speech: "The frequency of the word for 'great' (*megistos* in its various forms) in the present chapter [64] is remarkable: five times in lines 18–31 of the Oxford text" (I.339). In the previous section of this chapter, we observed how often Thucydides as narrator used this same adjective to describe the war between the Athenians and Spartans. Here is another parallel, then, between Thucydidean and Periklean pride. The pride of Perikles, as the parallel references to Homer and to the word "great" suggest, has an uncanny resemblance to the pride of Thucydides. Thus, if Thucydides is criticizing Perikles, he must also be criticizing himself. Thucydides would surely have bristled at the suggestion that, in his representation of Perikles, the historian was also criticizing himself. In view of this imagined bristling of Thucydides, the question then becomes, "Just how self-aware was this allegedly most self-aware of historians?"

There is another similarity between Thucydides and Perikles that bears mention in regard to the theme of this book, and this has to do with the attitude of these two Greek men toward women. At the conclusion of his eulogy in praise of the Athenian men who were killed in the first year of the war, Perikles at last mentions the women of Athens who must now face life as widows. The rather grudging address to the women is preceded by direct addresses first to the parents of the victims, then to the sons and brothers. The direct address to the women comes last and it is very brief in comparison:

> If I must say anything on the subject of female excellence to those of you who will now be in widowhood, it will be all comprised in this brief exhortation. Great will be your glory in not falling short of your natural character; and great as well will be hers whose reputation [*kleos*] is least mentioned, whether in praise or in blame.

The appeal to the women begins with the following rather remarkable phrase: *Ei de me dei kai gynaikeias ti aretês*. Crawley translates this as follows: "If I must say anything on the subject of female excellence." Kenneth Dover has questioned just how grudging is the tone of the

Greek. The phrase *ei de me dei* may also, perhaps, be less offensively translated as "if I may speak."[110] What we are dealing with here, however, is a question of degree rather than of substance. Gomme remarks that Perikles' words are "brief and priggish," consisting not of consolation but of advice, "and advice that is most of it not called for by the occasion."[111] Women, and especially wives, do not rank highly as active participants in Perikles' view. He addresses them last and only very briefly. *Kleos* (fame) of any kind is unbecoming to women, even favorable *kleos*. Judging from his derogatory, rather condescendingly Thucydidean, remarks about Homer, we can perhaps infer that Perikles did not delight in Homeric poetry. But if he did admire Homer, it is clear that Perikles would have preferred the male-centered *Iliad* to the *Odyssey*, with its intention of undoing the influence of the bad *kleos* of Klytaimnestra in favor of spreading the word about the noble *kleos* of Penelope.

Like his protagonist Perikles, Thucydides finds little space in his narrative for women. Simon Hornblower goes so far as to say that his disregard of women is one of the things that distinguishes the "single-sex world of Thucydides"[112] from that of his predecessor Herodotus. Since the feminine is often associated with the participationist dimension of experience, we would suggest that the grudging interest that Thucydides and Perikles pay to women has philosophical implications that are highly relevant to the theme of this book. As we will discuss in Part III, the symbolism of the feminine is extremely important both to Plato and to the Daoists, who wish to emphasize the irrefutably participationist dimension of consciousness, a dimension that is ignored at our peril.

The intentional consciousness views reality in an objectifying way. It intends reality as an object of the consciousness. The danger in emphasizing this aspect of consciousness too exclusively is the oblivion into which that overemphasis casts the participatory dimension, for the consciousness is itself part of the reality that it is attempting to understand. Objectivizing is necessary, but carried to an extreme it will obscure the reality of the participatory dimension. And it was the intention of the great historian Thucydides to see reality as objectively as possible, so much so that he sometimes appears tragically to forget the ways in which he is himself implicated in the very process he is analyzing. When these spots of oblivion surface as moments of unwitting kinship between subject and object, as is the case in the instance of the "subject" Thucydides and its Periklean "object," it is incumbent upon those who are sensitive to the damage done by such acts of imaginative oblivion to point out such tragic kinship. That is what we are doing at the present time. Perhaps those who read this book will have the patience to point out the blind spots that motivate the present analysis. We certainly would not presume to exempt ourselves from this process of an oblivious objectifying of the participatory dimension of reality.

Thucydides, then, attempted to render reality as objectively as possible. He is often remarkably successful. His knowledge of human nature and of psychology is powerfully perceptive. His analytical skills are exceptionally keen. There is an ineluctability to the events he narrates that strikes even the contemporary reader as possessing the undeniable solidity of objective truth. At moments, however, this attempt at almost complete objectivity, this effort to remove his own subjectivity from the text, has a rather bizarre feel.

We might recall here how Sima Qian concludes his history with his own autobiography, including a mention of the personal disaster that resulted in his personal mutilation and fall from favor. In the postface to the *Records of the Historian*, Sima Qian presents his theory that literary composition is often born of suffering and disaster, and he cites many previous authors who exemplify the theory, such as King Wen, Confucius, and Hanfeizi. Thucydides too suffered an unjustified fall from favor, and his great work is the result of some twenty years' exile following his dishonorable and unmerited dismissal from military duty. He does not speak about his own misfortune as openly as does Sima Qian, and the Greek historian's reserve is admirable. But the reserve verges on the bizarre when the narrator, in discussing the Spartan general Brasidas's assault against the Athenian-allied city of Amphipolis in the eighth year of the war, suddenly refers to himself in the third person. Thucydides does not say, "I arrived too late to save the city, whose inhabitants had already decided to surrender." What the historian in fact says is, "In this way they gave up the city, and late in the same day, Thucydides and his ships entered the harbor of Eion" (IV.106.3). And in the next several chapters, the narrator likewise objectifies himself by talking about what "Thucydides" did. Of this stylistic device, Hornblower (1. p. 333) in his commentary remarks:

> Thucydides can surely have had few or no precedents for mentioning himself as an agent in a narrative work. ... When speaking of himself as an agent in the present section he invariably uses the third person, thus conferring detachment on the narrative.

Thucydides' detachment achieved through his reference to himself in the third person is a bit bizarre, but perhaps rather harmlessly so. At other moments, however, the narrative achieves a degree of icily objective detachment that is positively unnerving. One such moment is the famous dialogue between the Melians and Athenians. It is the

141

summer of the sixteenth year of the war. The people of the island of Melos do not wish to be subjugated to Athenian rule. This is not acceptable to the Athenians, who argue that an independent Melos will weaken Athens' reputation and power. The idealism of Perikles has narrowed to a purely pragmatic policy of imperial domination. The Athenians had been known for their idealism, foolish and extreme though it may at times have been. As the Corinthian envoy had observed of the Athenians in Book I, "they alone [*monoi gar*] are enabled to call a thing hoped for a thing got, by the speed with which they act upon their resolutions" (I.70.7–8). That Athenian idealism has now turned to an icy pragmatism for, as the now callously pragmatic Athenians advise the idealistic Melians sixteen years later, "you are the only men [*all' oun monoi ge*] who regard future events as more certain than what lies before your eyes, and who look upon that which is out of sight, merely because you wish it, as already realized" (V.113.1). In crushing the Melians, the Athenians are murdering their formerly idealistic selves.

In his funeral oration, Perikles had praised the freedom enjoyed by Athenian citizens. We find none of that rhetoric here. What is at stake is not principle, but power. The question of justice, the Athenians argue, is quite beside the point. The Melians believe that they have justice on their side:

> We trust that the gods may grant us fortune as good as yours, since we are just men fighting against unjust, and that what we lack in power will be made up by the alliance of the Lacedaemonians, who are bound, if only for very shame, to come to the aid of their kindred. Our confidence, therefore, after all is not so utterly irrational.

To which the Athenians reply:

> When you speak of the favor of the gods, we may as fairly hope for that as yourselves, neither our pretensions nor our conduct being in any way contrary to what men believe of the gods, or practice among themselves. Of the gods we believe, and of men we know, that by a necessary law of their nature they rule wherever they can. And it is not as if we were the first to make this law, or to act upon it when made: we found it existing before us, and shall leave it to exist after us; all we do is to make use of it, knowing that you and everybody else, having the same power as we have, would do the same as we do. Thus, as far as the gods are concerned, we have good reason not to be afraid [*ou phoboumetha*] that we shall be at a disadvantage. (V.104–5)

For the Athenians, "justice" is simply a word. The reality to which the word refers does not exist. It will remain for Plato, in the *Republic*, to make the case that justice is indeed preferable to injustice and more in tune with the divine measure. But where does Thucydides, who wrote "before philosophy," himself stand on this issue? What he presents us with in this "dialogue" (if dialogue it can truly be called when one side has not the slightest interest in engaging in a meeting of minds), however, is the objective fact of the encounter. We must draw our own conclusions.[113]

The Melians will not capitulate, and their fate is sealed. In two brief, dispassionate sentences, Thucydides records the Melians' fate. That winter the Melians are forced, finally, to surrender:

> The Athenians thereupon slew all the adult males whom they had taken and made slaves of the children and women. The place itself they peopled with new settlers from Athens, subsequently sending at a later time five hundred colonists. (V.116.4)

Were we to read of an incident such as this in *Records of the Historian*, Sima Qian would surely have registered a sigh or a groan. Thucydides' silence is chilling. How are we to interpret the Greek historian's icy objectivity? Is he rendering an adverse judgment on the cruelty and cynicism of the Athenians, or are we simply to see and to accept that this is the way things work in the world of power politics, of *realpolitik*?

Thucydides is most surely a subtle analyst who carefully and clearly presents his materials so as to reveal the events that shaped the forces that were unleashed in the great upheaval (*kinêsis*) of his day. The blind spot in the enterprise, however, is precisely the consummately intelligent historian's unwitting complicity in the very tragic story that he is telling. King Oedipus of Thebes at first deeply resisted, and then tragically accepted, the idea that he was himself the cause of the plague that was destroying his city. Oedipus may be taken as a symbol of the mind of fifth-century Athens, as a symbol, that is, of an intentionality that refuses to see itself as participating in a greater whole that defies intentionalist control and domination. The intentionality of Thucydides, likewise, blinded the great historian from seeing the ways in which his own rationalism, his own quest for almost total objectivity, participated in the very phenomena he so brilliantly and tragically analyzed. We might call this the unwitting tragic irony of Thucydides' analysis of the tragedy of Athens.

Thucydides' story of the tragic demise of Athens, then, is even more tragic than Thucydides believed. Oedipus' blindness is precisely the blindness of Thucydides. As Simon Hornblower observes, Thucydides' "vocabulary for [his own] intellectual inquiry has affinities with that of the Sophocles of the *Oedipus Tyrannus*."[114] Like the Sophists and King Oedipus, Thucydides is concerned with probability, evidence, establishing the certainty of objective truth. Sophocles has his Oedipus appropriate the technical vocabulary of the Sophists of his day, with their Protagorean doctrine, "Of all things, man is the measure," in order to *critique* their rationalism.[115]

Let us look briefly at two of the fragments of Protagoras, who informs the critical background of Sophocles' play. We have already alluded to the opening sentence of the fragment (B 1) from the treatise *On Truth*. Quoted at somewhat greater length, it reads: "Of all things, the measure [*metron*] is man, of the being that they are, of the not being, that they are not."[116] Another passage, from a treatise *On the Gods*, reads:

> About the gods I am not able to know either that they are, or that they are not, or what they are like in shape, the things preventing knowledge being many, such as the obscurity of the subject and that the life of man is short. (B 4)

In the first fragment, the emphasis is upon the ability of the intentional consciousness to measure the "objective," empirical, material world. In the second, the luminous experience of divine mystery is reduced to the seen and the empirical. The gods are too obscure to be objects of certain knowledge. Perhaps if life were longer and we could develop more sophisticated instruments, Protagoras implies, we would be able to say something more definite and accurate about what Laozi calls "the *dao* that cannot be put into words." But in the present state of science, Protagoras implies, skepticism is the only rational course.

In the *Oedipus Tyrannus*, which was produced in 428 BCE, in the fourth year of the war, Sophocles vigorously calls into question the Protagorean notion that "of all things, the measure is man." As a supposed foreigner, Oedipus achieves success by virtue of his quick-witted intelligence, his cleverness or *gnômê*, a favorite word of Thucydides. Oedipus becomes king of Thebes by solving the riddle of the Sphinx: "What is it," the riddle asks, "that walks on four legs in the morning, on two at noon, at three in the evening?" Oedipus gets the objectively right answer, which is "man," but the play reveals that Oedipus in truth does not know who he is.

The rationalism of King Oedipus, which Sophocles sees as a pathology that characterizes his contemporary Athens, is precisely the rationalism of Thucydides. Like Oedipus and especially like Iokastê in the *Oedipus Tyrannus*, Thucydides is impatient with seers and oracles. The historian criticizes the great Nikias, whom he admired in so many other ways, because the general was "somewhat given to divination and the like" (VII.50). In Sophocles' play, Oedipus is a symbol of the rationalist desire to master reality, to know it from the outside rather than patiently participating in it. The *Oedipus Tyrannus* (together with the later, posthumous *Oedipus Colonus*) is a plea for a participationist notion of reason that Plato will make increasingly explicit throughout his work, as we shall discuss in Part III. Oedipus wished to save Thebes, but ironically he was himself the cause of the very plague he wished to eradicate. Thucydides, likewise, exemplifies and is deeply implicated in the very rationalist ethos that is the subject of his analysis and that resulted in the catastrophe of Athens' demise in the Peloponnesian War. In Part III, we shall see how the sages Confucius, Laozi, Zhuangzi and the philosopher Plato articulate the participatory dimension that Thucydides' intentionalist rationalism had eclipsed.

Summary and conclusion

In our analysis of the Homeric symbolism of the Siren and the Daoist figuration of the sage in the introduction to this book, we observed that Homer worries more than does Laozi about the threat to the intentional consciousness that is posed by the allure of the experience of complete participation in the *dao*. In Part I, we traced the emergence of the intentional consciousness in two roughly contemporary works, the *Odyssey* and the *Classic of Poetry*, and we suggested how the Chinese poets worry more than does Homer about the dangers of eclipsing the experience of participation. In the present part, we noted a similar pattern in our comparison of the works of Thucydides and Sima Qian. We focused our comparison on the topics of (1) how these two historians viewed tradition; (2) how they structured their works; and (3) to what degree they were aware of the ways in which they were themselves necessarily implicated in the stories they were relating.

1. Sima Qian sees himself as a filial son who is deeply embedded in tradition. Thucydides, on the other hand, is rather contemptuous of his literary fathers. Sima Qian, in other words, far more than Thucydides, sees himself as fully participating in a tradition.
2. Despite the fact that his historical work was an unpublished fragment at the time of his death, Thucydides' *History of the Peloponnesian War* has a single-minded narrative thrust and a clear structure which we have shown to be indebted to Greek tragedy – although Thucydides nowhere explicitly acknowledges this debt. Sima Qian structures his large and sprawling work, in part, around the categories and numerology that he derived from the social and cosmological thought of his time. If Thucydides' work has the rigorous and severe outline of Greek tragedy, Sima Qian's evokes the emotionalism of the Chinese lyric tradition as epitomized by the *Classic of Poetry*, a work we discussed at length in Part I. In Sima

Qian we do not find the firm and unambiguous clarity of purpose that characterizes Thucydides' history.

3. In the preceding two sections of Part II, we discussed how Sima Qian, far more self-consciously than Thucydides, sees himself as personally involved in the issues and events that his narratives present. As his account moves closer to his own era, the recounting of which makes up the greatest portion of *Records of the Historian*, readers can sense Sima Qian's even greater investment and involvement in the stories he is telling. Sima's own personal experiences, which the Chinese historian movingly relates in his history and in his "Letter to Ren An," often color his analyses of historical events and personages. Sima Qian does not shy away from such personal entanglements with his material.

Thucydides, in contrast, attempts to erase his own subjectivity from the story he is telling. When he must refer to his own involvement in the war, he detaches himself from the narrative and speaks of himself in the third person. Thucydides does not, as we have mentioned, explicitly acknowledge his debt to Greek tragedy. Such acknowledgment is perhaps not to be expected from an author who has an antagonistic relation to the many traditions from which his own work derives. We have tried to uncover some of the significant ways in which the "subject" Thucydides, which the historian has tried to suppress, nevertheless emerges in the historian's attempt to write as "objective" an account as he could manage. Readers of this book might note that we have discussed Sima Qian at somewhat greater length than Thucydides. This is due, in part, to the fact that Sima Qian asks us to see the historian in his work and that he thus invites his readers to undertake the very kinds of exegeses we have attempted. Thucydides has tried to absent himself from his own history, and he has, for the most part, succeeded remarkably well.

The essence of Greek tragedy, on the paradigm of Sophocles' *Oedipus Tyrannus*, is tragic irony: the protagonist is unaware of how he has prepared his own demise. Thucydides' *Peloponnesian War* is more tragic than its author intended, for the historian's relentless quest for objectivity is emblematic of the very rationalism, as embodied in the Athenian character, that was the cause of the conflict. We shall return to Greek tragedy in the third part of this book, specifically to the play that, for Nietzsche, defined the essence of tragedy, Euripides' *Bacchae*. Platonic philosophy, with its strong Dionysiac element so clearly evoked by Plato in the *Symposium*, is an attempt to recover the participatory dimension that had been eclipsed by the objectivizing intentionalism so relentlessly pursued by Thucydides, who wrote before the philosophy of Plato. We will conclude by discussing how Laozi and Zhuangzi attempt – as does Plato, and at roughly the same historical moment – to recover and explicitly articulate the luminous, participatory dimension of consciousness.

Notes

1. See Stephen W. Durrant, *The Cloudy Mirror: Tension and Conflict in the Writings of Sima Qian* (Albany: State University of New York Press, 1995), esp. chapter 2 ("Sima Qian's Confucius"), pp. 29–45, in which the author suggests that "Confucius is the central character in *Records of the Historian*" (p. 29). Sima Qian believed that Confucius "can indeed be called 'the ultimate sage' " (*Shi ji* 47.1947).

2. "Little Gidding," ll. 234–5 of *The Four Quartets*.

3. Cf. James Joyce's Vician view of history in *Finnegans Wake*. History is not a matter of dates and a parade of external events, but is rather constituted by the individual, experiencing consciousness (particularly in the mode of imagination) in defining moments of attunement with reality. See Donald Phillip Verene (ed.), *Vico and Joyce* (Albany: State University Press of New York, 1987).

4. For the philosophy of history implied by the *Dao de jing*, see Seon-Hee Suh Kwon, "Eric Voegelin and Lao Tzu: The Search for Order," Ph.D. dissertation, Texas Tech University, 1991.

5. The phrase "before philosophy" was given currency by Henri Frankfort in his well-known book of that name, which he wrote with Mrs. Henri Frankfort, John A. Wilson, and Thorkild Jacobsen. The volume first appeared, with a different title (*The Intellectual Adventure of Ancient Man*), in 1946 and was issued as *Before Philosophy* by Pelican Books in 1949. In the title of this chapter ("Before and after Philosophy"), we mean "philosophy" in its decisive, Platonic embodiment. Thucydides, it is true, postdates most of the pre-Socratics, is a contemporary of Democritus and the Sophists, and is clearly influenced, as we shall discuss later in this chapter, both by the Sophists and by the Hippocratic writers. Indeed, it is precisely the Sophistic influence on Thucydides that contributes to making its author a perhaps less than completely self-aware ally of the very kinds of Sophistic attitudes that provoke Sophocles' anti-Sophistic play, the *Oedipus Tyrannus*.

6. For a comparative study of Thucydides and Plato, see David Grene, *Greek Political Theory: The Image of Man in Plato and Thucydides* (Chicago: University of Chicago Press, 1965), originally published as *Man in His Pride: A Study in the Political Philosophy of Plato and Thucydides* (Chicago: University of Chicago Press, 1950).

7. Alfred North Whitehead, *Process and Reality: An Essay in Cosmology* (New York: Macmillan, 1929), p. 16.

8. A number inflated a bit from the 47,000 given approximately twenty years ago in the critical study of David N. Keightley, *Sources of Shang History: The Oracle-Bone Inscriptions of Bronze Age China* (Berkeley: University of California Press, 1978), p. 138.

9. *Sources of Western Zhou History* (Berkeley: University of California Press, 1991), pp. 1–4.

10. *Ibid.*, p. 181.

11. On this issue, with regard to the bone inscriptions, see Keightley, *Sources of Shang History*, p. 45.

12. In this distinction, Ban Gu is presumably following an early conception that there were once two court historians: a "historian of the left," who recorded words, and a "historian of the right," who recorded affairs (*Han shu* 10.1715). The *Li ji* [Records of Ritual] also makes this distinction but assigns the recording of words to the historian of the right and affairs to the historian of the left (*Li ji* 13/1).

13. The fifth-century BCE philosopher Mozi refers to annals from the states of Zhou, Yan, Song, and Qi. See *Mozi*, ch. 31. We know from other evidence that such records were maintained, at least, by the states of Qin, the state of Chu, and the state of Wei.

14. Thus, the Qin destruction of all state annals other than their own, ordered as a part of the famous book-burning of 213 BCE, was as much a symbolic act of political consolidation as a mean-spirited attempt to efface the past. For a translation of the proposal to burn books and the result, see *The Records of the Grand Historian: Qin Dynasty*, trans. Burton Watson (Hong Kong: Research Centre for Translation, Chinese University of Hong Kong, and Columbia University Press, 1993), pp. 54–5.

15. The *Shuo wen jie zi* [Explaining Simple Graphs and Analyzing Compound Graphs], China's earliest etymological dictionary, says that the character *shi* "comes from a hand holding the rectifying principle" (*Shuo wen jie zi zhu* IB.11). This explanation of the historian as the judge of right and wrong may reflect Sima Qian's understanding of the essential responsibility of his office, but most modern scholars have rejected this explanation of the shape of the character. For alternative views, see the articles by Hu Shi, Shen Gangbo, and Dai Junren in *Zhongguo shixue shi lunwen xuanji*, Vol. 1, ed. Du Weiyun and Huang Jinxing (Taipei: Huashi, 1980), pp. 1–29.

16. See the exceptionally insightful article of Xu Fuguan, "Yuan shi – you zongjiao tongxiang renwen de shixue chengli" [The Original Scribe – From a Religious toward the Establishment of a Humanistic Historiography], in *Zhongguo shixue shi lunwen xuanji* [A Collection of Essays on the History of Chinese Historiography], Vol. 3, ed. Tu Weiyun and Chen Jinzhong (Taipei: Huashi, 1980), pp. 1–72. Much of what follows is influenced by Xu's study.

17. The development of this notion of the great power of *Spring and Autumn Annals* is described in Qian Mu's "Kong zi yu *Chun qiu*" [Confucius and *Spring and Autumn Annals*], *Liang Han jingxue jin-guwen pingyi* [A Critical Discussion of New and Old Script Schools in Han Dynasty Classical Studies] (Taipei: Dongda, 1983), pp. 235–83. For a short, English-language discussion of this issue, see Durrant, *The Cloudy Mirror*, pp. 50–1, 57–8, and 61–7; and Sarah A. Queen, *From Chronicle to Canon: The Hermeneutic of the Spring and Autumn According to Tung Chung-shu* (Cambridge: Cambridge University Press, 1996), pp. 115–26.

18. On the "praise and blame" interpretation of *Spring and Autumn Annals*, which has dominated traditional views of this text, see the masterful study by George Kennedy, "Interpretation of the Ch'un-ch'iu," in *The Selected Works of George A. Kennedy*, ed. Tien-yi Li (New Haven: Far Eastern Publications, Yale University, 1964), pp. 79–103.

19. Xu Fuguan, "Yuan shi," p. 26.

20. This is Mencius's characterization of the popularity of Mohism in his own day. See *Mencius* IIIB.9. The sudden decline and disappearance of Mohism after the Qin is a

fascinating issue in the history of Chinese thought.

21. On this issue, see A. C. Graham, *Disputers of the Tao*, pp. 267–9, and Roger T. Ames, *The Art of Rulership: A Study in Ancient Chinese Political Thought* (Honolulu: University of Hawaii Press, 1983), pp. 1–27.

22. *Ibid.*, p. 271.

23. All *Shi ji* references, unless otherwise noted, are to the Beijing Zhonghua punctuated edition of 1992.

24. Michael Loewe, "The Former Han Dynasty," in *The Cambridge History of China*, Vol. 1: *The Ch'in and Han Empires, 221 B.C.–A.D. 220* (Cambridge: Cambridge University Press, 1986), pp. 123–7.

25. Derk Bodde, "The State and Empire of Ch'in," in *The Cambridge History of China*, Vol. I (Cambridge: Cambridge University Press), p. 84.

26. On the growth of Confucian infuence in the early Han, see Homer H. Dubs, "The Victory of Han Confucianism," in *History of the Former Han Dynasty*, Vol. 2 (Baltimore: Waverly Press, 1944), pp. 341–7.

27. *Han shu*, Zhonghua punctuated edition, 56.2523.

28. Robert P. Kramers, "The Development of the Confucian Schools," in *The Cambridge History of China*, Vol. 1 (Cambridge: Cambridge University Press), pp. 752–9.

29. *Han shu*, 32.2737–8. See the translation of Burton Watson in *Ssu-ma Ch'ien: Grand Historian of China* (New York: Columbia University Press, 1958), pp. 67–9.

30. See Durrant, *The Cloudy Mirror*, pp. 1–45.

31. The term "heavenly offices," in this context, is a reference to the astronomical and scribal duties of the historian.

32. The commentator in this case is the Tang scholar Sima Zhen (fl. 713–42).

33. For an excellent Chinese-language treatment of this subject, see Jin Dejian, *Sima Qian suojian shu kao* [An Investigation of the Books Seen by Sima Qian] (Shanghai: Renmin, 1963).

34. Translations of passages from Herodotus are adapted from the version of A. D. Godley in the Loeb Library Edition, 3 vols (Cambridge, MA: Harvard University Press, 1996). For Thucydides, we have adapted the translations of Richard Crawley (New York: Modern Library, 1982) and of Charles Foster Smith in the Loeb edition, 4 vols (Cambridge, MA: Harvard University Press, 1986). The Crawley translation is now available in a wonderful new edition, revised and complete with maps and helpful headnotes, by Robert D. Strassler, entitled *The Landmark Thucydides* (New York: Free Press, 1996). In our interpretation of the relation between Herodotus and Thucydides, we have profited from Eric Voegelin's discussion in *The World of the Polis* (Baton Rouge: Louisiana State University Press, 1957), which is Vol. 2 of *Order and History*, 5 vols (1956–87).

35. The fragment from Heraclitus is translated from the Greek text in *The Presocratic Philosophers*, ed. G. S. Kirk and J. E. Raven (Cambridge: Cambridge University Press, 1964), pp. 182–215.

36. *Herodotus: The Histories*, translated by Aubrey de Sélincourt, revised by A. R. Burns (Harmondsworth: Penguin, 1954; rpt. 1983), p. 173.

37. See his treatise entitled *Ancient Medicine*.

38. *A Commentary on Thucydides*, 2 vols (Oxford: Clarendon Press, 1991, 1996), vol. 1: p. 58.

39. *A Historical Commentary on Thucydides*, 5 vols (Oxford: Clarendon Press, 1945–81), vol. 1, p. 149. Gomme then goes on to cite some examples of Herodotean excursions into the fabulous (*to mythôdes*): "Candaules and Gyges, Croesus and Adrestos, Polykrates and his ring, Xerxes' dream before the sailing of the armada and Hippias' dream before Marathon, Themistokles and the allied admirals before Salamis."

40. *The Anxiety of Influence: A Theory of Poetry* (Oxford: Oxford University Press, 1973).

41. There are numerous problems with the way Sima Qian has sorted his material among these sections. Some of these issues will be mentioned below but cannot be studied in great detail here. For a good survey of these issues, see Zhang Dake, *Shi ji yanjiu* [A Study of Records of the Historian] (Lanzhou: Gansu Renmin Press, 1985), pp. 203–29. An excellent English-language study is that of Burton Watson, *Ssu-ma Ch'ien: Grand Historian of China* (New York: Columbia University Press, 1958), pp. 101–34.

42. For some trenchant comments on this hierarchical organization and the way it is reflected in tomb art of the same general period, see Wu Hung, *The Wu Liang Shrine: The Ideology of Early Chinese Pictorial Art* (Stanford, CA: Stanford University Press, 1989), pp. 148–58. Sima Qian's brief description of his five sections, quoted here, is found in *Shi ji* 130.3319 and is translated in Watson, *Ssu-ma Ch'ien*, pp. 56–7.

43. On the way in which the world was organized around schemes of five, see Joseph Needham, *Science and Civilisation in China*, Vol. 2 (Cambridge: Cambridge University Press, 1956), pp. 232–65, especially pp. 262–3.

44. *Science and Civilisation*, Vol. 3 (Cambridge: Cambridge University Press, 1959), pp. 402–6.

45. These correspondences are suggested by Zhang Shoujie (fl. 737) and others. See "Lun Shi li" ("A Discussion of the Organizational Principles of *Records*), p. 13 of the appendix to *Shi ji*, Vol. 10. For a translation of Zhang's comments, with some cautionary comments, see Mark Edward Lewis, *Writing and Authority in Early China* (Albany: State University of New York, 1999), p. 313.

46. See Needham, *Science and Civilisation*, vol. 3, pp. 396–8.

47. Which seems to be the opinion of the great scholar Zhao Yi (1727–1814), who, among his extremely perceptive comments on Sima Qian, suggested that his work proceeded by "randomly getting [a chapter together] and randomly editing it into his text." See *Ershier shi zhaji* [A Notebook on the Twenty-two Dynastic Histories] (Taipei: Letian, 1973), p. 5.

48. See *Han shu* 6.2735. On this particular translation, see Durrant, *The Cloudy Mirror*, pp. 124, 125.

49. For a discussion of the interplay of heaven and man, as Sima Qian portrays it, in one critical moment in Chinese history, see Durrant, *The Cloudy Mirror*, pp. 129–43.

50. *Shi tong tongshi* [A Comprehensive Explanation of A Study of History] (rpt., Taipei: Liren, 1980), p. 19.

51. Originally published in *Diogenes*, 42 (1963): 20–43, and quoted here from Jaroslav

Prusek, *Chinese History and Literature: Collection of Studies* (Dordrecht: D. Reidel, 1970), pp. 17–34.

52. *Ibid.*, p. 31.

53. See *Han shu* 62.2735. These historiographic principles are discussed further in Durrant, *The Cloudy Mirror*, pp. 124–9.

54. Ruan Zhisheng, "Shi lun Sima Qian suoshuo de 'tong gujin zhi bian'" [A Preliminary Essay on Sima Qian's Statement "To Penetrate the Transformations of Ancient and Modern Times"], *Zhongguo shixue shi lunwen xuanji*, pp. 185, 186.

55. To maintain the continuity, Sima Qian must fill in two gaps: first, the gap between the end of the Zhou dynasty in 256 BCE and the consolidation of the First Qin Emperor in 221 BCE; and second, the gap between the fall of Qin in 206 BCE and the proclamation of the Han dynasty in 202 BCE. The first of these is filled by creating a "Basic Annals of the Qin," which precedes the "Basic Annals of the First Qin Emperor," and the second by the "Basic Annals of Xiang Yu."

56. On the role of Sima Qian's historiography in the creation of a Chinese empire, see Michael Puett's forthcoming article, "The Tragedy of Creation: Sima Qian's Narrative of the Rise of Empire in Early China."

57. *Demystifying Mentalities* (Cambridge: Cambridge University Press, 1990), p. 122.

58. "To put aside the later kings and take as a model high antiquity is like putting aside one's own ruler and serving another man's ruler," *Xunzi*, Harvard–Yenching Edition, 13.5.30–1.

59. There are several excellent translations. We particularly recommend the most recent of these, which is by Stephen Owen: *An Anthology of Chinese Literature: Beginnings to 1911*, ed. and trans. Stephen Owen (New York: W. W. Norton, 1996), pp. 136–42. Our translations of this document follow Owen with minor adaptations.

60. "Thucydides and Tragedy," *Collected Essays* (Oxford: Oxford University Press, 1983). See also J. Peter Euben, *The Tragedy of Political Theory: The Road Not Taken* (Princeton, NJ: Princeton University Press, 1990), esp. pp. 172–3, n. 11. To Euben's bibliography, usefully cited in the footnote, should now be added Jacqueline de Romilly, *La Construction de la vérité chez Thucydide* (Paris: Juillard, 1990), esp. pp. 62–5. The Greek epic is itself imbued with tragic elements, and not only the clearly tragic *Iliad*, which has a tragic plot centered on the wrath of Achilles. Even the more "comic" *Odyssey*, the less elevated of the two Homeric epics, has tragic elements. For these, see Steven Shankman, *In Search of the Classic: The Greco-Roman Tradition. Homer to Valéry and Beyond* (University Park: Pennsylvania State University Press, 1994), ch. 4. In *Pindar's Homer: The Lyric Possession of an Epic Past* (Baltimore: Johns Hopkins University Press, 1990), Gregory Nagy views Herodotus's *Histories* as embodying a critique of imperialist Athens as tragic *tyrannos* (pp. 308–13).

61. Our translation of passages from Aristotle's *Poetics* is based on the Greek text in *Aristotle's Theory of Poetry and Fine Art* (New York: Dover, 1951).

62. See the Hellenistic critic Dionysius of Halicarnassus, *On the Style of Thucydides*, esp. ch. 24, where the Hellenistic critic speaks of the qualities of Thucydidean style, which is notable for its "harshness [*austêron*], gravity [*embrithes*], tendency to inspire awe and fear [*deinon kai phoberon*], and above all else the power of stirring the emotions [*pathêtikon*]," trans. W. Kendrick Pritchett, *Dionysius of Halicarnassus: On Thucydides* (Berkeley: University of California Press, 1975), p. 18.

63. On the word *hamartia* and its cognates in Thucydides, see J. M. Bremer, *Hamartia: Tragic Error in the Poetics of Aristotle and in Greek Tragedy* (Amsterdam: Adolf M. Hakkert, 1969), pp. 38–40, 46.

64. *Thucydides* (Princeton, NJ: Princeton University Press, 1984), p. 210.

65. The reference to Lao Peng is problematic. Some say Confucius has Pengzu in mind, a long-lived mythical figure of antiquity, others believe he is speaking of both Laozi and Pengzu, and still others think it is a reference to some other figure who is now lost to history.

66. On this issue, see also Michael Puett, "Nature and Artifice: Debates in Late Warring States China concerning the Creation of Culture," *Harvard Journal of Asiatic Studies*, 57 (2) (December, 1997), p. 474.

67. For two excellent translations, see *Songs of the South, An Ancient Chinese Anthology of Poems*, trans., annotated and introduced by David Hawkes (Harmondsworth: Penguin, 1985), pp. 54–60; and *Records of the Grand Historian*, Vol. 1, pp. 435–56.

68. Cf. 130.3300 and *Han shu* 62.2735. Part of the latter of these two references is translated on pp. 109–10.

69. On suicide in ancient China as a means of demonstrating sincerity or integrity, see Eric Henry, "The Motif of Recognition," *Harvard Journal of Asiatic Studies*, 47(1) (June, 1987): 13.

70. On this topic, see Stephen Owen, *Remembrances: The Experience of the Past in Classical Chinese Poetry* (Cambridge, MA: Harvard University Press, 1986).

71. Translation by James Robert Hightower in *The Columbia Anthology of Traditional Chinese Literature*, ed. Victor Mair (New York: Columbia University Press, 1994), p. 392.

72. As we have seen, Sima Qian "always weeps" when he visits the spot of Qu Yuan's suicide (84.2503). He also says that whenever he reads Yue Yi's letter in response to the King of Yan, he "always puts down the document and weeps" (80.2436). He "puts down the document and sighs" whenever he reads about King Hui's interview with Mencius (74.2343) and whenever he reads about the advancement of educational institutions in his own age (121.3115). "Alas, sad indeed," he groans about those "who are slandered by lesser men" (107.2856). "Alas, how sad" is his reaction to Guo Xie's execution (124.3189). "Alas, tragic indeed" is the fact that Chen Xi was misled by evil men (93.2642). And "Tragic indeed" is how he reacts to Wu Qi's death (65.2169), the story of Wu Zixu (66.2183), and the fact that some men's names vanish "like smoke" (61.2127). When Sima Qian visits the home and temple of Confucius, he tells us that he becomes so enraptured that he "is unable to depart" (47.1747). Many other similarly emotional reactions could be listed.

73. For more on Sima Qian's beliefs about *Spring and Autumn Annals*, see Durrant, *The Cloudy Mirror*, pp. 64–9. Mencius's comments are particularly important in later theories of Confucius and *Spring and Autumn Annals*. See *Mencius* 3B.9, translated by D. C. Lau in *Mencius* (Harmondsworth: Penguin, 1970), pp. 113–15. On Dong Zhongshu and *Spring and Autumn Annals*, there is now the excellent study by Queen, *From Chronicle to Canon*, esp. pp. 115–26.

74. *Mengzi* 6.14a (3B.9).

75. On Daoism during this period and the influence of Empress Dou, see Michael Loewe,

"The Former Han Dynasty," pp. 136–9, and "The Religious and Intellectual Background," pp. 693–7, both in *The Cambridge History of China*, Vol. 1. On the problematic content of Sima Qian's term "Huang-Lao," see the excellent summary and discussion in Lewis, *Writing and Authority in Early China*, p. 347.

76. On this theme, see Queen, *From Chronicle to Canon*, pp. 6–7.

77. *Wen xuan*, 48.1066 (Commercial Press).

78. *La Chine romanesque: fictions d'Orient et d'Occident* (Paris: Éditions de Seuil, 1995), p. 150. See also his historical novel *Le Fils du ciel et son annaliste* (Paris: Gallimard, 1992).

79. *Ershiwu shi*, *Shi ji* (Commercial Press edition), vol. 2, p. 130:30a (p. 1362). This is repeated later on in a text attributed to Ge Hong (283–343), *Xi jing za ji* (SBCK edition), pp. 6:19–20.

80. See, most notably, *Zuo zhuan*, Duke Xiang 25.2, translated by James Legge in *The Chinese Classics*, Vol. 5 (Oxford: Clarendon Press, 1893), pp. 514, 515.

81. *La Chine romanesque*, p. 147.

82. This is the opinion of Zhang Dake. See his useful summary of the entire problem in *Shi ji yanjiu*, pp. 165–9. Watson also summarizes the problem judiciously: "Whether Sima Qian got around to writing his chapter on 'The Basic Annals of the Present Emperor,' or whether he wrote it and it was later lost or suppressed, we do not know" (*The Records of the Grand Historian*, Vol. 1, p. 318).

83. For a discussion of five general issues upon which Sima Qian speaks disapprovingly of Emperor Wu, see Shi Ding, "Sima Qian xie, 'Jin shang (Han Wudi)'" [Sima Qian's Writing of "The Present Emperor" (Emperor Wu of the Han)], in *Sima Qian yanjiu xinlun* [New Essays in Sima Qian Studies] (Zhengzhou: Henan renmin, 1982), pp. 143–60.

84. *Han shu* 62.2732.

85. For example, in "The Letter to Ren An," Sima Qian bemoans the fact that "The rich and noble of ancient times whose names have perished are too numerous to count" (*Han shu* 62.2735).

86. On the development of this tradition, see especially Joseph Needham, *Science and Civilisation in China*, Vol. 5.3 (Cambridge: Cambridge University Press, 1976), pp. 1–50.

87. On the *fangshi*, see Isabella Robinet, *Histoire du Taoisme: des origines au XIVe siècle* (Paris: Les Éditions du Cerf, 1991), pp. 43–5. Robinet translates *fangshi* as "homme à techniques."

88. Certainly he would seem to agree, for example, with the harsh characterization of the First Qin Emperor that he puts in the mouth Wei Liao, a minister of the state of Han (see 6.230).

89. On this use of ironic juxtaposition in the narrative of the First Qin Emperor's life, see Stephen Durrant, "Ssu-ma Ch'ien's Portrayal of the First Ch'in Emperor," in *Imperial Rulership and Cultural Change in Traditional China*, ed. Frederick P. Brandauer and Huang Chun-chieh (Seattle: University of Washington Press, 1994), pp. 28–50.

90. We have followed here the translation of Tsai-fa Cheng, Zongli Lu, William H. Nienhauser, Jr. and Robert Reynolds in *The Grand Scribe's Records*, Vol. 1: *The Basic Annals of Pre-Han China*, ed. William H. Nienhauser, Jr. (Bloomington: Indiana University Press, 1994), pp. 154–5.

91. Needham notes that "Since metallic gold was the most beautiful and imperishable metal, it naturally came to be associated with the imperishability of the immortals, and if the mortal was to put on immortality it must somehow associate itself with the metal or its inner principle or nature. ... Later it was felt that the human body itself must somehow be transformed to a goldlike state, and later again that this could be effected by drinking or absorbing preparations of some kind of 'potable gold.'" *Science and Civilisation in China*, 5.3, p. 1.

92. For a discussion of these issues as they appear in the biographies of Bo Yi and Shu Qi, see Durrant, *The Cloudy Mirror*, pp. 19–26.

93. Such a position had been argued as early as the text *Mencius* and should be understood as an attack upon the Confucian construction of history. See *Mencius* IB.8, Lau, p. 68.

94. On this translation of *jiaren*, see Qian Zhongshu, *Guan zhui bian*, Vol. I (Hong Kong: Zhonghua, 1979), p. 372.

95. Certainly the Simas knew Gongsun Hong well. Sima Tan was at court as Prefect Grand Historian during these years, so he had an opportunity to view Gongsun at close distance. It is difficult to ascertain precisely when Sima Qian became a "Court Gentleman." Zheng Haosheng assigns this to 124 BCE, the year Gongsun became chancellor, in his *Sima Qian nianpu* [A Year-by-Year Chronology of Sima Qian] (rev. edition, Shanghai: Commercial Press, 1956), p. 42.

96. The Prefect Grand Historian served under the Grand Master of Ceremonies (*taichang*), who received a salary of 2000 piculs (*shi*), a term that originally referred to an actual payment in kind but later was a simple marker on a scale. The Prefect Grand Historian received 600 piculs, about one-third the salary of his superior. See Hans Bielenstein, *The Bureaucracy of Han Times* (Cambridge: University of Cambridge Press, 1980), pp. 17–22.

97. Sima Qian notes that his father "did not participate in governing people" (130:3293). Moreover, a careful reading of Sima Qian's words in the postface leads to the possible conclusion that Sima Tan was left behind on the Emperor's procession to Mount Tai either because he had displeased the Emperor, perhaps with theories about the *feng* and *shan* sacrifices incompatible with those of the "Masters of Method", or because he was not considered important enough to continue (130.3293). Finally, a passing reference to the Grand Historian's participation in a debate in 113 BCE concerning a sacrifice to the Earth does not make it sound as if Sima Tan was on the winning side of this issue (12.461).

98. Carrying a higher salary of 1000 piculs.

99. On the narrowing of specialization for those entering the bureaucracy as erudites, see the excellent study of Qian Mu, "Liang Han boshi jiafa kao" [An Investigation into the School System of the Erudites during the Han Dynasty], in *Liang Han jingxue jin gu pingyi* [A Critical Discussion of New and Old Script Schools in Han Dynasty Classical Studies] (Taipei: Dongda, 1983), pp. 171–82.

100. "When the Sima family left Zhou, they went to Jin. Then they split up, so that some were in Wei, some were in Zhao, and some were in Qin" (130.3286).

101. This was Sima Cuo, whom King Hui of Qin (*c*. 337–306 BCE) sent on an attack against the southwest state of Shu (see 130.3268).

102. This informs his discussion of the rise to power of the state of Qin in *Qin Han shi* [A History of the Qin and Han] (Taipei: Dongda, 1985), pp. 4–12.

103. Ji An is himself a very interesting case. He was a follower of Huang-Lao Daoism, Sima Qian says, and came from an old family of officials who had served in the state of Wei. He was exceedingly honest but was quite harsh, although he was always direct and only denounced people to their faces. He disparaged Confucian scholars and especially Gongsun Hong as men "harboring deceit and making a show of learning" (120.3108). Sima Qian declares him "worthy" (*xian*) and finds his ultimate decline in power "tragic" (120.3113).

104. Translated by James Robert Hightower in "The Fu of T'ao Ch'ien," *Harvard Journal of Asiatic Studies*, 17 (1954): 198.

105. On this rather quaint term, see n. 96 above.

106. Sima Qian provides Wei Qing with a rather lackluster biography (ch. 111) and seems to agree with a comment he quotes from another: "The worthy gentlemen of the empire did not praise Wei Qing" (111.2946).

107. On the pride of Thucydides, see K. J. Dover, *Thucydides, Greece and Rome: New Surveys in the Classics, No. 7* (Oxford: Clarendon Press, 1973), p. 44, who writes that Thucydides possessed "a sense of intellectual superiority which did not allow him seriously to consider that his verdicts might need to be reconsidered by others."

108. See Simon Hornblower, *A Commentary on Thucydides* (Oxford: Clarendon Press, 1991), Vol. 1, p. 309.

109. See Euben, *The Tragedy of Political Theory*, pp. 192ff., for other affinities between Thucydides and Perikles.

110. See Hornblower's *Commentary*, vol. 1, p. 314. For Dover, see *Classical Review*, 12 (1962): 103. Dover cites parallels from Plato, *Symposium* 173c 1, and Isocrates vi.42.

111. *A Historical Commentary on Thucydides*, vol. 2, p. 143. Gomme goes on to remark, "There is a *personal* consolation of the parents, children and widows of the fallen (from 44.3 to 45) which is in marked contrast to the warmth and splendour of all the rest of the speech in which the greatness of the city and the opportunities and qualities of the citizens are lauded. But this is in accordance with Perikles' character, at any rate as many of his contemporaries saw him; he was, unlike Peisistratos, whom in other respects he was said to resemble, not at all *dêmotikos* ("democratic," "folksy") in manner, nor, like Kimon, generous and hospitable, but unsociable, reserved, even haughty" (*ibid.*).

112. *Thucydides* (Baltimore: Johns Hopkins University Press, 1987), p. 14.

113. Jacqueline de Romilly, in *Thucydide et l'impérialisme* (Paris: Société d'Édition Les Belles Lettres, 1947), views Thucydides' representation of the Melian dialogue as a critique of Athenian imperialism. We are less sure of the nobility of Thucydides' intentions.

114. *Thucydides*, p. 108.

115. See Bernard Knox, *Oedipus of Thebes* (New Haven: Yale University Press, 1957). On Sophocles' play as a critique of fifth-century Athenian rationalism, see also Christopher Rocco, *Tragedy and Enlightenment: Athenian Political Thought and the Dilemmas of Modernity* (Berkeley: University of California Press, 1997), ch. 2 ("Sophocles' *Oedipus Tyrannos*: The Tragedy of Enlightenment"), pp. 34–67.

116. The Protagorean fragments are translated from Herman Diels, *Die Fragmente der Vorsokratiker*, 3 vols (Berlin: Weidmann, 1922), Vol. 2, pp. 228–30.

PART III

The philosopher, the sage, and the experience of participation

Philosophy does not arise in a vacuum. It is a response to concrete, historical events. Both Chinese and Greek philosophy emerge from periods of social crisis: in China, from the last century of the Spring and Autumn period and the subsequent two centuries of the Warring States period; in Greece, and specifically in the work of Plato, from the period of the Peloponnesian War. In the persons of sages such as Confucius and Laozi – whose actual lives, especially in the case of Laozi, remain shrouded in mystery – philosophy becomes a force in Chinese culture. By the end of the fourth and third centuries BCE, the old social order had largely broken down and the Zhou court no longer exercised any meaningful power. The feudatories that once loyally served the Zhou state were now independent states that fought with one another incessantly. Chinese philosophy arose in this atmosphere of political and social conflict, with the various Chinese thinkers each offering their solutions to this constant strife.

In our introductory remarks to Part II, we discussed the relation between history and philosophy and suggested how philosophy creates history by persuasively, and thus authoritatively, articulating a person's relationship to being, as the Greeks would have it, or to the *dao*, in the distinctive articulation of the Chinese sages. Historical or temporal existence, thus, will have meaning precisely in relation to how fully, or how poorly, human beings live in accordance with the insights achieved by the sages or philosophers. In responding to the narrow rationalism of his day, Plato develops figurations that articulate a balanced awareness of the relation between human intentionality and that intentionality's participation in a comprehensive structure of reality that can never be known as a whole. We have been associating the word "knowledge" with intentionalism and "wisdom" with an awareness of how that intentionalism is experienced as part of a mysterious whole that can never be mastered as an object of knowledge.

Confucius, in the *Analects*, reacts to the individualism of his day by suggesting that the *dao* can be found by experiencing one's identity as a participant in society. Laozi and Zhuangzi, perhaps reacting to the Confucian emphasis upon human beings as creatures who participate in society by developing their intentional, ethical consciousness, remind us that both the individual consciousness and society exist within a mysterious cosmic whole that we obscure to our peril.[1] The history of Chinese culture can, in fact, be viewed as attempting to achieve a balance between the intentionalist, ethical seeking of Confucius and the receptive, participatory awareness so beautifully and consistently expressed in Daoist thought and later enriched through the complex Daoist–Buddhist dialogue that went on in China during the late Han and post-Han period.[2] Western philosophy, while dominated in the past several hundred years by intentionalist rationalism, likewise can trace its roots to the balance achieved, in Platonic thought, between intentionality and the awareness, often achieved by Plato through his use of myth, of the intender's receptive participation in a larger cosmic whole.

Before we proceed to our consideration of the emergence of philosophical thought in these two cultures, an important caveat is in order. Throughout this chapter we shall speak of "philosophy" with reference to both Greece and China. The term "philosophy" means literally "the love of wisdom" and derives, of course, from the Greek word *philosophia*. Traditional China has no equivalent term. In fact, the modern Chinese word for philosophy, *zhexue*, was borrowed by Chinese from a nineteenth-century Japanese translation of the Western term. The formative thinkers of ancient China apparently had no general word for their activity at all. These thinkers were known as *zi* ("masters"), a word which is appended to the names of almost all of these figures and was sometimes rendered by the early missionary sinologists with the Latinate suffix *-cius* (Confu*cius*, Men*cius*, but Mo*zi*, Lao*zi* and Xun*zi* – who, if we wished to be consistent, might be called, respectively, Mocius, Laocius, and Xuncius). The use of this term "master" points to an important characteristic of early Chinese thought: it tends to develop around certain authoritative figures or teachers who then initiate an intellectual lineage. These lineages are called in Chinese *jia*, which usually is translated as "school" but literally means "family." The use of *jia* to describe an intellectual lineage, as well as a physical lineage, stresses the father–son-like characteristic of the teacher–student relationship in China and explains, in part, the conservative nature of much Chinese thought that some have contrasted so sharply with a more innovative Greek tradition.[3]

1 Contexts for the emergence of the sage and the philosopher

The emergence of the sage

The thirty-one hymns of Zhou constitute perhaps the earliest layer of the *Classic of Poetry*. As products of the first centuries of the reign of the Zhou kings,[4] a time when Heaven's Charge still rested squarely on the shoulders of the new dynasty, these hymns sing repeatedly of the greatness of the kings and are flush with confidence:

> Oh! August was King Wu,
> With no peer in glory.
> Truly cultured was King Wen,
> Opening the way for his posterity!
> His successor, Wu, received [the Charge],
> Conquered the Yin and slew them,
> And so established the task.
>
> (Mao 286)

Kings Wen and Wu provide a model of glorious and successful governance, and the later kings, these hymns make clear, are expected to sustain the new Zhou order. The institution of the king stands at the pinnacle of this order and provides the cohesion to keep a diverse assemblage of clans and regional interests bound together in a single polity. The Chinese written character for the word "king," *wang* 王, is made up of three horizontal lines joined in the middle by a vertical line. Xu Shen (30–124 CE), China's earliest and most influential lexicographer and etymologist, explains the character *wang* as follows:

The king [*wang*] is he to whom all under Heaven proceeds. Dong Zhongshu said, "He who in antiquity fashioned characters traced three lines, united them at the center, and called this 'king.' The three [lines] represent Heaven, Earth, and Humanity. He who communicates with all three is the 'king.'" Confucius said, "The one who joins the three is the king."[5]

It is unusual for Xu Shen to quote two earlier authorities, Confucius and Dong Zhongshu in this case, in a single definition. Perhaps he does this to lend authority to an etymology of which he himself is not entirely certain. In the past century or so, Xu Shen's explanation of the character *wang* has been challenged on the basis of script forms that appear on the oracle bones and probably were not known in Xu Shen's time. A current theory that takes these earliest forms into account is that the character *wang* originally included a symbol for "male" and an additional mark to indicate that this was the "virile male *par excellence*." To quote Leon Vandermeersch, "The king is called the virile *wang* because he is considered to be the father of the ethnic group and the inheritor of the power of the founding ancestor."[6]

Even an incorrect etymology from an ancient scholar of Xu Shen's stature, if he is indeed incorrect, is of value because it preserves a highly educated guess as to what would make sense historically. What is particularly interesting in both explanations of *wang* noted above is that they share a common emphasis upon the king as the central player in what we may call "a grand unity." In the first case, Xu Shen's etymology, the cosmic nature of this unity is underscored; the king links heaven, earth, and humanity. In the second etymology, which stresses the king's status as virile father, the emphasis is upon a genealogical unity that extends through the king's lineage and embraces virtually the entire ethnic group. Regardless of which etymology might be more accurate within the context of the history of early Chinese writing, we believe that each reflects important aspects – that is, the cosmic and the genealogical – of the institution of early Zhou kingship.

We have already discussed, in Part I, the early Zhou kings' claim that they ruled by means of Heaven's Charge (*tian ming*) and could maintain power only so long as they ruled with "shining virtue" and acted in accord with "the kingly way" (*wang dao*), which one early text describes as "true and straight."[7] To maintain Heaven's Charge, the Zhou rulers were expected to emulate their original ancestor, Hou Ji, who is portrayed in one of the Zhou hymns as "capable of being a full partner with that Heaven" (*ke pei bi tian*).[8]

Whether the Zhou kings or their immediate predecessors of the earlier Shang dynasty were themselves priests or shamans remains an issue of controversy among sinologists, but it is certain that they "formulated their legitimacy by linking the throne to a higher authority; they constantly aspired to the divine."[9] In other words, the first Zhou kings performed a religious as well as a secular function, if we may make an intentional distinction between two realms that the ancient Zhou people almost certainly would have seen as one. A bronze inscription from approximately 900 BCE speaks of this link of the throne to a higher authority in the following words: "Accordant with antiquity was King

Wen! [He] first brought harmony to government. The Lord on High sent down fine virtue and great security. Extending the high and low, he joined the ten thousand states."[10]

The first Zhou kings also "parceled out sovereignty among their kinsmen," a practice which "provided a formidable symbolic basis for both a feudal and later a bureaucratic system."[11] Even after the central Zhou government weakened in the ninth and eighth centuries BCE, this kin-based political structure, which Cho-yun Hsu calls "familiastic," continued in the individual states throughout much of the Spring and Autumn period.[12] Because of the importance of ancestor worship to the Zhou nobility, a topic we have discussed earlier, the familiastic organization embraced not just the living, but the dead as well.

As the head of a kinship-based polity, the Zhou king was indeed "the virile man *par excellence*." The power of his office and, in a sense, his own virility as a dynastic father were enhanced by emulating the pattern established by his most distinguished predecessors. Constance A. Cook has explained that "The king, as central pillar connecting the present Zhou authority to the primal event, had to prove through warfare and ritual action that he 'modeled' himself upon the behavior of his ancestors who received the Charge or Mandate of Heaven."[13] That is, the later Zhou kings derived legitimacy from emulating the pattern set down by the founder of the Zhou dynasty, King Wen, whose very name actually means "pattern."[14]

The early Zhou unity, reflected in the institution of kingship and portrayed powerfully in the oldest layers of the *Classic of Poetry*, preceded the era of classical Chinese thought and became for many of the later masters, particularly the Confucians, a utopian ideal. Thus, it is with some despair that Confucius once admitted that he seemed to have lost touch with one of the great figures of the early Zhou: "Extreme has been my decline! Long it has been since I dreamt of the Duke of Zhou" (*Analects* 7.5). And elsewhere, the Master proclaims quite proudly that "I follow the Zhou" (*Analects* 3.14).

It is interesting that an early Zhou hero like the Duke of Zhou exists for Confucius not just in history but in his own dreams as well. For much like a dream, the early Zhou culture virtually exists outside of time as a grand monument to an experience of complete participation and becomes an object of considerable nostalgia among early Chinese thinkers. As we noted in the first section of this study, many of the poems from the *Classic of Poetry* derive from this period and reflect a degree of social and political harmony that at times inspires hymns, such as the following, with a sense of ecstatic pride:

Seizing rivals, King Wu,
His power was unrivalled.
Greatly renown, kings Cheng and Kang,
God on high gave them splendor.
Since those Cheng and Kang,
We have held the realm.
So bright is their glory!
Bells and drums resound;
Stones and pipes clang.
Blessings descend, so rich;
Blessings descend, so vast;
Majestic rites so stern!
We are drunk, we are full,
For blessings and rewards come in return.

(Mao 274)

This grand unity, which brought "blessings and rewards" down from "God on high," began to decline within a century or so after its foundation. The culmination of this decline came in 771 BCE, when the Zhou rulers were driven from their old capital near modern-day Xi'an and relocated far to the east in the region of today's Luoyang. From that time until their final destruction in 256 BCE, the Zhou kings were little more than figureheads who possessed, at most, some residual ritual and moral power.

The age of Chinese philosophical thought dawns well after the decline of Zhou political power. Confucius (551–479) and Laozi, even if we accept the traditional sixth century BCE date for the latter, were active more than a full century after the weakened Zhou household moved to a new capital in the east. Indeed, the golden era of Chinese thought, as well as the period in which even *Analects* and *Dao de jing* probably took shape, is the fifth through third centuries, a period known as the Warring States (480–221). In other words, the first great flourishing of Chinese philosophy was not *immediately* precipitated by the fall of Zhou. Why is this?

Although the transfer of political power from the Zhou kings to the rulers of individual states did clearly produce trauma that can be traced, for example, in certain poems of the *Classic of Poetry*, it did not exert an immediate and far-reaching impact upon the social structure. To be sure, the feudatories could now act independently, but they continued to be dominated politically and economically by a hereditary nobility. In other words, the old familiastic structure, with its confident control of power and its assurance of ancestral blessing, persisted in dominating the political order. However, highly significant changes began to occur in the last century of the Spring and Autumn period and continued on into the Warring States. The hereditary nobility, who had dominated the political order up to that time, gradually lost power, and a system based upon contractual reciprocity gradually replaced the older structure of family relationships.[15] The new society that emerged was characterized by much greater mobility, and the lowest class of the earlier nobility, the *shi*, which we might loosely translate as "gentlemen," became "the most active social class of that time."[16] Detached from their hereditary obligations by the higher nobility's loss of power, many educated gentlemen, *shi*, began to wander from state to state marketing their talents quite freely. They gathered at the courts of men of power who appreciated them and became the basis of the emergent bureaucracies that were replacing hereditary officials in the larger and more successful states. Many of the philosophers, including Confucius himself, were to come from this class of detached gentlemen.[17]

Besides this fundamental change in the social order, other changes took place during these critical centuries. As the nobility lost land, private ownership became common, and a whole new class of wealthy landowners, who collected taxes and rent from poor peasants, began to appear. Moreover, the growth of cities, increased commercial activity, and the wider circulation of coinage meant that many merchants gradually accumulated wealth and, eventually, political influence. Warfare became much more brutal. The chariot, which had been the early Zhou equivalent of our tank, was replaced, for reasons that are not entirely clear, by large armies made up mostly of infantry with support from some mounted cavalry. The old code of "polite warfare" was supplanted by attitudes much closer to modern "total warfare" as "masses of tough foot soldiers, mostly hard-working peasants inured to hardship and toil, replaced the gallant chariot-riding noblemen."[18] Finally, there were important technological changes. One of these, the gradual but still expensive production of iron, tipped the balance of power even more in the direction of the most powerful states that could afford to produce and disseminate the more effective iron tools and weaponry.

Many of these enormous changes would seem, at least from a much later perspective, to have marked an advance over the ostensibly static years of the early Zhou. However, the thinkers who emerged in the wake of these changes generally felt a keen sense of loss. In the words of A. C. Graham,

> Their whole thinking is a response to the breakdown of the moral and political order which had claimed the authority of Heaven; and the crucial question for all of them is not the Western philosopher's "What is

the truth?" but "Where is the Way?", the way to order the state and conduct personal life.[19]

Among the various attempts in the world of philosophy to reconstruct order during this period of profound change two groups, we believe, deserve particular attention, the Confucians and the Daoists. Among the "hundred schools" that supposedly contended during the Warring States period, Confucianism and Daoism were not necessarily perceived as the most promising and prominent, but they have exerted a more widespread and enduring impact upon Chinese civilization than any of their rivals.

The emergence of the philosopher

We have discussed how many of the earliest Chinese philosophers came from a class of detached gentlemen who tried to offer their services to the rulers of the various states of the Spring and Autumn and Warring States periods. In response to the gradual decline of an older aristocracy, both Chinese and Greek philosophy transmute an aristocracy of blood into a more democratic aristocracy of the spirit, although it would be misleading, of course, to refer to ancient China as in any contemporary sense "democratic," and even in the case of Greece, democracy included a slave population and did not grant citizenship to women. In the wake of the breakdown of the influence of hereditary nobility in China, a new system of contractual reciprocity was taking its place, as we have mentioned, and the Chinese masters were part of this process. We note a similar pattern in Greece, from the time of Thales (sometimes described as the first philosopher), in the sixth century, through Plato in the late fourth century BCE. In Greece, the process had begun even earlier, in the eighth and seventh centuries, as the kingships of the various *poleis* gave way to rule by elected officials. In some states, tyrannies were established – that is, rule by those who did not inherit power. These tyrannies also helped to break the long-standing hold of aristocratic rule.

In 508 BCE, Kleisthenes instituted a reform in Athens that furthered democratization. In the early organization of the *polis*, ancestral worship was an important unifying factor. Immediate families were all part of a *genos*, which conceived of itself as descending from a common ancestor. These various "clans" were themselves subdivisions of *phratriai*, of which you had to be a member if you were to be an Athenian citizen. In order to break the dominance of aristocratic families, Kleisthenes divided Attica into ten regions, the inhabitants of which were now distinguished by belonging to a number of *phylae*, and the ten *phylae* were further divided into ten districts called *demes*. After

Kleisthenes' reform, Athenian citizenship was based upon membership in a particular *dêmos*. In the work of Plato and Aristotle, the experience of "philosophy" emerged from this political structure. In some ways, in fact, it could be said that Greek philosophy is inconceivable apart from its emergence in the political culture of the time. Socrates resolutely considered himself an Athenian to the point of accepting, with equanimity and even with a kind of ironic superiority, the sentence of death imposed on him by the Athenian court. The notion of leaving Athens in order to escape his sentence was inconceivable to him, as Plato has suggested in the *Phaedo*. In the *Politics*, Aristotle defines a person as "a living being that inhabits a polis" (*zôon politikon*, 1253a3).

The problem with contemporary Athenian democracy, from Plato's perspective, was that it depended for its success upon a high level of cultivation in the souls of the *dêmos*, but such cultivation was not to be seen in the Athens that chose Alcibiades as its leader and then later sentenced Socrates to death. Only in a *polis* governed by those with a truly philosophical temper, Plato believed, could the city survive. This is the theme of the *Republic*. The democratic Athenian *polis* was in a state of relative health in the glory days of the tragedies of Aeschylus (525–456 BCE). Under the rule of Peisistratus (d. 528), the cult of the god Dionysus was introduced as a means of breaking "the power of the hereditary priesthoods of the noble clans."[20] It was from this Dionysiac cult, with its hymns in honor of the god, that tragedy evolved. The tragedies were performed at two annual festivals before the citizens of Athens. The *dêmos* would be worthy of its newly found autonomy if it could act in a principled manner.

A tragedy such as the *Suppliants* of Aeschylus, performed sometime around 463,[21] can be viewed as an ethical and spiritual training ground for the people. The play presents a moral dilemma. A group of suppliant maidens, the Danaids, have left the Nile Valley in order to seek asylum in Argos. They have been betrothed, despite their protestations, to a brutal group of suitors who are the sons of the recently victorious King Aegyptus. The conflict between the Danaids and the sons of Aegyptus is, essentially, a foreign dispute and the king must worry over whether or not he is willing to confront the distinct possibility that his granting exile to the young women will result in a war that will no doubt badly hurt his own city. The king is thus faced with a profound dilemma, as he himself recognizes:

> There is a need here for deep, salvific counsel –
> in the manner of a diver, I must plunge into the depths
> with a seeing eye, not too much disturbed.
>
> (407–9)

The king ultimately decides to protect the suppliant maidens. The Athenian spectators attending the play would have made the sympathetically imaginative dive "into the depths" (*es bython*, l. 408) with the diver (*kolymbêtêr*, also l. 408) King Pelasgus of Argos in order to decide what was the truly just action to take. The king, moreover, did not take the just action he finally decided upon without first consulting the people. The spiritual health of a democracy, Aeschylus is suggesting, is determined by the willingness and ability of its citizens to dive into the depths in order to seek justice (*dikê*, *Suppliants* 343, 395).

The Athenian spectators thus descended into the depths with King Pelasgus and imaginatively experienced the meaning of justice (*dikê*). The achievement was short-lived, however, for by the year 435 BCE, the Athenians were engaged in the conflict of the Peloponnesian Wars that would eventually destroy their city. We have seen, in Part II, that by the year 416 the Athenian *dêmos* was no longer willing to dive into the depths to seek justice. By the time of the summer of the sixteenth year of the war, as Thucydides vividly suggests in his characterization of Athens in the Melian dialogue, justice is, for the Athenians, simply a word that is evoked by the powerless in order to flatter themselves with the illusion of their own integrity. The Athenian embassy to Melos is hardly impressed with the argument of the Melians that, since the besieged islanders are devoutly religious and god-fearing (*hosioi*), and since the Athenians are unjust (*ou dikaious*), divinity will therefore be on the side of the just (V.104). The gods, the Athenians answer, are no different from men in their concern, not with justice, but rather with ruling over others (*archein*) wherever they can. That is simply an undeniable law (*nomos*) of nature; it has always been true and will continue to be so.

The dialogue between the Melians and the Athenians proceeds via the *stichomythiai* – the quick, back-and-forth conversations – of Athenian tragedy, but without the moralizing we so often encounter in the choral sections of the plays. Missing is an authorial voice of adverse ethical judgment on the actions of the Athenians. There is in Thucydides, however, a perhaps implied critique of the callous arrogance of the Athenians in this episode, since they are incapable of experiencing the tragic emotions of fear and pity, as discussed by Aristotle in the thirteenth chapter of the *Poetics*. As we mentioned in Part II, Thucydides applauds Perikles for the statesman's ability – like a good tragedian – to evoke the emotion of fear in the souls of the Athenian citizens, and thus to keep them humble. The Athenians of the Melian dialogue are beyond experiencing such emotions. They now claim that they do not fear the gods: "We are not afraid [*ou phoboumetha*] of provoking the wrath of the gods," they tell the Melians. Nor do they feel pity for their Melian victims, whom they soon rather perfunctorily put to death (in the case of the men) or sell into slavery (in the case of the women and children). In their arrogance, the Athenians are incapable of experiencing a *katharsis* of the emotions of pity and fear.

The inability of the Athenians to experience such a *katharsis* of the two quintessential tragic emotions is a disturbing measure of how far the *êthos* of the people has departed from the glory days of Aeschylean tragedy when, moved with compassion for the plight of the suppliant maidens and fearful about making an unjust decision, the Athenian audience was able to dive into the depths, with King Pelasgus of Argos, to search for justice.

It is clear, from Thucydides' analysis, that the Athenians who interrogated the Melians were incapable of experiencing a *katharsis* of the emotions of pity and fear. What is far less clear is whether Thucydides is criticizing the Athenians for this moral insensitivity; for the historian, as we have suggested in the previous chapter, is himself implicated in the very degenerative process that he is analyzing. Thucydides has himself perhaps not quite made the descent, like the Aeschylean diver, into the depths to search for justice. We saw in Part II how, with a kind of tragic foreboding, Thucydides had described the descent to the Piraeus (i.e. the port of Athens) of the Athenians and their allies just before they made their fateful departure for Sicily. "The Athenians themselves and the allies that were present," Thucydides writes, "went down to the Piraeus [*es ton Peiraia katabantes*]." He then repeats the ominous verb *katabainein* ("to go down") at the beginning of the following sentence (adding the prefix "*syn*," meaning "with"), as he remarks, "with them also went down [*syngkatebê*] all the general throng – everyone, we might almost say, who was in the city, both citizens and strangers" (VI.30.2). The verb *katabainein*, we suggested, recalls Homer's description of the *katabasis* – the descent to the underworld – of Odysseus in the eleventh book of the *Odyssey*. We noted, however, that it was difficult to know just how intentional was Thucydides' allusion to Homer and thus just how infernal were the connotations of Thucydides' representation of the Athenian departure for Sicily. Thucydides, after all, did not think that the expedition was necessarily a bad idea. Socrates, however (if we are to believe Plutarch, *Nic.* 13.9 and *Alc.* 17.5), was one of the few doubters, and his pupil Plato perhaps shared the master's serious qualms.

The *Republic* of Plato also begins with the word *katebên* ("I went down"), and here the allusion to Homer appears to be unmistakable. Just after he reveals himself to Penelope, Odysseus tells her of the future that Teiresias had prophesied for him "on the day that I went down [*katebên*] into the house of Hades" (XXIII.252). The Homeric *katebên* becomes the first word of Plato's *Republic*, as Socrates says:

> I went down [*Katebên*] to the Piraeus [*eis Peiraia*] yesterday with Glaucon, son of Ariston, in order to make my prayers to the goddess and wishing to see, at the same time, how they would celebrate her rites, since they were doing this for the first time. The procession of our own citizens seemed beautiful to me; no less decorous, it appeared to me, was the procession of the Thracians. (327)

Thucydides had painted for his readers a scene in which throngs of Athenian citizens and foreigners could be viewed going down to the Piraeus [*es ton Peiraia katabantes*] to marvel at the departure of the huge and magnificent Athenian fleet for far-off Sicily. Plato tells of Socrates' descent to the Piraeus (*Katebên eis Peiraia*) in order to make his prayers to a goddess, Bendis, whose cult was imported from Thrace and who was associated with both Persephone and Hecate, who accompanied souls to the underworld.[22]

Socrates, in other words, at the beginning of the *Republic*, is in the underworld that is Athenian culture, sometime between 411 and 405 BCE, when Sparta decisively defeated Athens to end the Peloponnesian War.[23] Thucydides also appears to believe that the descent to the Piraeus was the beginning of a nightmare in hell, although part of the nightmarish quality for readers of the Thucydidean passage is the sense that we, as readers, are not quite sure, are somewhat in the murky darkness ourselves, in regard to our perceptions of just how nightmarish the historian perceived the situation to be. With Plato's unusual elimination of the article *ton* ("the") in his phrase *es Peiraia*, he turns Thucydides' literal port of the Piraeus into "Beyond-Land" of the philosopher's myth: "I went down yesterday, with Glaucon, to Beyond-Land." As Eva Brann remarks, this curious phrase "to Piraeus"

> is to be heard in a special way. Now it happens that the Athenians did hear a certain meaning in this name – it meant the "beyond-land," *hê Peiraia*, the land beyond the river that was once thought to have separated the Peraic peninsula from Attica.[24]

Hence, *hê Peiraia* [*gaia*] (with the word "country" [*gê* or *gaia*] gapped) means "the country *on the other side*." This "Beyond-Land" is the Hades that is contemporary Athenian society, whose recently crushed imperial policy of economic and military expansion was launched from this very harbor of the Piraeus. "Beyond-Land" is also, however, that place in the depths from which the philosopher can rise to clarify the meaning of justice that had been so conspicuously absent from the consciousness of the Athenians in Thucydides' Melian dialogue. Immediately following this opening passage from the *Republic*, a group of young men anxiously pursue Socrates in hopes that he will engage with them in a dialogue about the meaning of justice, and whether it has any meaning at all. Since the young men, surrounded as they are by the corruption of contemporary Athens, wish to engage in inquiry, there is still hope, but the philosophical ascent toward participation in the "Beyond-Land" of the idea of justice must begin in the depths of the "Beyond-Land" of Hades.

Thus, in both ancient Greece and ancient China philosophy emerges from a period of considerable distress and disillusionment. However, the two cultures experience the crisis differently. In China there is a deep sense of loss that permeates almost all the schools of thought. The Confucians, for example, looked back longingly to the political unity of the early Zhou, while the Mohists felt nostalgia for the still earlier, legendary time of the hard-working Emperor Yu and the Xia dynasty he supposedly founded. The Daoists, for their part, idealized a more primitive time before such institutions as ritual and writing shattered the original unity with the *dao*. There is a clear nostalgia in early Chinese thought for a period of more complete participation, whether with the state, as in Confucianism, or with the *dao* itself, as with Daoism.

In Greece, the crisis is a more immediate and sudden one that culminates, as we have seen, in the total defeat of Athens by Sparta in 405 BCE. The problem among Greek thinkers is expressed not so much in terms of how to recuperate the past as how to think one's way toward a new and more just society. Plato's *Republic* is the most ambitious and famous attempt to do just this. Plato does not present his ideal polity as a recovery of some earlier order but rather as a new product that emerges from the rigorous application of reason in both its discursive and visionary modes. Contradiction, Plato tells us, is essential to this reasoning process, for it spurs the soul "to make search, setting the intelligence within it in motion" (*Republic* 524e). The Chinese, less enamored of contradiction and a visionary, forward-looking kind of rationality, felt that their utopia could be found largely through remembering the past, and so they turned, much more consistently, to studying the precedents of history rather than exploring the uncharted frontiers that could be discovered by reason.[25] In a famous analect (2.15), Confucius says that one should balance studying (*xue*), which almost certainly means studying the texts from the past, and thinking (*si*). Whatever balance the Master himself might have advocated, the emphasis of his disciples, and of many other Chinese thinkers as well, fell on the side of studying the texts of the past. The Greek emphasis, at least as one sees it in Socrates and Plato, while not necessarily minimizing the importance of such study, rather stressed thinking for oneself.

2 From poetry to philosophy

Both Confucius and Plato, in the words of the former, "warm up the old so as to know the new" (*Analects* 2.11). Philosophy in both Greece and China emerges out of the earlier poetic tradition. At least on the surface, Confucius has a less ambivalent attitude than does Plato toward the poetic tradition that preceded him. We do not hear Confucius explicitly state, as we do in the case of Plato, that there is an "ancient quarrel between philosophy and poetry" (*Republic* 607c). This appears to be another instance of the antagonistic attitude of Greek authors to their literary forebears, an attitude which stands in sharp contrast to that of the more reverential Chinese. The views of both Confucius and Plato toward their respective poetic traditions may, however, have more in common than a superficial first glance might suggest. Both the Chinese sage and the Greek philosopher worry, for instance, about the dangers poetry poses to maintaining a stable social order, although in the case of Confucius the worry is less explicit. For both thinkers, in other words, the considerable affective power of poetry should be enlisted in the interests of heightening a person's *participation in society*. In the case of Plato, moreover, the quarrel is not so much with poetry itself as it is with the way poetry was understood, in the rationalist climate of his day that we have alluded to in Part II, to reflect reality understood chiefly as an object of the human consciousness. What had been lost, and what needed to be (in Confucius's phrase) "warmed up," was poetry's luminous capacity for conveying a person's experience of participation in a comprehensive reality that included the human consciousness itself.

Confucius and the *Classic of Poetry*

Chinese poetry, as we have seen, begins in the early years of the Zhou dynasty with religious hymns and odes in praise of the dynastic founders. As Zhou power declines and political power passes to the states, the poetic voice becomes more lyrical and, we should add, much less uniformly optimistic in tone. This first great era of Chinese poetry culminates in the *Classic of Poetry* about the time of Confucius, who may or may not have been the editor, as Sima Qian later claimed, but who presumably did know of a collection of about "three hundred poems" (see *Analects* 2.2).[26] The next important flowering of Chinese poetry is initiated by the disaffected politician Qu Yuan (340?–278?), although most of the pieces in the collection *Songs of the South* (*Chu ci*) are almost certainly from the century following Qu Yuan's death. Poetry, to be sure, was written in the two centuries between Confucius and Qu Yuan, and some pieces have been preserved,[27] but it almost seems as if the poetic voice during this interval, insofar as it continued to exist, became primarily the handmaiden of philosophy and is to be found most notably, as we shall see later, in the evocative writings of Laozi and Zhuangzi.

One reason for this decline in the production of great poetry may have been the need to process and assimilate the *Classic of Poetry*, which obviously had gained a very lofty status by the time of the "Hundred Schools." The challenge of digesting this earlier text was complicated by the fact that it frequently reflected a unified world that had been fractured by the social and political upheavals that we noted above. The first major figure to respond to this challenge was Confucius, who might rightly be considered not just China's most influential thinker but also China's most influential literary critic.

Our source for considering Confucius' attitude toward the poetry that preceded him is the *Analects*. None of this text was authored by Confucius himself. It is only as reliable as the memories and traditions of the disciples in the Confucian scholarly lineage who recalled and recorded the Master's words. There is little doubt that *Analects* contains layers of greater and lesser authenticity and that much of the text responds to philosophical issues and debates that took place well after Confucius' death. Still, we find merit in treating the text as a unity. Such an approach, to be sure, minimizes the significance of the development in early Confucian thought that can doubtless be traced within *Analects*. But the Confucius we speak of here is more the Confucius of traditional China than a "real" Confucius who might be recoverable from the few sayings that can, with varying degrees of probability, be unearthed by the spade of modern philology.[28]

Confucius regarded himself as a transmitter of earlier learning (*Analects* 7.1). He denied that he possessed any innate knowledge but claimed to be "one who loves antiquity and seeks after it with diligence" (7.20). Certainly one part of the antiquity Confucius loved most fervently is preserved in the collection that he called simply *Shi* (Poetry), which we have considered in some detail in Part I of this book. There are fourteen direct references to the *Classic of Poetry* in *Analects*, whereas *Historical Documents* (*shu*) is mentioned three times and *Changes* only twice. While Robert Eno, in his study of Confucian instruction, argues that Westerners have tended to overemphasize the role of textual study in the early Confucian curriculum, he does agree that "the most discussed text in all Ruist (= our 'Confucian') texts is the *Poetry*."[29]

Confucius clearly regards the poems contained in the *Classic of Poetry* not simply as written texts, such as we have them today, but as a part of a highly ritualized musical performance. Thus, the rival philosopher Mozi, who probably studied among the second or third generation of Confucian scholars, is quoted as saying that when the Confucians are not "in mourning," which is one activity he thought they engaged in excessively, they "chanted the three hundred poems, they strummed the three hundred poems, they sang the three hundred poems, and they danced the three hundred poems."[30] The performance of these poems as both music and dance must have greatly increased their affective power, which is precisely the aspect of the *Poetry* that Confucius seems to appreciate most.

In a passage from *Analects* that we have already discussed in another context, Confucius urges his students to "Be stimulated [*xing*] by poetry" (8.8), and elsewhere he says that one should study poetry because "it can be stimulating [*xing*]" (17.9). At one point, Confucius makes a statement that sounds very much like Aristotle on *katharsis*, so long as we understand *katharsis* not as an extirpation of the emotions but rather as their purification in the sense of maintaining, in good working order, emotions that are essential to moral health. "In the 'Guan ju' [the first poem of the *Classic of Poetry*]," Confucius says, "there is joy without wantonness, and sorrow without self-injury" (3.20). A poem like the "Guan ju" stimulates (*xing*) emotions such as joy and sorrow in the listener. It allows the person who is hearing the poem to experience these powerful emotions of joy and sorrow in a balanced, moderated state – that is, as a sage should experience them.[31]

Confucius was not, however, about to set the powerful affective force of poetry loose without some counterbalancing restraint. As we have explained in Part I, *xing*, which we have translated as "stimulate," also carries the connotation of "begin." That is, one begins study with the *Poetry*, which is precisely what happened in the formal education of most Confucians. Immediately after telling his students to "be stimulated by *Poetry*" or "to make a beginning with *Poetry*," Confucius says they should next "take a stand in rites [*li*]" (8.8). The rites are the appropriate social forms and serve to restrain the potentially dangerous effect of literature. Confucius' most perceptive disciple, Yan Hui, once said that the Master had "broadened me with literary culture and restrained me with ritual" (9.11).

If ritual forms are so important and constitute a necessary restraint upon emotion, why set loose the potentially dangerous affective power of poetry at all? And why should such study precede ritual restraint rather than the other way around? In other words, would Confucius not have been more circumspect to say, "Take a stand in ritual, be stimulated by *Poetry*" rather than the reverse? We can perhaps begin to answer this question by examining one of the most important and puzzling uses of a poem in the Confucian *Analects:*

Zixia asked,
   " 'Her artful smile so dimpled,
   Her lovely eyes so bright!
   To plain silk is added adornment.'
What is this saying?"
   The Master said, "The painting comes after the plain
silk background."
   [Zixia] said, "Ritual comes after!"
   The Master said, "Shang (= Zixia), you have stimulated me!
Now I can begin to discuss the *Poetry* with you!"

(3.8)

This is a discussion between Confucius and Zixia, one of his best-known disciples. As others have suggested, the passage may derive from disciples of Zixia who are anxious to establish the special prescience, and hence preeminence, of their teacher.[32] The passage begins with a quotation of three lines of poetry. The first two lines apparently come from a famous description of female beauty found in the *Classic of Poetry* (Mao 57 – see p. 66 above). The derivation of the third line is unknown but may simply be an edition of the *Poetry* somewhat different from the current received version.[33] When Zixia asks for the meaning of these lines, Confucius appears to provide little more than a somewhat simpler and clearer restatement of the third line of the poem. However, Confucius' summary provokes Zixia to provide a parallel from the world of Confucian ethics: "Ritual comes after," he says. Confucius boils the poem down to a single line and Zixia then treats the summary as a metaphor and supplies an apt underlying meaning. Clearly, the Master is impressed. He commends Zixia and says that the latter has "stimulated" him. The word that we have translated as "stimulated" is not the usual *xing*, but the character *qi*. However, we have chosen our translation advisedly; *xing* and *qi* have almost the same range of meanings and are equated with one another in the earliest Chinese dictionary.[34]

What we have here is a rapid exchange in which Zixia proves able to move between the interlocking worlds of aesthetics, with its powerful affect, and Confucian ethics. Obviously, poetic "stimulation" is itself a kind of background, like "plain silk," that then best moves in the direction of patterned ethical formulation. But what of the insightful interpretation Zixia provides, that "Ritual comes after?" What *does* ritual come after? The great Song dynasty commentator Zhu Xi (1130–1200) has provided one possible answer: "Ritual must take loyalty [*zhong*] and truthfulness of speech [*xin*] as its substance."[35] Others have suggested that ritual comes after "humaneness [*ren*] and duty [*yi*]."[36] We believe that it is not necessary to specify precisely *which* Confucian virtues should precede ritual. The point is that ritual, like adornment, comes after the world of affect, which is precisely what the *Poetry* stimulates. In other words, ritual shapes and gives appropriate form to our emotional and ethical inclinations. A consequence of this view, and one that might be disturbing to the ethical formalists who dominate later Confucianism, is that such inclinations are a necessary background for ritual. Without the proper affect, the type of ritual Confucius advocates cannot exist.

There is evidence for such an interpretation elsewhere in *Analects*. In the following passage, for example, Confucius asserts the ethical priority of humaneness over ritual: "A human being but not humane, of what use is ritual?" (3.3). Elsewhere the Master says that he cannot "look upon" ritual acts that "do not show respect" (3.26). And in yet another passage, the disciple Zilu asks Confucius about the "complete man" (*cheng ren*). The Master refers to the "wisdom" (*zhi*) of one man, the "lack of covetousness" (*bu yu*) in another, the "courage" (*yong*) of a third man, and the "skillfulness" (*yi*) of a fourth. These men all have the right stuff, but they need something more: "If you were to adorn them with ritual and music, then they could also become complete men" (14.12). The word we have translated "adorn" is *wen*, which, as we have previously noted, literally means "pattern." Ritual, then, is one of the means of imparting pattern to ethical feeling and behavior.

To put ritual in this secondary position is by no means to diminish its critical importance to Confucius. We agree with Eno's contention that "self-ritualization" – that is, turning one's every action and spoken word almost into a ritual dance – is the essence of Confucian training.[37] Moreover, without the restraint that ritual imposes, our best inclinations easily become excessive or even ridiculous:

> The Master said, "If, being respectful, one is without ritual, then he will be tiresome. If, being cautious, one is without ritual, then he will be tedious. If, being courageous, one is without ritual, then he will be rebellious. If, being straightforward, one is without ritual, then he will be pitiless. (*Analects* 8.2)

Poetry thus plays a central role in the Confucian vision. It stimulates an array of emotions and actions. Under the guidance of a teacher, the response to poetry can be channeled toward greater ethical understanding, such as in Zixia's insight that one poem could lead, by a clever application of a metaphorical reading, to an important ethical insight ("Ritual comes after!"). But there is a danger in feeling, even essentially moral feeling, and that is the natural tendency toward excessive, inappropriate and socially destructive expressions. To provide the proper restraint, one must be steeped in ritual. To summarize and perhaps simplify: poetry without ritual is dangerous; but ritual, without those qualities poetry can stimulate, is empty.

Much more is at stake in the vision of Confucius, however, than the status of poetry. As critical as the study of the *Poetry* may have been to the Master, it was only one part of his attempt to reestablish order. The old kin- and king-based harmony of the Zhou was gone, and it was left to the "Hundred Masters," one of the most important of whom was Confucius, to find a new order. It was their task to apply a newly emerged intentional consciousness to the task of recovering the sense of participation they felt had been lost. There is, of course, a paradox here, one realized and exploited by Daoist thinkers, but before we discuss two early Daoists, we shall turn our attention to Confucius and his attempt to reinvent social order. First, however, we wish to take a brief look at Plato's relation to the poetic tradition that, as in the case of Confucius, preceded his own philosophical speculations.

The reduction of poetry to depicting the "ten thousand things" and Plato's critique

We mentioned earlier that, at least on the surface, Plato has a less positive view of the poetic tradition that preceded him than does Confucius. The Greek philosopher's most famous critique of poetic representation – that is, of *mimêsis* – occurs toward the end of the *Republic* (595a–608b). Socrates has by this time discussed the so-called theory of the forms and the tripartite division of the soul, and his criticism of poetry here gains additional force when it is viewed from the perspective of these important discussions. In order to suggest the illusory nature of poetic representation, Plato draws upon an analogy from the visual arts. Only the forms or "ideas" of things have absolute being. A bed made by a carpenter reflects the world of becoming rather than of being.[38] It is a particular example of a bed, but it is not bedness itself. As Socrates says to Glaucon, "Didn't you say just now that it isn't the category itself that he [the carpenter] makes – which we agree is what "couch" really *is* [*ho esti klinê*] – but one particular couch [*klinên tina*]?"[39] The artist who depicts a bed on a canvas is, therefore, a step further removed from bedness. His image exists at a third remove from true being.

Socrates goes on to say that the painter is like a person carrying a mirror and turning it around in all directions, thus producing images of the sun, stars, and earth, and oneself and all the other animals, plants, and lifeless objects (596e). As Friedländer suggests, Plato may be referring here not to an old master such as Polygnotos – the "good artist who paints a model of what might be the most beautiful human being" (472d). What Plato "had in mind," Friedländer continues,

> was the younger generation of painters, who in their manners as well as their products are rightly compared to the "Sophists": Apollodorus, for example, the inventor of the illusionistic paintings with shadows (*skigraphia*) rejected by Plato as deceitful; Zeuxis, who in Aristotle's judgment lacked the "ethos" of Polygnotos, and who took delight in the portrayal of the individual, concrete object, painting grapes with such an illusion that birds came to pick at them; or Parrhasios and Pauson.[40]

Nor was Plato referring to the Egyptian statues, which he loved. As the citation from Friedländer suggests, Plato may well be alluding to the younger generations of painters,[41] those illusionists who, through their extremely realistic depictions, thereby implicitly suggested – as sophists such as Protagoras said quite explicitly – that man was the measure of all things. Both the Sophists and these painters of mundane and literal realism, whose attention was riveted wholly upon the world of appearances, would – from Plato's perspective – be closed to the investigation of more general truths. What Plato is objecting to is the mimetic literalists of fourth-century Greece and to the kind of viewer who admires a particular painting only for its achievement of a remarkable degree of mimetic accuracy. Aristotle, in the *Poetics* (ch. 9), will say that poetry depicts the universal, history the particular; and that poetry is therefore more philosophical than history. What Plato is suggesting here is that art has, in effect, become "history" in the sense of its being a mere recording of objective, material reality. It is not the generalizing or philosophical power of art that is appreciated by the populace. They enjoy only that which confirms the manner in which they see things.

Such mimetic literalism had also invaded the high art of tragedy. Much of the work of Euripides, when compared with the drama of Aeschylus or even a Sophoclean tragedy, is approaching a kind of mundane realism, a tradition that was continued by the successors of Euripides. The Homeric poems are profoundly philosophical and are certainly not mere mirror images of mundane reality. But since the prevailing style of the arts during Plato's time was naturalism, there was a tendency to read the Homeric poems (and tragedy) as if they, too, were merely naturalistic. Their philosophical implications, their ability to point beyond themselves, had been lost. They were now often experienced as realistic adventure stories, or they were ransacked for extraliterary reasons. It was said that the Homeric poems could teach various technical skills and that students could extract useful maxims from them. Plato perhaps feared that those who were not philosophers would not be capable of understanding the meaning of Homer's poetry. What was necessary now was a historical understanding of Homer from the perspective of the philosopher, with his myth of the human soul. Plato must have felt that this truly historical understanding of Homer was, because of the pressures of the contemporary climate of opinion, very difficult to achieve. Rather than run the risk of having poetry misunderstood, he may have felt that it was better to take the "official" position that poetry itself was – from a philosophical perspective – a suspect medium.[42]

The prevailing trend in the arts of Plato's time, then, was toward naturalism. It might be helpful to return here to Laozi's analysis of consciousness as we described it in our Introduction. The consciousness must be aware of the two ways in which it simultaneously interacts with reality. The consciousness intends objects, and in this capacity of intentionality, reality consists of the "the ten thousand things" (*wan wu*) intended by the consciousness. But a thinker will be engaging in what Eric Voegelin calls an act of "imaginative oblivion" if she or he takes thing-reality for the whole picture.[43] For the consciousness has its participatory dimension as well. It not only, as a subject, intends objects, but is itself a participant in the *dao*. A flattened naturalism, with its exclusive emphasis upon reality in its mode of thingness, may seduce the soul into performing an act of imaginative oblivion by suggesting that reality is equivalent only to the world of the "ten thousand things." Indeed, that which distinguishes the tales or stories narrated in Plato's dialogues from much of the literature written in his own time is the lack of a flattened naturalism in such myths as the concluding myth of Er, which describes the rewards and punishments for the good and bad souls in Hades, as well as the consequences which their previous development and nurturing of *aretê* ("virtue" or "human excellence") has for the choice of a future life.

The so-called attack upon poetry in the tenth book of the *Republic*, then, must be read in the context of the work as a whole, and this means reading the *Republic* itself as a symbolically evocative work of prose-poetry culminating in the myth of Er. Er the Pamphylian ("Every-man"), at the conclusion to the *Republic*, descends to the Underworld, is revived, and brings back an account of how the dead choose their next life in the cycle of reincarnation. Socrates, at the beginning of the *Republic*, descends from Athens into the "underworld" of the Piraeus in order to help save the souls who desire to ascend to the light.[44] The *Republic* should not be misread, moreover, as a literalist blueprint for establishing a political utopia. Plato's construction of a paradigmatic *politeia* is, to a large extent, a metaphor through which he could print out a draft in enlarged type, as it were, of the possible contours of the human soul. Many of the rather outrageous suggestions Socrates makes in the dialogue – such as the abolition of the family, the banishment of the poets, the recommendation that women compete (as did the men) in athletic events in the nude – are designed to be provocative, to stimulate spirited discussion about how to cure Athens' severe contemporary ills. They are not "positions" comprising a political platform in the modern sense.

The Platonic philosopher and the Confucian sage thus both emerge out of the poetic traditions that precede them. It looked at first glance as though we had, in Plato's "ancient quarrel between poetry and philosophy," yet another instance of that scorn for tradition that we saw displayed in the bad manners of Thucydides in the opening section of his history. We have been arguing that Plato's critique of poetry has more to do, however, with the philosopher's belief that, in the rationalist climate we discussed in Part II, poetry had been reduced to a mimetic and objectivist literalism. Poetic figurations had, in other words, lost their luminous capacity for exploring and conveying an experience of participation in a greater whole. In section III.1, we discussed Plato's artful rewriting, in the *Republic*, of Homer's *Odyssey*. In the following section we shall reflect on the philosopher's rewriting of Greek tragedy in the *Symposium*. If Plato, the supreme literary artist of dialogues such as the *Republic* and the *Symposium*, is clearly not the enemy of art that he is so often accused of being, neither is Confucius the narrowly moralistic literary critic of Chinese tradition. The remarks of the Chinese sage on poetry are extremely brief and fragmentary in comparison with the speculations of Plato and Aristotle. We can nevertheless clearly detect in these Confucian writings the articulation of an affective view of poetry that has much in common with the affective literary theory of Aristotle's *Poetics*. Poetry is not simply a didactic tool, although Confucius obviously hopes that affect will lead to appropriate ethical formulations. But much of poetry's importance, for Confucius, resides in its capacity to stimulate (*xing*) the emotions.

3 The sage, the philosopher, and the recovery of the participatory dimension

Confucius and participation in society

There is in the thought of Confucius a "deep sense of alienation from the way things are."[45] As we have noted, Confucius lived in an age of political and social upheaval, and he was distressed that in his own age "the Way [*dao*] does not prevail" (*Analects* 5.7). He looked to the past as a guide. On one occasion he described a teacher as someone who "understands the new by reviewing [or warming up] the old" (2.11), and the old that he reviewed, transmitted and took as a model for his Way was the early Zhou.

Ritual is at the center of Confucius' attempt to resuscitate the lost Zhou spirit. "In the application of ritual," Confucius once said, "harmony is most precious" (1.12), but the old harmony of Heaven and man that had once provided a foundation for correct behavior had collapsed and "the task was to find the 'real' values, ones that restored to Tian (= heaven) its prescriptive perfection."[46] Confucius, we believe, found a "real value" that could be the basis for a new harmony in the individual human being's capacity for empathy and potential for self-actualization. "Is humaneness distant?" asked Confucius. And then he continued, "If I desire humaneness, then humaneness arrives" (7.30). Confucius admired an old order, but he knew the revival of that earlier ritual-based system required a foundation other than the aristocratic structure that had largely collapsed. He therefore turned to the individual human being and the human capacity for *ren*, which he once defined simply as "to treat other people well" (12.22).

The virtue of *ren*, which Confucius says is so close at hand, is mentioned in *Analects* far more than any other virtue. *Ren* has most often been translated as "benevolence," although more recently the translations "humaneness" or "humanity" have also become quite common. Writing several decades ago, Peter A. Boodberg stated his preference for "humaneness" or "humanity" over the older tradition on the grounds that *ren*, " 'humanity,' is not only a derivative, but is actually the same word, though in distinct graphic form, as the common Chinese vocable *ren*, 'man,' *homo*."[47] The virtue *ren* is the highest distinctive quality of a human being, also pronounced "*ren*" – it is "human" in the best sense of the word. Thus, in *Analects* 3.3 Confucius is engaging in etymological word-play when he says, "A human but not humane [*ren er bu ren*], of what use [to him] is ritual? A human but not humane, of what use [to him] is music?" The point, we suppose, is that only someone who is fully human – that is, possesses humaneness – can truly benefit from ritual and music.

This raises the question of precisely what constitutes this particular quality of humaneness. Traditional Chinese scholars made much of the fact that the written character for *ren* (humaneness) contains the graph for "two." The latter graph 二, they maintain, indicates the interpersonal nature, the "twoness" as it were, of this virtue. *Ren* can only develop, one might say, through the relationship between one person and another. As an accurate explanation of the derivation of the character, such an etymology is suspect, but it does capture an essential feature of this virtue, for Confucius seems to have believed that our highest humanity can develop only through our relationship with other human beings.

In the first three verses of *Analects*, chapter 12, the Master is asked about the virtue of "humanity" by three successive disciples, Yan Yuan, Ran Yong, and Sima Niu. Since the first of these three was clearly Confucius' premier student, we should pay particular attention to his exchange with the Master:

> Yuan asked about humanity. The Master said, "To overcome oneself and return to ritual constitutes humanity. If one day one overcomes oneself and returns to ritual, then the realm will turn to humanity. Practicing humanity comes from oneself; could it come from another?"
>
> Yan Yuan said, "May I ask about its details?"
>
> The Master said, "If it is not in accord with ritual, do not regard it; if it is not in accord with ritual, do not pay heed to it; if it is not in accord with ritual, do not speak of it; if it is not in accord with ritual, do not set it into motion."
>
> Yan Yuan said, "Although I, Hui, am not clever, may I act upon this teaching!" (*Analects* 12.1)

This passage may date from a time when the Confucian disciples had begun to debate the question of whether moral qualities were innate within human beings or somehow developed only through outside influence, an issue contested, for example, in *Mencius*.[48] In the passage above, the Master indicates that while humaneness comes from oneself – from within, we might say – it is realized only when one "overcomes oneself" and engages in the ritual forms that organize social life. Herbert Fingarette, in a highly controversial but important study of the Master's thought, has argued that Confucius is not much concerned with inner, psychological states.[49] We would qualify this somewhat to argue that he is concerned with psychological states *only* as they are revealed in concrete human action. And this action must be social in nature. As Hall and Ames have explained, "authoritative humanity is attainable only in a communal context through inter-personal exchange."[50] This point is reiterated in the subsequent passage, *Analects* 12.2, where Confucius tells us that a feature of *ren* is "not to impose upon others what one does not desire for oneself." This indicates that *ren* is the ability to use one's inner disposition as a guide to interpersonal behavior.

To Confucius, participation in human society is the only way our humanity *can* be actualized. There were other voices in ancient China – agriculturists and some Daoists – who challenged this assumption. In a late layer of *Analects*, probably deriving from a time when the conflict between Confucians and other philosophical schools had become acute, Confucius' disciple Zilu encounters two farmers who ask him why the Master does not flee the "turbulent waves" that are disrupting society and that no one has the power to change. Later, Zilu reports the former's question to his Master, and Confucius, "crestfallen," replies, "I cannot associate with birds and beasts. If I do not associate with human beings, with whom would I associate?" (18.6). This Confucian passage has an interesting parallel in Socrates' statement to Phaedrus, in the dialogue that is named after that particular interlocutor, in response to Phaedrus' invitation to Socrates to leave the city for the countryside in order to have a conversation. "I am a lover of learning," Socrates tells Phaedrus, "and the countryside and the trees will not teach me anything, whereas men in the town do" (230d).

Confucianism is a philosophy of social and political participation. The virtue of humanity cannot be realized in society with "birds and beasts," and Plato's "the countryside and the trees" likewise have nothing to teach Confucius. Indeed, a human being is only constituted as such, according to Confucius, *through* interpersonal relationships. These relationships should be harmonious. Hence, the Confucian is wary of any form of competition. The Master says, "The True Gentleman has no occasion to compete. If he must, let it be in archery. Bowing and deferring, he mounts [the platform]; descending, he drinks. Such is the competition of the True Gentleman" (3.7). In this passage, drawn from the earliest layer of *Analects*, Confucius speaks out against competition in general. Although he does allow for archery contests, even in such an activity the competitor's real concern should be with the proper performance of rituals. And, as always, these rituals have a social dimension; they entail bowing and deferring to the other competitors and then joining them in drink.

The well-known Confucian attack upon seeking material profit (*li*) may derive from a notion that such pursuit always puts human beings in sharp competition with one another and thereby disrupts social harmony. The Master says, "He who acts by giving himself up to material profit will bring about much resentment" (4.12). Mencius, the second great Confucian philosopher, addresses this issue in even more explicit words:

> If a king asks, "How can I profit my state?" and the high officials ask, "How can I profit my clan?" and the gentlemen and common people ask, "How can I profit myself?" then those above and those below will struggle with one another for profit and the state will be imperiled. (1A.1)

The Confucian virtue of "deference" or "yielding" (*rang*) may also be seen as a strategy to avoid the appearance of competitiveness. Confucius speaks of deference as an essential component of ritual behavior (*li*): "Can he govern with ritual and deference? What else is there? If he cannot govern with ritual and deference, of what use is ritual?" (4.13). Elsewhere, Confucius commends Taibo, a legendary Zhou ruler, for three times declining the realm when he was offered it (8.1).

Ironically, such acts of deference and noncompetition do have a competitive dimension: one competes in self-sacrifice and modesty and thereby gains a certain power over others. The very fact that Taibo would refuse the realm three times obligates his followers to keep offering the prize and to admire him all the more when he finally does accept. David Nivison has discussed this aspect of Confucian civilization with regard to the concept of *de*, "virtue," which he explains as the power A has over B because B feels some debt of gratitude. *De*, he suggests, "is generated by, or given in reward for, acts of generosity, self-restraint, and self-sacrifice, and for an attitude of humility."[51] Thus, acts of apparent diminishment actually can be acts of self-enhancement. However, the point we would like to stress is that such acts, by their ostensibly noncompetitive, nonaggressive nature, are less likely to disrupt the social harmony so central to Confucian concern. Moreover, the early Confucians, however much they might have competed in modesty, would have been profoundly distressed at "the informal and extempore competitive struggles and rivalries that permeated Greek life."[52]

There is no reason to assume that Confucius' plea to his age "to overcome the self and return to ritual," which he apparently believed was within the capacity of each human being, had immediate, significant impact. Confucius himself despaired that he "had never met one as fond of virtue as of sensual beauty [*se*]" (9.18 and 15.13), and late in his life, according to Sima Qian, Confucius turned to scholarly work that he hoped would have an impact on some later age.[53] Two and a half centuries after the Master's death China was unified, and within another century after that, Confucianism became a state-supported ideology. It is doubtful whether Confucius himself would have recognized this later Confucianism, which was neatly tailored to serve the legalistic needs of the Han state. But before that age, despite the efforts of Confucius and his disciples, society continued to be racked with conflict and violence. The Confucian program for social harmony went largely unheeded. It was within this milieu that the Daoists proposed a quite different solution to the question, "Where is the Way?"

Laozi's return to the *Dao*

The *Dao de jing* is one of the most perplexing and difficult texts to come to us from ancient China. We know virtually nothing of its purported author, Laozi. In fact, some have even argued that "there is no evidence that he was a historical figure."[54] *Dao de jing* is certainly much later than the sixth century BCE, which is when some traditional Chinese scholars believed it was written, but new manuscript evidence indicates that it may be earlier than the post-*Zhuangzi* date favored by a number of modern scholars. Whatever its precise date, *Dao de jing* does seem to address, although never mentioning other thinkers or schools by name, a variety of philosophical issues and arguments current in the Warring States period. For example, the first two sentences of the *Dao de jing*, which we have discussed briefly in our "preamble," have a philosophical context that we can, at least in part, reconstruct:

> If a way can be spoken, it is not the constant Way.
> If a name can be named, it is not the constant Name.
> *(Dao de jing* 1)

Confucius frequently mentioned the existence of a "way" or *dao*. For him this meant a proper path for ethical action that he thought was rooted in the traditions of the early Zhou. Confucius said much less of "names," but he does speak in *Analects* 13.3 of "rectifying names" (*zheng ming*) or "setting names right" as an important task of good leaders. This concern with names as normative categories becomes important in later Confucian thought, particularly in Xunzi (*c.* 305–235). Moreover, a "school of names" (*ming jia*), as it was later to be called, arose during the Warring States period and attempted to examine language and the world of linguistic representation through a careful, and sometimes paradoxical, analysis of words.

Laozi's first two sentences are a broadside against those who employ language in an attempt to surround and somehow capture truth. Hence, says Laozi, "The sage . . . practices teaching that does not require words" (*DDJ* 2). Elsewhere, he attacks quite emphatically those verbal formulations which Confucians and others advance as wisdom: "Throw away knowledge [*zhi*]" (*DDJ* 19).

Thus, the Way of Laozi escapes precise verbal formulation. And yet, *Dao de jing* is a book made up of words, an apparent paradox that is sometimes brushed aside with a delightful, although surely fictitious, story that Laozi was required to write this book by a "keeper of the pass," a sort of customs agent, who would not allow the Daoist sage to pass by until he had made a record of his wisdom.[55] But there is no paradox if we understand that *Dao de jing* is composed primarily of a highly poetic and symbolic language that is meant to inspire us about the Way rather than to teach us in some prescriptive and intentional fashion. In other words, although Laozi does not find a utopia in the political and social ritual of the early Zhou, he does attempt to revive a mythic world of participation in the cosmos that shares much with the rural world of harmony with nature that is found in the *Classic of Poetry*.

In fact, *Dao de jing* is best read, we believe, not as a work of analytic philosophy that propounds anything like a coherent and paraphrasable creed, but rather as a collection of suggestive poems that all point in a similar direction. It has been more than fifty years since the distinguished historical linguist Bernhard Karlgren presented evidence, building upon earlier Chinese research, that approximately three-quarters of *Dao de jing* is in rhymed verse. As Karlgren noted, "it may seem astonishing that many sentences start in prose, then continue with a couple of rhythmical and rimed lines, and then, again, wind up with a line or two in prose."[56] Yet none of the many recent translations, so far as we know, attempts to capture this critical feature of *Dao de jing*, so that it is easy to forget, unless one either knows Karlgren's article or is oneself knowledgeable in the historical reconstruction of early Chinese, how formally poetic this text actually is.[57]

In addition to its use of rhyme and evocative rhythms, *Dao de jing* is filled with metaphors and symbols. It is this quality that provides Laozi's classic with much of its appeal and sense of mystery. Since the most important principles, Laozi claims, cannot be reduced to clear formulation, they are best pointed at with metaphor and symbol:

The highest good is like water. (*DDJ* 8)

The highest virtue is like a valley. (*DDJ* 41)

The Way in respect to all-under-Heaven is like the relationship of rivers and valleys to the Yangtze and the sea. (*DDJ* 32)

Could it be the Way of Heaven is like a stretched bow?
The highest is pressed down, and the lowest is raised up. (*DDJ* 78)

In contrast to the early Confucian texts, much of the imagery of this highly poetic text is feminine. This should not be construed to mean that Laozi is an early Chinese harbinger of feminism. One of his purposes is to challenge us to reassess our notions of power and prestige, and so he is fond of asserting that what appears weak is really strong and vice versa. Laozi is not challenging women to question their roles as much as he is encouraging his readers to recognize the tremendous power of submissiveness and flexibility (see *DDJ* 28 and 61). Of course, quite beyond this, Laozi apparently finds in the feminine aspect apt imagery for the mysterious, inexhaustible fecundity of the Way:

> The spirit of the valley does not die –
> We call this "the mysterious female."
> The gate of the mysterious female –
> We call this "the root of heaven and earth."
> Continuously unraveling it seems to exist,
> But use it and it will not be spent.
>
> (*DDJ* 6)

What we must do is return to this "root of heaven and earth," and that, for Laozi, is very much a return to the mother:

> After you have known the son,
> Go back and protect the mother.
>
> (*DDJ* 52)

> I alone am different from others,
> For I value being fed by the mother.
>
> (*DJJ* 20)

Laozi, like Confucius, believes that we have fallen from an earlier unity, but for him that unity is not some era in human history when a political and social order gave us our proper place.[58] Instead, Laozi looks to a time before history when humanity rested in harmony with the natural order like a baby nestling in the arms of its mother. The Confucian agenda, which consists of such practices as ritual, duty, learning, wisdom, and humaneness, is explicitly rejected because these only lead to yet greater levels of intentionalism and hence exile us yet further from the Way, which "takes as model what is so of itself" (*DDJ* 25):

> After the great Way has been thrown aside,
> There is humaneness and duty.
> After cleverness and knowledge [*zhi*] appear,
> There is great falseness.
>
> (*DDJ* 18)

> Therefore, one loses the Way and then there is virtue.
> One loses virtue and then there is humaneness.
> One loses humaneness and then there is duty.
> One loses duty and then there is ritual.
> This thing "ritual" is but the wearing thin of
>   truthfulness and loyalty.
>
> (*DDJ* 38)

> Eradicate sageness and throw away knowledge [*zhi*],
> And the people will benefit a hundredfold.

> Eradicate humaneness and throw away duty,
> And the people will return to filial piety and kindness.
>
> (*DDJ* 19)

Despite this last attack on "sageness" (*sheng*), Laozi's ideal person is designated as a "sage" (*sheng ren*). But this is not the Confucian sage who masters the details of ritual and who reflects the virtue of humaneness in all interpersonal dealings. Laozi, indeed, tells us directly that "the sage does not behave with humaneness" (*DDJ* 5). Instead, the Daoist sage simply "embraces the One" (*DDJ* 22). The sage in *Dao de jing* also possesses understanding, but this understanding does not derive from "knowledge" (*zhi*), which implies for Confucius and his followers a constant struggle of the intentional consciousness to master the texts and practices of the past. Laozi uses another term for the insight or enlightenment sought by his sage, and that is *ming*, which literally means "bright" and is a kind of "luminosity" not unlike the *satori* of the much later Zen tradition. Laozi defines this "luminosity" as simply "to know the constant" *(zhi chang, DDJ* 16 and 55). Elsewhere in *Dao de jing*, luminosity is linked with the constant:

> To perceive the small is called "luminosity."
> To preserve the supple is called "strength."
> Use the light to return again to luminosity,
> And your body will not be left in peril.
> This is considered practicing the constant.
>
> (*DDJ* 52)

Let us now look more closely at Laozi's use of the words for "knowing" in the *Dao de jing*.

Often in Laozi the word *zhi*, in the two related graphic forms of 知 and 智, refers to knowledge in the purely intentionalist, discursive mode.[59] Laozi employs verbs, such as *ming* 明 and *guan* 觀, in order to suggest an awareness of what we have been calling the participatory dimension of the human consciousness. The luminous quality of this experience of participation is suggested by the very word *ming* 明, which is composed of two characters that represent the sun 日 and the moon 明.

In the first chapter of the *Dao de jing*, the verb *zhi* does not appear. Intentionality is, rather, associated with the bodily experience of desire (*yu*).[60] *Yu* can mean "to seek" or "to intend." As Shigenori Nagatomo observes, *yu* refers to "a directionality within a noetic act; I seek *something*; I intend *something* or desire *something*."[61] Such intentionality must be constantly negated if one is to perceive (*guan*) the mystery (*miao*) of *dao*. Couvreur defines *guan* as "To consider from afar, to observe from a high place" ("*Considérer de loin, observer d'un lieu élevé*"),[62] while others have suggested that *guan* originally meant to look "with wide-open eyes" and, hence, "to take a broad view."[63] Rather than use the verb *zhi* in this context, Laozi has chosen instead a verb that implies the contemplation of a whole, which is perceived at a great horizontal or vertical distance from the viewer.

The second chapter begins with the statement, "The whole world understands [*zhi*] that which makes beauty beautiful, and thus the concept of ugliness arises. Everyone understands [*zhi*] that which makes goodness good, and thus the concept of badness arises." Laozi here seems to be questioning the reality status of opposites in favor of achieving an awareness of what these supposed opposites in fact share. Once beauty or goodness is conceptualized and put into language, then people will begin to categorize and therefore limit their experiences. As soon as people create the artificial category of the beautiful or the good, then there will arise the opposite category of the ugly or the bad. Thus, reality is manipulated through language and one's experience of unity is ruptured. "Knowing," in the sense of *zhi*, is thus associated – as it will be by Zhuangzi – with understanding from one's limited individual perspective rather than with an awareness of how that perspective is situated within a greater whole. In chapter 22, the true sage, who "embraces unity" (*bao yi*), does not focus on himself – that is, does not view reality from his own limited perspective – and therefore he experiences luminosity (*bu zi jian, gu ming*).[64]

In the third chapter, we find Laozi remarking that the good ruler constantly ensures that his people are without knowledge or erudition (*wu zhi*) and without desires (*wu yu*). He also prevents the gratuitously clever (*zhi zhe*) from initiating activities. *Zhi* refers to knowledge that is "artificial and contrived" and that thus "inhibits any true understanding of the Tao."[65]

In the following chapter, Laozi speaks of the emptiness, the intangibility of *dao*. Because of its extraordinary depth, "it resembles the ancestor of the ten thousand things." If it is itself like the ancestor of the visible universe, however, what was responsible for generating *dao*? Knowledge of this question is impossible: "I cannot know [*zhi*] whose son it is." The coming-into-existence of the *dao* cannot be "known" as an intended object of the consciousness because such a process cannot be conceived in spatio-temporal terms. The *dao* is itself the very ground of existence, including the existence of divinity: "It seems God's predecessor" – if we take the word *di*, in the phrase *xiang di zhi xian*, as meaning "God," as does Lau.[66]

We have provided enough examples to make the point that Laozi often uses the verb *zhi* to refer to knowledge in the subject–object mode. For the subject's awareness of his luminous participation in the whole,

Laozi sometimes uses the word *ming*, as he does in chapter 22, which we discussed above, and as he does in chapter 10, to which we now turn our attention. Chapter 10 is constructed as a series of statements followed by questions. The last of the series is the following: "When a sense of luminous awareness [*ming*] shines through and clarifies the four quarters, are you capable of not knowing [*zhi*]?" The sense here is that only when one refrains from pursuing knowledge in the relentlessly intentionalist mode can luminosity manifest itself.[67] True enlightenment, *ming*, is "knowing the constant" (*DDJ* 16).

In chapter 52 Laozi makes the curious statement, which we quoted earlier, that "Seeing the small is called luminosity [*ming*]." The statement becomes less curious if we take it to mean "Seeing *what the world considers* insignificant is, in fact, luminosity." The following line ("*shou rou yue qiang*"), which contains four characters that perfectly parallel the preceding line ("*jian xiao yue ming*"), can be taken in a similar sense of choosing a path that seems paradoxical because it goes against conventional wisdom: "Clinging to [what is conventionally thought of as weakness or] gentleness is called strength." Laozi once again depicts knowledge, in the sense of *zhi*, as the opposite of this. We can only *zhi* the manifestations of *dao*, not its essence. "The world has its beginning," Laozi begins this chapter by saying, and "this genesis is the mother of the world. Having found the mother, we know [*zhi*] her children. When we reach the knowledge [*zhi*] of her children, we can return and cling to the mother." As in the first chapter, we cannot *zhi* the experience of *dao* (despite the contemporary Mandarin word *zhidao*, meaning "to know"!). But we can, through an awareness of how we participate in the *dao*, "return to its luminosity" (*fu gui ming*, 52.15). And, once again, such luminosity is associated with the constant, for experiences such as returning to luminosity are, Laozi says, "inheriting constancy" (*xi chang*, 52.19).

Let us meditate, for a moment, on the phrase *fu gui ming*, which means "return to its luminosity." We titled this section "Laozi's Return to the Dao." The experience of returning to luminosity has its parallel in Greek philosophy in the very word for reason, *nous*, which Douglas Frame believes is derived, through a common Indo-European root, from the Homeric word *neomai*, which means "to return home." The Indo-European root (*nes-*), according to Frame, had an early, sacred meaning of returning from darkness and death to light and life.[68] Hence, Plato's and Aristotle's view of noetic participation, which we shall discuss later in this part, may well contain in it an experience of returning to the light that is not unlike Laozi's *fan qi ming*.

Laozi's search for a return to a luminous awareness of "the constant," his pursuit of "the One," the Mother, the *dao*, on one level reflects a nostalgic yearning for some simpler, rustic life. The Daoist utopia painted in *Dao de jing*, chapter 81, is a "small state with few people." It has tools, weapons, boats, and carriages, but no one makes use of them. Most significantly, people communicate by "knotting ropes," which is a system of transmitting short messages that early Chinese thinkers believed existed before the advent of writing. The inhabitants are so satisfied in their happy lives that they "reach old age and die" without ever even having the urge to visit a neighboring village. No philosophy could be further removed from the restlessness and, indeed, the inventiveness of the Warring States period in which *Dao de jing* presumably took shape. A. C. Graham, in a surprisingly negative characterization of Laozi, says that "At the root of the thinking, pervading this book of evasions and retreats disguised by a pseudonym, is one dominant emotion, fear."[69] Perhaps. But *Dao de jing* also is a daring attack on all those constructs and beliefs that Confucians and many other early Chinese thinkers might have regarded as leading to a more orderly and content society. Laozi avers that we will not overcome our sense of alienation from the *dao* through ever more intentional striving. We must, somehow, recover a lost spontaneity, what is "so of itself," and in such a participatory consciousness we will once again "be fed by the mother."

Zhuangzi's participationist response to Huizi's intentionalism

The word *philosophos* ("philosopher"), Eric Voegelin observes, arises as the symbol of an experience of resistance against the climate of opinion in the Athens of Plato's day. The word "philosopher," the lover of wisdom, emerged as one of two paired terms, the other being "philodoxer," "the lover of opinion."[70] Similarly, the speculations of Zhuangzi, who probably lived sometime in the last half of the fourth century BCE and felt a close affinity with Laozi, arise in opposition to the views of an antagonist and friend, Huizi. Zhuangzi's particular form of Daoism is a clearly participationist response to the intentionalism of Huizi.

A. C. Graham tells us about how, in the fourth century BCE, there appears for the first time in China the phenomenon of thinkers who are obsessed with the mechanics of argumentation and the paradoxes that arise through a literalistic manipulation of language.[71] The manipulations of these Chinese "sophists," who were originally known as "those who make distinctions" (*bian zhe*) and later as "the school of names" (*ming jia*), produced allegedly provable propositions that were

189

nonsensical and counterintuitive. One of the most famous of these sophists was Hui Shi (= Huizi), who was a contemporary of Zhuangzi and rose to serve King Hui of Liang (c. 370–319 BCE) as chief minister. Unfortunately, none of Huizi's writings have been preserved, and he is largely known through the writings of his philosophical rivals, chiefly in the text *Zhuangzi*, which is itself an anthology stemming from the philosopher Zhuangzi and his later followers. A series of Huizi's paradoxes, some of which bear a striking similarity to those of the fifth-century BCE Greek thinker Zeno, appears in chapter 33 of *Zhuangzi*. It is difficult, if not impossible, to know precisely what the point of these paradoxes might have been, but it is clear that they are based upon a highly literalistic and somewhat mechanistic notion of language.[72]

As we observed earlier, Laozi worries over the reduction of language to flattened, true or false propositions. The act of naming will thus separate us from the very experiences that the naming is meant to evoke. Since language participates in both the intentional and the participatory poles of consciousness, language should reflect this fact. A relentlessly intentionalist naming appears to be the path down which Huizi headed, and the sophists followed him, with propositions even more outlandish than his, such as "Fire is not hot," "A wheel does not roll on the ground," and "Swift as the barbed arrow may be, there is a time when it neither moves nor is at rest."[73] Language, which can reveal reality by reflecting both its intentionalist and participatory dimensions, here obscures the *dao* through a reductively intentionalist discourse. In the concluding chapter, which is not the work of Zhuangzi himself but rather of one of his much later followers, the narrator remarks that Huizi had "devised strange propositions."[74] Zhuangzi wished to reveal the *dao* that had been obscured by Huizi's narrowly intentional focus upon what ancient Chinese call "*wan wu*" (the ten thousand things). Since Huizi did not "honor the Way," Zhuangzi says, "he scattered himself insatiably among the myriad things, ending up being famed as a skillful debater."[75]

Huizi is Zhuangzi's alter ego, his philosophical sparring partner against whom his own uniquely participatory vision of the world is articulated. In chapter 24 of the *Zhuangzi* we read:

> When Zhuangzi was once part of a burial procession, he passed by the grave of Huizi. Looking back, he said to his followers, "There was a plasterer from Ying who, if he got a speck of mud on the tip of his nose as thin as a fly's wing, would get Carpenter Shi to slice it off for him. Carpenter Shi would whirl his hatchet, stirring up a wind, then he would proceed to slice it off. Every bit of mud was removed with no injury to the nose, while the plasterer just stood there completely unperturbed. Lord

Yuan of Song heard of this feat, summoned Carpenter Shi, and said, 'Could you try doing this for me?' But Carpenter Shi replied, 'I once was able to slice like that. Although that is so, the material I worked on has been dead for a long time.' Since you died, Master Hui, I have had no material to work on. There's no one I can talk to any more."[76] (24.6)

In this nostalgic description of the symbiotic relationship between the plasterer and Carpenter Shi, the analogy to Huizi and Zhuangzi remains unclear and ambiguous. Who is being compared to Huizi, who to Zhuangzi? On the one hand, the pinpoint precision of the whirling hatchet recalls the unerring, Daoist knife-thrusts of Cook Ding in the second chapter of the *Zhuangzi*. Carpenter Shi would then represent Zhuangzi. But the hatchet also might evoke the logic-chopping of Huizi. The analogy is thus ambiguous, which may be precisely Zhuangzi's point. Huizi, if asked, would probably have wanted the analogy clarified, but Zhuangzi appears content to have it remain ambiguous. Interpretation is, after all, for Zhuangzi, the result of one's particular "subject-position" in the whole of reality. What is not ambiguous about the statement, however, is that the feat described clearly requires the presence of *both* the plasterer *and* Carpenter Shi. They both must *participate* in the process, even if it is not clear whom they represent in Zhuangzi's parable.

And so we come to the famous little story about the happy fish from the "Autumn Floods" section of the *Zhuangzi*. "Zhuangzi and Huizi," Zhuangzi writes (ch. 17), "wandered [*you*] onto the bridge over the Hao River." Zhuangzi says, "The Shu fish have come out to wander [*you*] and move freely about. This is the peculiar happiness of fish." Huizi asks how [*an*] Zhuangzi can possibly know [*zhi*] that the fish are happy, since he, Zhuangzi, is not a fish. Zhuangzi replies, "You are not I, so how do you know that I don't know what fish enjoy?" Huizi concedes that he is not Zhuangzi and that he therefore certainly doesn't know what he, Zhuangzi, knows. But by the same token, Huizi adds, "You (Zhuangzi) are certainly not a fish – so that still proves you don't know what fish enjoy." "Your asking of the question how did I know," Zhuangzi replies, "presupposed the fact that I did in fact know."

What is at stake here is, to a large extent, the meaning of "know" (*zhi*). For Huizi, *zhi* means *certain* knowledge from an intentionalist perspective. For Zhuangzi, *zhi* means the awareness, however proximate and imprecise, of his participation in the unity of the *dao*. Zhuangzi is clarifying the difference between the "knowledge" of the intentionalist thinker and the "wisdom" of the Daoist sage. How (*an*) does Zhuangzi know that the fish are happy? Zhuangzi chooses to understand "*an*" as meaning "from what perspective" (literally, "where").[77] He knows fish are happy, he concludes, from his perspective on the bridge overlooking the Hao River. A purely intentionalist thinker forgets that acts of intentionality occur within a comprehensive whole. There is no place to stand outside the process of reality. Zhuangzi is attempting to recover that insight, and his playful and ambiguous use of language reflects this fact. Huizi's question to Zhuangzi, "How do you know what the fish enjoy?" according to Zhuangzi presupposes this participationist understanding of knowledge. "You already knew [zhi] I knew [zhi] it when you asked the question," Zhuangzi replies.

Whether we can know if the fish are happy or not all depends on what is meant by knowing (zhi). As we have seen above, in Laozi zhi refers specifically to knowledge about the external world and the verb ming is reserved for the luminosity of the experience of participation. Ming is used in the Zhuangzi, as well, for this higher type of participatory awareness. For example, in the "Essay on Making Things Equal" (Zhuangzi, ch. 2), Zhuangzi offers a devastating and, at times, humorous critique of the ability of language, which is always perspective-bound, to resolve questions of "so" (shi) and "not so" (fei): "What one can say is so is infinite; and what one can say is not so is infinite. Therefore, I say nothing is equal to using illumination [ming]" (2.5). Later in the same chapter, we are told that a sage resolves apparent contradictions between the views of a variety of thinkers by using "illumination" (ming) (2.7).[78] In the passage concerning the happiness of the fish, Zhuangzi is pushing the experience of zhi, which in Laozi is associated with intentionality, toward the luminous dimension that both Laozi and Zhuangzi himself had elsewhere evoked with the verb ming.[79]

Zhuangzi and the fish, moreover, are not separate and purely self-interested entities. Indeed, their kinship is suggested by the repetition of the verb you 遊. Zhuangzi and Huizi have wandered (you) onto the Hao Bridge, the fish swim about (you) beneath them. Zhuangzi therefore can "know" or intuit what makes fish happy because he and the fish both participate in similar ways – i.e. they both wander about (you) – in the very same reality.

Later in the work, Zhuangzi clarifies the bond that living beings share with each other:

Zhuang Zhou was wandering in the park at Diaoling when he saw a strange magpie flying toward him from the south. ... It brushed against Zhuang Zhou's forehead and then settled down in a chestnut grove. ... Zhuangzi hitched up his robe, strode over, raised his crossbow, and paused for a moment. Just then, he spied a cicada that was enjoying a bit of shade and had forgotten the safety of its own body. Behind it, a praying mantis raised its legs to strike at it. The mantis saw a goal and forgot the safety of its own form. The strange magpie was close behind, ready to take advantage of the mantis. Seeing its advantage, it had forgotten the true situation. Zhuang Zhou, shuddering at the sight, said, "Ah! Things make trouble for one another – each creature bringing disaster upon another!" He threw down his crossbow and ran back out of the park with the park keeper running after him and shouting accusations.

Zhuang Zhou returned home and for three months looked unhappy. (20.8)

The park keeper is about to pounce on Zhuangzi, Zhuangzi is about to shoot the magpie, the magpie is eyeing a praying mantis, which is in turn eyeing a cicada. As Woody Allen once remarked, "the whole world is a restaurant," as creature looks to devour creature. Such is the purely intentionalist, self-interested view of reality. For Watson's "things do nothing but make trouble for each other," A. C. Graham prefers, "It is inherent in things that they are ties to each other, that one kind calls up another." Graham argues that Zhuangzi is here rejecting self-interested Yangist individualism and intentionalism in favor of an awareness of how living beings all participate in a cosmic whole and are linked with each other.[80] That kind of participatory awareness (*zhi*) is how the wandering Zhuangzi knows (*zhi*) that the analogously meandering fish are happy.

Plato's *Symposium*, Euripides' *Bacchae*, and noetic participation

We spoke in the Introduction about how Homer, in his characterization of the Sirens' song from the twelfth book of the *Odyssey*, worried more than did Laozi about the loss of human individuality and intentionality that would necessarily accompany the experience of complete participation in a mystical oneness with being. In order to hear the Sirens' song and yet avoid personal obliteration, Odysseus orders his men to tie him to the mast so that he can remain "upright" (*orthon*, XII.51) and maintain his sense of bounded individuality, his intentional consciousness. The loss of individuality is experienced as a threat.

In Plato's *Symposium*, the sage – in the guise of the Hellenic symbol of the "philosopher," the "lover of wisdom" – becomes the Siren. The *Symposium* is a recounting of a dinner-party given by the playwright Agathon following the victory of his play in a tradegy competition. It was Agathon's first such victory, and it occurred at the festival of the Lenaea in 416 BCE.[81] The dialogue contains a series of speeches on the nature of love given by five gentlemen who had been invited to

Agathon's house for the celebration. We first hear speeches by Phaedrus, Pausanias, Eryximachus, Aristophanes (the famous comic playwright), Agathon, and Socrates. The tranquility of the measured conversation is then interrupted by a loud and persistent knocking at the door, as the drunken Alcibiades suddenly appears. When Alcibiades hears that the party has been devoted to speeches on the nature of love, he decides to praise Socrates. He begins his encomium by describing how thoroughly enraptured he becomes whenever he hears Socrates talk. After first comparing Socrates to the satyrs Silenus and Marsyas, the latter famous for his rapturous flute-playing that fatally earned him the envy of Apollo, Alcibiades says he is sure that, if he heard Socrates speak now, he would once again be helplessly swept away. "If I lent him my ears [ta ôta], I could not refute him and I would be subject to the very same experience." Alcibiades continues:

> He forces [anangkazei] me to admit that, although I am sorely in need, I nevertheless neglect myself while managing, instead, the affairs of Athens. Forcefully [biai] shutting my ears [ta ôta], as if against the Sirens, I flee from him to prevent myself from growing old while sitting at his feet. (216a)

Alcibiades would have done better had he yielded to the Siren song of Socratic philosophy and grown old while sitting at the master's feet. As it turned out, and as Plato well knew when he composed this dialogue, Alcibiades' fate was disastrous, as was the fate of the Athens that eventually sentenced Socrates to death. Since Agathon's victory in the tragedy competition can be dated at 416 BCE, we are here presented with the Alcibiades who, just one year later, would passionately persuade the Athenians that it was their destiny to invade Sicily, an invasion that Socrates, according to Plutarch (Nic. 13.9; Alc. 17.5), considered sheer folly. Alcibiades' resistance to the Siren song of Socratic philosophy, then, was in some sense responsible for his success in seducing the Athenians with the "mad passion" – the dyserôs, in Nikias' memorable phrasing (Peloponnesian War, VI.13) – "to possess that which is out of reach." Alcibiades resisted the Siren song of Socratic philosophy in favor of the Siren song of the fame and power he felt he could achieve through leading Athens toward a policy of infinitely extending the empire.

Those reading the dialogue know the fate of Alcibiades. He would argue for invading Sicily. Just before the expedition was to set out from the Piraeus, he would be accused of mutilating many of the statues of Hermes that were found in Athens and of profaning certain mysteries. These "herms" were, as Thucydides remarks, "stone statues of Hermes in the city of Athens – they are pillars of square construction which, according to local custom, stand in great numbers both in the doorways of private houses and in temples" (VI.27.1). Nearly all of these statues in the city, Thucydides continues, "in one night had their faces [*ta prosôpa*] mutilated." The decorous and rationalistic Thucydides comments on the facial mutilation, but he suppresses the fact that, since these statues were often "ornamented with an erect phallus,"[82] the ancient hellraisers most likely knocked off the phalli as well. On the extreme decorousness of Thucydides, the commentators Gomme, Andrewes, and Dover remark: "it might seem that Thucydides in an anxiety to avoid *aischrologia* [obscene language] is falsifying the facts, and falsifying them unnecessarily, as he need not have specified the exact nature of the mutilation."[83]

It remains unclear as to whether or not Alcibiades was in fact a member of the party of probably drunken revelers who mutilated the statues. Soon after he arrived in Sicily, Alcibiades was recalled for trial in Athens. Rather than return, he defected to the Spartans. He later fled Sparta to become an adviser to the Persian satrap Tissaphernes. Miraculously, despite his treachery, Alcibiades managed to get himself invited back to Athens in 407 and, in triumph, was declared innocent of the charges of religious blasphemy and elevated to a position of supreme leadership. After a series of brilliant victories, he suffered a major military setback, fled to northern Greece and was eventually murdered, at around age forty-five. The facts of his murder are still not settled. Some believe the Athenians killed him, some the Spartans. Plutarch thought the deed was done by irate family members of a girl Alcibiades had seduced and taken with him to his property in northern Greece.[84]

The important point to be noted for readers of Plato's *Symposium* is that the dialogue ends with the vivid representation of a troublingly charismatic and ethically bankrupt figure who had met a tragic end that was intimately intertwined with the tragic fate of Athens. Readers of the dialogue, which was composed probably between 384 and 379 BCE,[85] would have been well aware of the fate of this Alcibiades, who would have been so much better off had he listened to the Siren song of Socratic philosophy, curbed his limitless political ambitions, and grown old while sitting at the feet of Socrates.

Alcibiades heard the Siren song but chose to stop up his ears. Plato sees this as a tragic mistake. Alcibiades rejected the erotic appeal of philosophy and succumbed, instead, to the erotic appeal of personal ambition. This highly attractive and charismatic man, the seducer of many lovers of both sexes, wishes to possess Socrates carnally, as if the consummation of his physical desire will eradicate the experience of *erôs* from his soul and relieve him of his philosophical yearning, his aching sense of incompleteness. As we have mentioned, Alcibiades sees

Socrates as a kind of Dionysiac spirit, as Alcibiades' comparison of Socrates to the satyrs Marsyas and Silenus suggests. "Whenever anyone hears you," Alcibiades tells Socrates, "or hears your words from someone else – no matter how poor a speaker he might be, and whether the listener be a woman, man, or schoolboy – we are awestruck and inspired. ... Whenever I hear you, far worse than is the case of the Korybantes, my heart throbs and tears pour down my face in response to his words" (215d). The Korybantes are associated with Dionysus. In the *Bacchae* (*Korybantes*, l. 125) these nature spirits are depicted as dancing around a drum in celebration of the birth of Zeus in Crete. According to the Euripidean chorus (ll. 125–34), this drum was then passed on to Rhea, the mother of Zeus; the satyrs stole it from Rhea and it was then passed on from them to the Bacchantes, who use it to accompany their dancing in celebration of Dionysus.

Socrates himself concurs with Alcibiades' view of Socrates' Dionysiac spirit. In the *Phaedo*, Socrates is facing his imminent death, that moment when the Greeks believed our speech was most prescient, and it is at this moment that Socrates declares himself a Bacchante, one of those enraptured religious followers of Dionysus, the god of wine and of ecstasy, who was associated with fertility and with the life impulse itself. "Those who bear the thyrsis [the rod of fennel, sacred to Dionysus, that is held by the Bacchantes] are many [i.e. those who exhibit the mere outward appearance of religious devotion]," Socrates says,

> but the true Bakkhoi are few. In my opinion, those true devotees of Dionysus are none other than those who have philosophized rightly [*orthôs*] – a group of which I, my whole life long, have done everything in my power to make myself worthy, and of which I, in every way, have been a zealous participant [*prothymêthên*]. (69d)[86]

The true philosopher, according to Socrates, is a devoted follower of Dionysus. We shall be arguing that, in the work of Plato, the Dionysiac experience of complete participation in the cosmos is resuscitated as an ecstatic experience of participation in the reality of the ideas. In order to make this case, we must turn to the play from the fifth century that so vividly depicts Dionysiac experience, Euripides' *Bacchae*.

Euripides (480–406 BCE) was fifty years older than Plato (429–347), but their lives overlapped by twenty-five years. They both lived through the disaster of the Peloponnesian Wars. At least one of Euripides' plays, *The Trojan Women* (*c.* 415), appears to be a comment on that conflict. The *Bacchae* was produced in Athens some time after the poet's exile to Macedonia in 408 BCE and his death in 406. Euripides' analysis of the decay of Athenian civilization in the *Bacchae* seems rather close to our own in the sense that the play records the devastating effects of

Athenian rationalism, which was characteristic, in Charles Segal's words, of "the general tendency ... of the fifth century ... to assert man's independence from nature, a tendency since then stamped on all of Western thought."[87]

Like Thucydides, Euripides himself, in his rationalist questioning of the nature of the gods,[88] for example, participates in the very rationalism that he sees, in plays such as the *Medea* and the *Hippolytus*, as responsible for the disintegration of Athenian culture. Unlike Thucydides, however, Euripides, the great tragic playwright – the most tragic of the poets, in Aristotle's view (*Poetics* 1453a29) – has not shied away from the problems that arise from the suppression of those experiences that are beyond the purview of a narrow intentionalism. In the *Bacchae*, Euripides contemplates what a return to a predifferentiated state of unity with the natural world would look like, and it is not a pretty picture. The alternative to a narrowly intentionalist rationalism, as represented by Pentheus, however, is equally unsatisfactory. Euripides thus leaves his audience with an *aporia* that cannot be resolved.

The play begins with a prologue in which Dionysus announces he has returned to the land of Thebes, where he was born. He is in truth the son of Zeus and Kadmos' daughter, Semele, but his divinity was denied by Semele's sisters, who slandered Dionysus by claiming that the explanation of Semele's pregnancy was a ruse created by her father, King Kadmos of Thebes, to protect his daughter's reputation. The true father of Dionysus, Semele's sisters maliciously maintained, was no god at all. The true father, Zeus, was angered by the denial, and this supreme Olympian deity, apparently without regard either for Semele's own wishes or for her physical well-being, came to Semele in the form of a lightning blast, reducing the unfortunate girl to ashes but resulting in the birth of the child Dionysus. Because Semele's sisters denied the divinity of Dionysus, the god has now returned to exact his revenge. He has stung all the women of the city with madness (32–3), turning them into ecstatic devotees who wander the hills around Thebes performing Dionysiac rites. Kadmos has abdicated and been replaced by the young Pentheus, who resolutely continues to deny the divinity of Dionysus. The scene for the tragedy is set.

In our analysis of the Sirens episode in *Odyssey* 12, we noted that, according to the editors of the recent Oxford commentary, "both the conception and the portrayal of man–beast hybrids ... are influenced by oriental models,"[89] probably from the ancient Near East. The Sirens, as symbols of that which endangers the integrity of the intentional consciousness, are thus associated with Asia – not with China, of course, in the case of fifth-century Athens, but with the Near East. So, in the *Bacchae*, the Maenads devoted to Dionysus are represented as coming to Thebes, where the play is set, from Asia. Dionysus mentions the word "Asia" in the prologue (17), as the god traces his journey to Thebes, to which he came from as far east as Bactria (15), which is not a great distance from the Indus River in present-day India and Pakistan. Dionysus first established his power, then, among those who had never been Hellenized; he next made his way to Asia Minor where "barbarians" (18) lived mingled with Greeks; he has now finally come to Greece, beginning with Thebes, the city in which he was born. The symbol "Asia" is thus clearly used by Euripides to allude to the very same experience of the obliteration of the intentional consciousness that Homer had earlier associated with the Sirens. *Asias* is indeed the first word uttered, in the ecstatic ionic rhythms so characteristic "of Dionysiac cult-hymns,"[90] in the first ode of the play: *Asias apo gas* ("From the land of Asia"), the Bacchantes ecstatically sing, "have we come" (64–65).

After the ecstatic poetry of the Maenads comes the dialogue, in prosy iambics, between the surprisingly now prosy Teiresias, the famous seer, and Kadmos, the Theban king who had only recently abdicated rule to his grandson, Pentheus. We are thus brought back, from the ecstatic realm of the Bacchantes' lengthy and lyrical ode, to the intentionalist world of discourse. And we are reminded, at the same time, that Athenian tragedy has always lived, as Nietzsche perceptively saw, in the tension between Apollonian reason and Dionysiac ecstasy. Tragedy, that is, traditionally preserved the tension between what we have been referring to throughout this book as the experiences of "intentionality" and "participation." That tension, however, has now reached the breaking point in the last play composed by the very tragedian, Euripides, whose rationalistic spirit Nietzsche saw as embodying the destruction of the genre.[91]

In *The Birth of Tragedy*, Nietzsche criticized Euripides for the "anti-Dionysiac tendency" that "led him towards inartistic naturalism" – that very naturalism, as we discussed earlier in this chapter, to which Plato objected and against which he revolted. "The Euripidean prologue," Nietzsche suggests, may be taken as a prime illustration of the playwright's "rationalistic method."[92] From Nietzsche's perspective, the prosy prologue that begins the *Bacchae* would be a paradoxically Apollonian representation of the very Dionysus to whose ecstatic trance the audience, upon viewing a play, should submit. As an audience, then, we move from prosy prologue, to ecstatic poetry, and then back again to prosy dialogue. Euripides makes the attempt to move from the Apollonian to the Dionysiac mode and then back again, but, from a Nietzschean viewpoint, the all-too-self-conscious Euripidean manipulations have destroyed the very Dionysiac spell which the dramatist is supposed to cast on his audience.

We come then to the scene which is crucial to our understanding precisely how seriously the audience is to contemplate accepting the divinity of Dionysus as the alternative to a narrowed Hellenic rationalism. Teiresias and Kadmos appear and announce their allegiance to the god. There is something undeniably grotesque about two elderly gentlemen proclaiming their recently discovered devotion to a cult that emphasizes the necessity of a youthful abandonment to physical and sensual ecstasy. Teiresias becomes the spokesman for his adherence to the new religion:

> We do not play sophistic games with spirits.
> The customs we have inherited from our fathers
> and which have been in place from the beginning of
> time – no argument [*logos*] will topple these,
> not if some piece of sophistry [*ton sophon*] is discovered
> by the loftiest mind. Someone will ask if I am not
> disgracing old age by wreathing my head with ivy and
> preparing to dance. But the god did not decide [*diêirch'*]
> that either the young or the older person would be
> exempted from the necessity of dancing. He rather
> wishes to have his rites observed by all and wants
> to be exalted, making no fine distinctions [*diarithmôn*]
> in regard to any potential worshiper.
>
> (200–9)

These lines are a devastating critique of the rationalistic, sophistic spirit of fifth-century Athens. If we recall the contrasting characterization of the Spartans and Athenians from the Corinthian envoy's speech in the first book of Thucydides' history, it will be observed that the qualities admired by Teiresias are Spartan traditionalism rather than Athenian inventiveness. Indeed, the attitude toward tradition enunciated here is more consonant with the reverence for the ancestral past that we have been associating with much of ancient Chinese thought rather than with Greek. There is a rejection here of rationalistic intentionality. The truth of Dionysus, Teiresias proclaims, is impervious to the subtleties of rational argument (*logos*, 202). Dionysus rejects fine distinctions: he never decided, or made the distinguishing point (*diêirch'*, 206), that only the young must dance; "putting none in a class apart"[93] (*diarithmôn*, 209) – that is, making no categorical distinctions, he wants to be exalted by everyone. The problem with taking these lines as a transparent critique of Athenian rationalism, however, is that the credibility of the speaker is itself questionable. As William Arrowsmith suggests in the stage directions to his translation, Teiresias "is incongruously dressed in the bacchant's fawn-skin and is crowned with ivy."[94] The incongruity to which Arrowsmith alludes is a function of the fact that the sincerity of Teiresias' devotion is questionable. Teiresias clearly understands the practical necessity of accepting the divinity of Dionysus, but he and Kadmos hardly seem comfortable with the experiential dimension of Dionysiac religion.

Euripides' critique of rationalism is more convincing in the form of his representation of the repressed and repressive figure of the young Pentheus, who continues to reject the reality of Dionysus. This young rationalist is hardly convinced of the divinity of Dionysus by the fact that, as the god (disguised as a stranger whom Pentheus' henchmen have seized) explains to him, "All foreigners [pas barbarôn, 482] now dance the [Dionysiac] rites." Pentheus responds by brashly asserting that such foreigners "are less intelligent, by far, than Greeks" (483). Euripides then brilliantly reveals just how closely allied is such rigid rationalism to a fascination with the very experiences that are being repressed, for once Dionysus offers Pentheus the chance to see for himself the Maenads engaged in their orgiastic rites, Pentheus seals his own doom. In order to see the rites, the aggressively male young rationalist must, according to the commands of Dionysus, dress in the women's clothes worn by the Bacchantes. Pentheus then himself becomes the sacrificial victim of the raging Bacchantes, who tear him to shreds. The play ends with Pentheus' own mother, Agave, at first unwittingly holding her son's head impaled upon the point of her thyrsus and proudly displaying it to the onlookers. Agave had originally denied that Dionysus had been the offspring of her sister Semele's illicit love affair. Dionysus has now exacted his revenge. Agave, in her Dionysiac frenzy, believed that the head in her hands was that of an animal she had hunted down in celebration of Dionysus. As she slowly returns to reality, she discovers the truth. The result of Agave's Dionysiac union with nature has been the loss of ethical awareness that results in her brutally slaying her own son.

Kadmos now sees Dionysus for what he is. He is a powerful god, indeed, but he is also vengeful, petty, and completely devoid of compassion. When Dionysus hands down his final, harsh judgment against the very Kadmos who had earlier in the play announced his devotion to Dionysus, Kadmos complains that the god's punishment is too severe (1346). Dionysus replies with the following uncompromising and unforgiving pronouncement: "I am a god and I was blasphemed by you." Kadmos, anticipating Plato's critique of Homer's representation of the gods in the *Republic* and elsewhere, responds that gods should not stoop to the level of humans in trying to exact petty vengeance (1348). All Dionysus can answer is that his father Zeus decreed this outcome long ago. For Euripides, Olympian Zeus is ultimately responsible for the tragic events we have just witnessed. The tragedian thus indicts the Olympian gods.

The chilly voice of Dionysus asserts itself one last time as the play is about to end. The Olympian gods have been revealed as heartless and cruel. Human beings may be powerless, but they are at least, Euripides is suggesting, uniquely capable of compassion, a trait notably lacking in the divine Dionysus.[95] Here is the scene the playwright paints as Kadmos and his daughter Agave are about to part forever:

> *Agave*: I groan [*stenomai*] for you, father.
> *Kadmos*: And I for you, child, and I weep for your sisters.
> *Agave*: Terribly [*deinôs*] has Lord Dionysus visited a brutal outrage
>   against your house.

> (1372–6)

Euripides then stresses the pettiness of Dionysus by having him inappropriately appropriate Agave's adverb "terribly" (*deinôs*), as the god then replies,

> But I suffered terrible things [*deina*] at your hands, my name
>   dishonored in Thebes!

> (1377–8)

The notion of a god "suffering" at the hands of mortals is, from Euripides' perspective, clearly an absurdity. Human suffering, on the other hand, is an obvious and terrible fact of life.

The playwright then returns to the human plane, as father and daughter bid each other adieu:

> *Agave*: Farewell, my father.
> *Kadmos*: Farewell, O unhappy daughter. I fear, however, that your
>   faring shall hardly be well.

> (1379–80)

It will take a religious genius such as Plato to revive a positive experience of the divine in the wake of Euripides' devastating critique of the gods.[96]

The play thus leaves its audience in a state of dreadful *aporia*. There is no way out of the dilemma. We can either return to a state of undifferentiated participation in the natural world, as dictated by Dionysus; or we can take the rationalist and narrowly intentionalist route of Pentheus and resist the participationist threat. Nor will it do to become a kind of latitudinarian Bacchant, like Kadmos or Teiresias, pragmatically offering doctrinal adherence to the creed in order to avoid civil and personal disorder. Judging from his treatment of Kadmos,

Dionysus clearly regards such Brooks Brothers Dionysianism as completely wanting. We must look to Plato for a philosopher's revival of the Dionysiac experience of participation in oneness.

Plato's *Symposium* is, in fact, filled with allusions to Dionysus. Greek tragedies were performed during the Dionysiac festivals at the theater of Dionysus that was located at the foot of the Akropolis in Athens.[97] We can assume that the tragedy of the victorious Agathon, who is hosting the banquet that is the subject of the *Symposium*, was performed there. Agathon is, however, a rather vacuous character, as readers will readily infer from the fatuous, rhetorically overblown speech on love he delivers in this dialogue. If Agathon won the tragic competition, Plato is clearly suggesting, then the once glorious genre of Athenian tragedy is moribund. The *Symposium* is thus, in part, a work that attempts to determine who is the true heir of the glory days of tragedy.[98] Athenian tragedies were performed as entries in a competition. That agonistic atmosphere is re-created within the dialogue itself, as the reader must decide which of the speeches is most persuasive and is most deserving of the coveted first prize, which will be determined, as Socrates says, by Dionysus himself, who will be the judge (175e). Is the winner the vapid and self-satisfied Agathon, or is it Socrates, the character who so deeply inspired the poet-philosopher Plato himself, who in this dialogue stages a competition – an *agôn* in the genuinely competitive tragic mode – between various explicators of the meaning of love?

Let us look at the speech of Socrates, although "speech" is probably the wrong word. All the previous speakers had given set speeches, but Socrates' contribution is different. He presents, instead, a dialogue in which he claims he once participated with "a woman of Mantinea, Diotima" (201d). Readers can infer from these names that Diotima (meaning "honored by Zeus") of Mantinea (chosen by Plato no doubt because of the verbal association of Mantinea with "mantic," that is, prophetic) will have special revelatory powers. Agathon had depicted love as being the most beautiful of all the gods. Socrates says to Agathon that this was precisely his understanding, until he met the "foreign woman" who "questioned" (201e) him about the truth of the matter. While Socrates' level of understanding was once on a par with that of the rather complacent Agathon, he nevertheless had an intuition that something was lacking in his earlier conception. "The reason I have come to talk with you," Socrates says to Diotima, is that "I recognized that I am in need [*deomai*] of your instruction" (207c).

Love, as Diotima explains, is not itself beautiful, for if it were, it would not desire the beautiful, and the essence of love is desire, the awareness of one's incompleteness. Nor could love be a god, as Agathon had suggested, because gods are immortal and therefore they do not desire immortality. We do not desire that which we already possess. No, Diotima says, love is a great force or spirit (*daimonion*) that exists "between" (*metaxy*) wisdom and ignorance (202a), between mortality and immortality (202e).

A purely intentionalist discourse, however, could hardly evoke, for Plato, the true nature of *erôs*, of the erotic nature of the philosophical experience. Not that this dialogue has in any way been restricted to such intentionalism. The very narrative structure of the dialogue makes it purposely difficult to attribute its referents to the projections of any single and inviolable intentional consciousness. To describe a very complicated narrative frame in a fairly streamlined manner: the dialogue consists of a certain Apollodorus (a rather foolishly sycophantic follower of Socrates) telling an unidentified inquirer what he (Apollodorus) had told Glaucon that Aristodemus, who was actually at the banquet, had told him (Apollodorus). It is in this series of Chinese boxes that Socrates' recounting of his dialogue with Diotima is nested.[99] And within that dialogue nested within that series of Chinese boxes, we encounter the myth of the birth of Love. Plato clearly feels he must use the luminous language of myth, at this point in the dialogue, in order to explore and articulate the nature of philosophical experience, of *erôs*.

The following passage is crucial to the central argument of this book, and therefore we will cite it at length. Socrates asks Diotima, "Who is the father and who is the mother of *Erôs*?" Diotima answers:

> That's a rather long story to recount ... but I'll tell it to you. When Aphrodite was born, the gods were feasting along with some others, including the son of Cunning [*Mêtis*], Can-Do [*Poros*]. And when they had eaten, Poverty (*Penia*) had come along begging, since there was a great feast going on, and she was standing at the door. Now Can-Do, having gotten completely drunk on nectar – there was no wine then – and feeling weighed down, went to the orchard of Zeus and fell asleep. Here Poverty, having contrived – because she herself was without a way [*aporian*] – to make [*poiêsasthai*] a child with Can-Do [*Poros*], lay with him and conceived Love [*Erôs*]. For this reason Love has been Aphrodite's attendant and servant, since he was conceived on the festive day of her birth, and at the same time he is naturally a lover of beauty because of Aphrodite's being beautiful.
>
> Since, therefore, he is the son of Can-Do and Poverty, Love exists in the following condition. First of all, he is always poor, and he is far from delicate and beautiful, as many people think, but he is rugged and dusty and barefoot and homeless and he sleeps in doorways and along the sides of roads, lying on the ground without a proper bed. Having his mother's nature, he is always associated with need [*endeia*]. Then again, however,

because of his father, he is a contriver of beautiful and good things, is courageous and ready for anything and intense, an awesome hunter, always devising some kind of scheme or other, and eager of understanding and inventive, loving wisdom throughout his life, an awesome sorcerer and a healer and a verbal trickster.

And so he was born as neither immortal nor mortal, but rather sometimes he blossoms and lives, whenever he can find a way, and at other times he is dying – but he comes to life again through his father's nature, yet his finding of ways and means is always ebbing, so that Love is neither without ways and means nor is he wealthy, but rather he exists in the middle of wisdom and ignorance. (203b-204a)

As we discussed in Part II, Thucydides had articulated the intentionalist nature of the Athenian character, although the historian fell short of recommending the necessary therapy for curbing the excesses of such intentionalism. In this passage, through the voice of Diotima, Plato likewise acknowledges the brilliant, inventive, constantly striving nature of Athenian intentionalism, which is represented by Love's father, Can-Do (*Poros*). As Dover remarks in his commentary, the word *poros*,

etymologically cognate with *peirein* "pierce," is applied to any means (e.g. a path or a ferry) of getting across or over land or water; then of any means which enable one to cope with a difficulty, or of the provision of monetary or other resources. (141)

Not only does the trait of resourcefulness recall the Athenian character as depicted by Thucydides, but the word itself was often associated by Homer with his hero Odysseus, an association that Plato strengthens by imagining the mother of Can-Do (*Poros*) to be *Mêtis* (or Cunning), the Odyssean trait *par excellence*, as we discussed in Part I.[100]

This Platonic passage from the *Symposium*, then, recounts the history of the emergence of the intentional consciousness that we have traced in Parts I and II of this book. What Plato is careful to point out, however, is that such intending must be accompanied by the experience of poverty and need and emptiness, which is figured as feminine in this passage, like the equivalent experiences in Laozi, as we discussed earlier in this chapter. The philosopher exists in the tension between fullness and emptiness. All acts of intending, in other words, occur within a constantly shifting and yet luminous reality that can never be mastered as an object of the intentional consciousness. Philosophizing is as much the product of a profound awareness of one's ignorance as it is of an intentionalist seeking. Indeed, the Socrates who reports this conversation to the guests assembled at Agathon's house had earlier recognized himself as someone who profoundly needed the instruction of Diotima in order to clarify his understanding of the nature of love.

This now brings us to the difficult but central question of the relation of language itself to the philosophical experience of a simultaneous recognition of the intentional and participatory awareness of reality, such as we saw articulated in the first chapter of the *Dao de jing*. Is Plato, like Zhuangzi and Laozi, concerned with the implications, for language, of these experiences of intending reality as an object, on the one hand, and of feeling oneself to be only a part of a larger whole, on the other? It is to a dialogue such as the *Cratylus* that we should turn for Plato's most explicitly stated views on the relation of language to reality, but Plato often reflects on language in his work, and the *Symposium* is no exception.[101] In his figuring of the resourceful father and needy mother, Plato might appear to be rigidly essentializing femininity and masculinity by symbolizing the feminine as lack and the masculine as fullness. He might appear to be locking his language in, to be attempting to assign unbendingly clear referents to signifiers that will perforce enter the flux of history.

A few observations should be made about this passage, however, before we jump to the conclusion that Plato's articulation of the philosophical experience is marred by the stereotypically "gendered" nature of his symbolic language.[102] For one thing, the scheming quality of the father (*epiboulos*, 203c4) is not quite absent in the mother, who Diotima says schemed (*epibouleusousa*) to seduce the father of Love. For another, Plato is rejecting the uninhibitedly "male" quality of aggressive self-assertion – embodied in Alcibiades[103] – and desire for mastery by depicting need as being essential to the philosophical experience. Most importantly, the participants in the dialogue reverse – one is tempted to say "deconstruct" – the gender roles of the allegory. Plato does not see need or lack as the lesser or dependent "term" in a hierarchical arrangement that would grant greater importance to the experience of fullness. In the allegory, it is the female who is lacking and needs the resourcefulness of the male. *In the narrative itself, however, it is the male Socrates who is in need and the female Diotima who is full.* One way to read this reversal of gender roles is to infer that Plato wishes the listener to understand that the philosophical experience he is describing is a universal one, not limited to men alone, that it is not necessarily gender-specific. It was, after all, Plato who in Book V of the *Republic* maintained, in a stunningly revolutionary passage, that women as well as men had the capacity to be philosophical rulers and should be trained as such, since "the only difference" between men and women is "that the female bears offspring, while the male begets" (454e).[104]

Our readers should not misunderstand what we mean, above, by "universality." The "universal," less historically restricted, meaning is an expression of a quest that is never finished, a quest in which the inquirer participates through articulating language symbols that, in Jürgen Gebhardt's words, "are distinguished by the precarious balance they strike between the finality of the language of truth experienced and articulated historically and the nonfinality determined by the language's position in an ongoing, open-ended process."[105] By having the narrative context reverse the gender roles of the narrative, Plato is experimenting with an open and responsive language that, through the kind of serious play we have observed in Zhuangzi, wishes to claim a freedom from the apparent "finality" of its historical utterance. This is another way of saying that *the dao that can be put into words is not the constant dao.* Plato, Laozi, and Zhuangzi need a language that will try to keep up with the flux, that will be self-conscious about its own historically emergent referents. All three thinkers, in other words, want a language that will be responsive to the luminously participatory dimension of reality, to the sense that the intending consciousness is itself always a part of the reality that it is attempting to know.

We have discussed how, for Laozi and Zhuangzi, the verb *zhi* is often associated with the intentional consciousness, *ming* with the participatory. We still have not, however, described precisely enough the meaning of "participation" in the Greek philosophical tradition. This task will return us to the Dionysiac context of Plato's *Symposium.*

Diotima is telling Socrates about the nature of love. Love is not the beautiful itself, but is rather the *desire* for the beautiful. Human beings, because they are mortal and transitory creatures, have a natural desire to experience what is lasting. This explains why people are concerned with fame, with having children, and with gaining knowledge. In this way, Diotima says, a person *metechei athanasias* ("participates in immortality," 208b) and experiences "the joy of immortality." The "beautiful" is lasting, which is why we mortals desire it. It exists "by itself, in itself, as a single form [*monoeides*], eternally, and all other beautiful things participate [*metechonta*] in it in such a way that, while they come into being and perish, it does not" (211b). For Diotima in this passage, humans are most fully themselves when they are seekers and thus *participate in* the idea or form of the beautiful.

The verb Plato uses to describe the experience of noetic participation is *metechein*, which means to have (*echein*) a part in (*meta*), to share in, to partake of, to participate in. In the Platonic context, the verb *metechein* means to participate in the ideas or forms, in that which is lasting or universal. In the *Metaphysics*, Aristotle recognizes the Platonic coinage of the term "participation" when he says that, for Plato, "the many existed by participation [*kata methexin*] in the ideas that have the same name as they" (987b10). The many participate in the one.

It is often said that Plato emphasizes the "transcendent" and his pupil Aristotle the "immanent" nature of the eternal forms. We shall return to this issue, but for now it is worth pointing out that even the usually sober and empirically grounded Aristotle shared Diotima's ecstatic experience of participation in the forms.[106] In the *Nicomachean Ethics* Aristotle describes the erotic appeal of the contemplative life (*bios theôretikos*). Such a life, Aristotle remarks, is the most satisfying of all the various kinds of existence, since it is its own reward, as the contemplator experiences a sense of his own self-sufficiency (*autarkeia*, 1177a). Here is how Aristotle describes "self-sufficiency":

> If reason [*nous*] is divine in comparison with man, then the life lived in accordance with reason is divine in comparison with human life. But we must not follow those who tell us that, since we are men, we must have merely human aspirations, and since we are mortal, we must have mortal aspirations, but we must, so far as we are able, make ourselves immortal [*athanatizein*], and do everything we can to live in accordance with the best thing in us.[107] (1177b30)

For an equivalent figuration from roughly the same time period in China, we might recall the passage from the first chapter of the *Zhuangzi*, when the sage remarks on the remarkable freedom of the "spiritual person" (*shen ren*):

> As for the one who mounts the true principles of Heaven and Earth and rides upon the transformations of the six breaths in order to wander in the limitless, on what would he rely? Thus it is said, "The perfect man is without self, the spiritual man is without accomplishment, the sage is without a name." (*Zhuangzi* 1.1)

Both Aristotle and Zhuangzi recognize the importance of what the Greek philosopher calls "self-sufficiency" (*autarkeia*).

It is often remarked that Confucius does not indulge in the reification of transcendence, as Greek thought allegedly does. Such reification, we have suggested and shall continue to suggest in this chapter, is surely characteristic of Western thought, particularly after the founding of the philosophical schools in the third and fourth centuries BCE, but it should not be imputed to Plato and Aristotle. The human soul's loving quest for participation in lastingness is, however, often experienced and thus figured by both Plato and Aristotle as a loving, upward movement, and we find a similar figuration in Confucius. In *Analects* 14:35, Confucius tells Zi Gong, "No one understands me!" Zi Gong replies, "Why is it you say that no one understands you?" The Master answers, "I do not complain against Heaven; I do not blame men. I study below and then penetrate above [*xia xue er shang da*]. That which understands me is Heaven." Even Yang Bojun, a modern commentator who generally provides an entirely materialist interpretation of the Master, translates the phrase *xia xue er shang da* in a fashion that points upward: "I study common things and then clearly understand the highest doctrines."[108] We would go even further and suggest that the phrase *xia xue er shang da*, with its terse juxtaposition of "below" (*xia*) and "above" (*shang*), suggests a clear directional movement that parallels the Platonic ladder of being.

If Confucius has more in common with Plato's transcendentalism than has been conventionally assumed, it is also true than Plato is closer to Confucian antitranscendentalism than tradition would have it. It is often said that Plato's ideas or forms exist in a realm that is separate from the human, and that Plato has hence been responsible for introducing a dualistic manner of thinking into the West. It is surely true that Plato, especially in his earlier work, posited a realm of ideas that was permanent and eternal. His positing of a world of eternal forms must be understood in part, however, as a rhetorically conceived response to a concrete historical situation which witnessed the great popularity of the contemporary Sophists, whose relativistic doctrines are summed up in the statement of Protagoras, which we discussed in Part II, that "Man is the measure of all things." As we observed in the previous chapter, such a statement, refuted by Sophocles in the *Oedipus Tyrannus*, conceives of reality purely in the intentionalist, subject–object mode. The Platonic "ideas," as the Greek word suggests, are, however, perhaps best understood as the "pictures" or "visions" of a psyche that is grounded in the material world. The forms inform empirical reality. They are not to be thought of as existing independent of an experiencing consciousness. In his later work, Plato is careful to make this clear and, in this sense, the master's view of the relation between transcendent and immanent reality looks very much like what his pupil Aristotle will say on this important issue. In order to attempt to verify this claim, we will need to look briefly at some passages from Plato's dialogues the *Parmenides* and the *Sophist*.

The *Parmenides* is named after the great philosopher who was awestruck by his experience of the unity of being which is perceived by the human faculty of the *nous* ("reason" in the rich Platonic and Aristotelian sense of the word). So struck was Parmenides by this reality that in his now fragmentary hexameter poem (c. 485), he made a sharp distinction between "the way of truth" and "the way of delusion." In the prologue, the speaker is transported by a chariot of "wise horses" (4) to the gates of Night and Day. There the Daughters of the Sun receive him and the goddess Justice (*Dikê*) expounds to him the nature of truth. In the first part of the poem proper, Justice reveals that "you cannot know that which is not [*to mê eon*]" nor can you speak it, for "knowing [*noein*] and being [*einai*] are the same."[109] Later, she warns our mystic traveler: "For never shall this be proved, that things that are not are; but you must keep your thought away from this road (*hodou*) of inquiry." Hence, Parmenides, awestruck by the capacity of thought to participate in eternal Being, in this poem relegated the world of appearances, of *doxai*, to nonbeing. As Eric Voegelin – in his otherwise extremely positive account of Parmenides' great achievement – comments, "Parmenides juxtaposes Being and Delusion without touching the problem that the reality as given in the 'Is!' [i.e. the experience of the eternal oneness of Being] and the reality of Delusion must somehow be ontologically connected."[110]

In his dialogues the *Parmenides* and the *Sophist*, Plato takes it upon himself to connect these two realms of Being and Delusion, of Reality and Appearance, and he does so by means of articulating the philosophical experience of participation (*methexis*). One consequence of Parmenides' assertion that "knowing and being are the same" is that it makes the world of appearances totally unknowable, since such appearances do not truly exist and thus cannot be known. Such an assertion can lead to a rigid dualism that belies the very experience of oneness that engendered the word "Being" in the first place. In the dialogue *Parmenides*, Plato implicitly rejects the monopolizing of the word Being by those, such as Parmenides, who argue that only the One is real.

In this dialogue that bears his name, the philosopher Parmenides first establishes the existence of the two realms of the intelligible and the human. "The significance of the things in our own experience [*en hêmin*]," Parmenides tells the young Socrates,

> is not with reference to things in that other realm [*pros ekeina*], nor do the things of that other realm [*ekeina*] have [*echei*] any significance for us [*pros hêmas*], but, as I say, the things in that realm are what they are with reference to one another and toward one another, and so likewise are the things in our realm. (134)

Before proceeding further, we must observe that Plato here has Parmenides' language paradoxically belie the very point he is making, for Plato has Parmenides linguistically link the very realms that he says are so separate. Parmenides, in other words, does not linguistically separate "our experience" and "the other realm," which would have been easy enough to have done in Greek. Rather, he rhetorically juxtaposes and thus connects the two realms through the *chiasmus* contained in the two balanced phrases *hêmin pros ekeina* ("our experience in regard to the other realm") and *ekeina pros hêmas* ("the other realm in regard to our experience"): *all' ou ta en **hêmin pros ekeina** tên dynamin echei oude **ekeina pros hêmas*** ("but the significance of things in our experience is not with regard to that other realm, nor do the things of that other realm have their significance in regard to our experience").

Parmenides then goes on to try to persuade the young Socrates that, since "we do not possess the forms [*ideas*] themselves, nor can they exist in our realm," we therefore do not possess the idea of knowledge. And if we do not possess the idea of knowledge or any of the other ideas, "we do not participate in [*ou metechomen*] knowledge itself" (134c). Plato's implication here is that, contra Parmenides, as philosophers we surely do – or at least should – participate in knowing to some degree. If the undeniable consequence of Parmenides' vision of the reality of Being is that participation in it is a logical impossibility, then as philosophers we must call Parmenides' thought into question. The dialogue *Parmenides* may thus be viewed as a critique of the dualism to which Parmenides' experience of mystical oneness can paradoxically lead if our language symbols do not reflect the differences between the intentional and participatory dimensions of consciousness.[111] Plato's critique of Parmenides, carried out in the interests of articulating the central importance of noetic participation, becomes more explicit in the *Sophist*.

In the *Sophist*, Plato goes down the path of nonbeing against which Parmenides had been sternly warned by the goddess Justice. It was a daring move. Indeed, for the Plato who was so deeply indebted to Parmenides' mystic vision of the unity of thought and being, such a move could look like philosophical parricide. The Athenian stranger begs his interlocutor Theaetetus not to judge him harshly if, in his attempt to redefine reality, he appears to be abandoning "Father Parmenides." If I pursue this path, the Athenian stranger says, "Don't take me to be, as it were, a kind of parricide." It will be necessary in defending ourselves, the Stranger continues, "to put the speech of our father Parmenides to the torture [*basanizein*] and force it [*biazesthai*] to say that 'that which is not' *is* in some respect, and again, in turn, 'that which is' *is not* in some measure."[112] We have noted the respect with which, as A. C. Graham has observed, Zhuangzi treats even his philosophical rival, Confucius.[113] We discussed, in Parts I and II, the ambivalence one often finds in the relations between fathers and sons in the Greek tradition. In Part I, we looked at how Odysseus, at the end of the poem, to some extent rather gratuitously put his father to the test. In Part II, we focused on the ambivalence of Thucydides toward his literary predecessors and contrasted this to Sima Qian's reverence for his actual father as well as for his literary fathers. The Athenian stranger here in Plato's *Sophist* wants to make sure that he not be taken for a parricide (*patraloian*), it is true, yet he still retains the aggressive vocabulary of torture (the word *basanizein* can also mean "cross-examination") and force. It is thus that Plato feels he must distinguish his own vision from that of Parmenides, to which he is so indebted. "We now must have the nerve to set our hands upon the paternal speech [*patrikôi logôi*]," says the Athenian stranger, "or dismiss it altogether, if a kind of reluctance keeps us from doing it" (242a).

The goal of the Athenian stranger in the dialogue is to hunt down the Sophist who claims, as had Parmenides, that "what is not" (*to mê on*, 258b) has no existence. The Sophist can hide and find shelter in the view that falsehoods have no real existence, for if a lie does not exist, then it cannot be refuted. We recall that Parmenides' arguments, in the Platonic dialogue of that name, led to a dualism between human experience and the reality of the forms themselves. The forms are, by this argument, different from human experience. Yet "difference" itself, according to the reasoning of the Athenian stranger in the *Sophist*, must have some kind of existence. Difference can only exist if it is different from something other than itself. That something is sameness. Ideas or forms, such as the idea of difference or of sameness, mingle with each other. If we do not admit the existence of sameness as well as difference, then discourse becomes impossible (259e). Thus we cannot argue, as did Parmenides and the Sophist, that "difference" has no existence. We must recognize the reality, according to the Athenian stranger, of *degrees of difference*. Hence, the stranger goes on to remark,

> difference, by partaking of existence, *is* by virtue of that participation [*methexin*], but on the other hand *is not* that existence of which it partakes, but is different, and since it is different from existence, quite clearly it must be possible that it should *be* a thing that *is not*. (259b)[114]

It is thus impossible for human discourse *not* to be participatory. Human beings, by their very nature, for Plato, participate with their noetic being (their *nous*, or "reason") in the ideas. The technical term for such noetic participation is *methexis* or *metalepsis*.

This experience of noetic participation, so passionately expressed in Diotima's speech in the *Symposium* and in Aristotle's description of the contemplative life in the *Nicomachean Ethics*, may be seen as the philosopher's recuperation of the Dionysiac experience of mystical participation in the unity of the cosmos.[115] That is surely what Plato meant when he had Socrates say (*Phaedo* 69d), as we mentioned above, that

> those true devotees of Dionysus are none other than those who have philosophized rightly – a group of which I, my whole life long, have done everything in my power to make myself worthy, and of which I, in every way, have been a zealous participant.

In his encomium to Socrates at the conclusion of the *Symposium*, Alcibiades refers to himself as one of those "who have shared in the madness and Bacchic frenzy of philosophy [*tês philosophou manias te kai Bakheias*, 218b]". The experience of return (in this case, to a sense of oneness) in the philosopher's *noêsis* is, moreover, perhaps implicit in the very word *nous* ("reason"). As we previously mentioned, Douglas Frame has argued that the word for "reason" (*nous*) in Plato and Aristotle is derived from the Indo-European root *nes-*, which is the root of the word *neomai*, meaning "to return."[116] We should add here that the philosopher's experience of noetic participation does not invalidate the experience of participation in the physical cosmos. Indeed, as Plato makes clear in the *Timaeus*, the philosopher well understands that noetic participation takes place in a physical cosmos that is experienced as divine.

Summary and conclusion

The Greek philosopher and the Chinese sage emerge at roughly the same time in their respective cultures. Philosophy ("the love of wisdom") is, in the work of Plato, a concrete response to the corruption of Athenian society in the wake of the Peloponnesian War that we discussed in Part II. Similarly, the writings of the Masters (*zi*) Confucius, Laozi, and Zhuangzi are responses to the breakdown of the Zhou order during the Spring and Autumn and Warring States periods.

The Platonic philosopher and the Confucian and Daoist sages arise out of the poetic traditions that precede them. In the case of Plato, it looked at first glance as though we had, in the "ancient quarrel between poetry and philosophy," another example of that scorn for the fathers and for tradition that was suggested in Odysseus' treatment of Laertes at the conclusion of the *Odyssey* and that was fully articulated in the opening section of Thucydides' history. On closer inspection, however, we saw that Plato's critique of poetry had to do with his belief that, in the rationalist climate we discussed in Part II, poetry had been reduced to a mimetic and objectivist literalism. Poetic symbols had, in other words, lost their luminous capacity for exploring and conveying an experience of participation in a greater whole. If Plato, the supreme literary artist of dialogues such as the *Republic* and the *Symposium*, is clearly not the enemy of art that he is so often accused of being, neither is Confucius the narrowly moralistic literary critic of Chinese tradition. Although the writings of the Chinese sage on poetry are extremely brief and fragmentary in comparison to the Platonic and Aristotelian texts that have come down to us, we can nevertheless detect in those Confucian writings an affective view of poetry that has much in common with Aristotle's literary theory. Much of poetry's importance, for Confucius, resides in its capacity to stimulate (*xing*) the emotions.

Both the philosopher and the sage attempt to recover the participatory dimension of consciousness in the wake of the crises of the Peloponnesian Wars, in the case of Greece, and the Spring and Autumn and Warring States periods, in the case of China. Confucius, looking back nostalgically to the time of Zhou order, focuses his attention on the importance of participation in society. This could be best achieved, Confucius believed, through the conscious, intentional striving of individuals to be worthy members of a social order conceived on the model of the family.

This conscious, intentional striving was perceived by Laozi to be part of the very problem of the sense of a lost wholeness. For Laozi, the Confucian emphasis upon knowledge in the intentionalist mode (which he associates with the verb *zhi* 知) had to be subordinated to or even ignored in the interests of developing and increasing an awareness (which Laozi associates with verbs such as *ming* 明) of how such intentionalist constructions occur within a greater, mysterious whole that he calls the *dao*.

Zhuangzi similarly views intentionalist striving, which like Laozi he associates with the verb *zhi*, as obscuring our relation to a comprehensive whole. For Zhuangzi, individuals too often take the objective reality constructed by their own subject positions as absolute truth and thus forget that such constructions take place within a larger whole. It is Zhuangzi's great friend, the logician and sophist Huizi, who embodies the intentionalism to which Zhuangzi responds with his insistent articulation of the necessity of realizing how such acts of intentionality in fact occur within a comprehensive whole. Huizi and Zhuangzi are a symbiotic pair and together they suggest that intentionality and participation cannot, in truth, be separated out as two distinct operations. As Laozi writes in the first chapter of the *Dao de jing*, "these two come forth together, but they have different names."

For Plato, the experience of noetic participation is a philosopher's recuperation of the Dionysiac experience of mystical participation in the oneness of the physical cosmos. It is for this reason that Plato, in the *Symposium*, draws constant analogies between Socrates and Dionysus. *Erôs* is the child of his father, Can-Do, and of his mother, Poverty. He is thus both eternally resourceful and eternally needy. In the person of Socrates, who is the embodiment of *Erôs*, philosophy in the Platonic sense thus combines intentionalist seeking with the experience of participation – with being part of a mysterious whole that can never be mastered as an intentionalist object of knowledge. To recall the vocabulary of Laozi and Zhuangzi, Platonic philosophy seeks knowledge (*zhi*) about reality while, at the same time, fully recognizing that such acts of knowledge occur within a comprehensive whole. This participatory awareness, often expressed in Zhuangzi and Laozi with the verb *ming*, has an equivalent figuration in the Platonic *methexis* and *metalepsis* (cf. *Parmenides* 131a). Both the philosopher and the sage articulate, with decisive and persuasive analytic precision, the nature of the relationship between knowledge and wisdom as this relationship had been more inchoately expressed by their predecessors.

Throughout this book we have noted the tendency in Greek thought to allow the participatory dimension of reality to be eclipsed by intentionality. In Part I, we observed an early adumbration of this process in Odysseus' testing of his father Laertes at the conclusion of the poem. In Part II, we pointed out how Thucydides had, analogously, tried to remove himself emotionally from the situation he was analyzing. The separation of intentionality from participation in an experience of mystical oneness becomes complete in Euripides' tragedy the *Bacchae*, which was produced in Athens some time after the poet's death in 406 BCE. If Plato had to restore the balance between human intentionality and the mystery of participation in an experience of divine oneness, it was because such a balance had been badly lost. Plato recovered the experience of participation by reconceptualizing – as *methexis* or *metalepsis* – the very nature of participation. And this reconceptualization, as we have shown, has equivalent figurations in both Confucian and Daoist thought. The experience of participation in the lastingness of the ideas, for example, has its rough equivalent in Laozi's expression of the experience of luminosity as knowledge of the constant (*Dao de jing* 16.55).

Notes

1. Perhaps, as Benjamin I. Schwartz suggests, some of the thought of Laozi and Zhuangzi arose as a reaction to the Mohist school. See *The World of Thought in Ancient*

China (Cambridge, MA: The Belknap Press of Harvard University Press, 1985), pp. 189–91. For example, in his discussion of the word *wei* (meaning "to act as," "to do for the sake of," "being for") in Mozi, Schwartz comments: "[t]he stress on intellectual analysis is obvious and the intuitive grasp of the whole is conspicuously absent" (p. 190). The famous Daoist phrase *wu wei* ("having no action") may thus be seen as a rejection of Mozi's relentless intentionalism in which, as Schwartz remarks, "the intuitive grasp of the whole is conspicuously absent."

2. For a survey of these later developments see, among other scholarship, Erik Zürcher, *The Buddhist Conquest of China*, 2 vols (Leiden: E. Brill, 1959).

3. For a very provocative discussion of the nature of a *jia* or "lineage" in the Chinese medical tradition, see Nathan Sivin, "Text and Experience in Classical Chinese Medicine," in *Knowledge and the Scholarly Medical Traditions*, ed. D. Bates (Cambridge: Cambridge University Press, 1995). There is no reason, as Sivin himself implies, to assume that the transmission of texts from teacher to student functioned any differently in the lineages of such masters as Confucius and Mozi.

For a stimulating discussion of the similarities and differences between Chinese philosophical lineages and Greek philosophical schools, see Lloyd, *Adversaries and Authorities: Investigations into Ancient Greek and Chinese Science* (Cambridge: Cambridge University Press, 1996), pp. 32–6.

4. For some recent comments on the early date of these poems, see Edward L. Shaughnessy, *Before Confucius: Studies in the Creation of the Confucian Classics* (Albany: State University of New York Press, 1998), pp. 165–95.

5. *Shuo wen jie zi zhu*, 1A.9.

6. *Wangdao ou la voie royale* (Paris: École Française d'Extrême-Orient, 1980), pp. 15, 16.

7. *Shang shu*, *Shisan jing zhushu* edition (Taipei: Yiwen, 1973), "Hong fan" chapter, p. 173.

8. *Shi jing*, Mao 275.

9. William E. Savage, "Archetypes, Model Emulation, and the Confucian Gentleman," *Early China*, 17 (1992): 3. The controversy on whether rulers "in a state of trance effected direct communication with the ancestral spirits" is summarized in Lothar von Falkenhausen, "Reflections on the Political Role of Spirit Mediums in Early China: The *Wu* Officials in the *Zhou Li*," *Early China*, 20 (1995): 279–80. For a new study that links the institutions of shaman and king in ancient China, see Julia Ching, *Mysticism and Kingship in China: The Heart of Chinese Wisdom* (Cambridge: Cambridge University Press, 1997).

10. Edward Shaughnessy, *Sources of Western Zhou History: Inscribed Bronze Vessels* (Berkeley: University of California Press, 1991), p. 3.

11. Schwartz, *The World of Thought in Ancient China*, p. 43.

12. See *Ancient China in Transition: An Analysis of Social Mobility, 722–222 B.C.* (Stanford, CA: Stanford University Press, 1965), pp. 1–2.

13. "'Scribes, Cooks, and Artisans: Breaking Zhou Tradition," *Early China*, 20 (1995): 244.

14. See William E. Savage, "Archetypes," pp. 2–7.

15. The social changes that occurred in this period have been brilliantly and thoroughly

analyzed by Cho-yun Hsu in *Ancient China in Transition: An Analysis of Social Mobility, 722-222 B.C.* (Stanford, CA: Stanford University Press, 1965). On this particular transition, see pp. 24–52 and esp. p. 179.

16. Yang Kuan, *Zhanguo shi* [A History of the Warring States] (1979; rpt., Zhonghe: Gufeng, 1986), p. 491.

17. *Ibid.*, pp. 488–90.

18. Hsu, *Ancient China in Transition*, p. 71.

19. *Disputers of the Tao: Philosophical Argument in Ancient China* (La Salle, IL: Open Court, 1989), p. 3.

20. See Eric Voegelin, *Order and History*, Vol. 2: *The World of the Polis* (Baton Rouge: Louisiana State University Press, 1957), p. 243. Our discussion of the structure of Athenian society before the reform of Kleisthenes is indebted to this same book, pp. 115–16.

21. See John Herington, *Aeschylus* (New Haven: Yale University Press, 1986), p. 186, and Voegelin, *The World of the Polis*, pp. 247–8, n. 5. For an analysis of the *Suppliants* of Aeschylus, see Voegelin, pp. 247–50.

22. See on this, and on the significance of the word *katebên*, Eric Voegelin, *Order and History*, Vol. 3: *Plato and Aristotle* (Baton Rouge: Louisiana State University Press, 1957), pp. 52ff.; John Sallis, *Being and Logos: Reading the Platonic Dialogues* (Bloomington: Indiana University Press, 1996), pp. 313ff.; and Eva T. H. Brann, "The Music of the *Republic*," *St. John's Review*, 39 (1966): 1, 2, 8ff.

23. See Brann, "The Music of the *Republic*," p. 9, for the dramatic date of the dialogue.

24. *Ibid.*, p. 8. On the meaning of *Peraia*, see also *Paulys Realencylopädie der classichen Altertumswissenschaft*, ed. G. Wissowa, W. Knoll, and K. Mittelhaus (Stuttgart, 1940), Vol. 19, Pt. 1, p. 78, as cited by Sallis, *Being and Logos*, p. 315.

25. Thus, an early Chinese utopia, portrayed in the *Rituals of Zhou* (*Zhou li*), is "an elaborately laid out and detailed description of what purports to be the governmental and administrative structure and organization of the royal state of Zhou" (William G. Boltz, "*Chou li*," *Early Chinese Texts: A Bibliographical Guide*, ed. Michael Loewe [Berkeley: Society for the Study of Early China and the Institute of East Asian Studies, University of California, 1993], p. 24). Whether or not this utopian vision was really a reflection of the historical Zhou is beside the point; it was presented as such, which shows the power of the Zhou idea.

26. In the "accretion theory" of *Analects*, argued in great detail by E. Bruce Brooks and A. Taeko Brooks in *The Original Analects: Sayings of Confucius and His Successors* (New York: Columbus University Press, 1998), 2.2 is considered to be a late passage and an indication that the *Classic of Poetry* assumed its present shape well after Confucius (see *op. cit.*, p. 255). We are speaking here, however, more of Confucius as a character presented in *Analects* than as an actual historical person. Moreover, even a late "accretion" to a text is not always based upon forgery or inaccurate recollection.

27. For a list of such works, see Fang Zidan, *Zhongguo lidai shi xue tonglun* [A General Discussion of Chinese Historiography across the Ages] (Taipei: Dahai, 1978), pp. 26–40.

28. We draw some comfort that in this regard we are following the lead of both Graham, *Disputers of the Tao*, p. 10, and Schwartz, *The World of Thought in Ancient China*, p. 62. See also the cautionary words of Simon Leys in *The Analects of Confucius*, trans. and

notes by Simon Leys (New York: W. W. Norton, 1997), pp. xix–xx. It does seem to us, however, that to consider much of the last five chapters (chs. 16–20) as genuinely reflecting the teachings of Confucius or his earliest disciples requires an act of faith that is difficult to summon for even the most liberal interpreter. A detailed and brilliant exegesis of the *Analects* which takes the opposite approach and subjects it to a historical "sorting" that goes well beyond anything published before is E. Bruce Brooks and A. Taeko Brooks, *The Original Analects: Sayings of Confucius and His Successors* forthcoming Columbia University Press book.

29. Robert Eno, *The Confucian Creation of Heaven: Philosophy and the Defense of Ritual Mastery* (Albany: State University of New York Press, 1990), p. 56.

30. Mozi, *Xin bian zhuzi ji cheng* edition, ch. 48, 12.274. Steven Van Zoeren, who traces Confucian attitudes toward *Poetry* as seen in the successive textual layers of *Analects*, demonstrates quite convincingly that "for the historical Confucius insofar as we can discern him in the earliest stratum of the *Analects*," the power of the *Poetry* derives from "the Odes as music, in their ritual setting." See *Poetry and Personality: Reading, Exegesis, and Hermeneutics in Traditional China* (Stanford, CA: Stanford University Press, 1991), p. 31.

31. For an interpretation of "Guan ju" along precisely these lines, see Steven Shankman, "*Katharsis, Xing*, and *Hua*: Aristotle and Confucius on Poetry's Affective Power" (unpublished paper).

32. Van Zoeren, *Poetry and Personality*, pp. 32–5.

33. See Yang Bojun, *Lun yu yi zhu* [A Translation and Commentary of Analects] (1958; rpt., Taipei: Huazheng, 1988), p. 28. For an argument that all three lines are from a lost poem, see *Shisan jing zhushu* 8.3.5.

34. See *Shuo wen jie zi zhu*, p. 105.

35. *Si shu jizhu*, SBBY edition (Taipei: Zhonghua, 1974), 2.3a.

36. See Yang Bojun, *Lun yu yi zhu*, p. 28.

37. *The Confucian Creation of Heaven*, pp. 68–70.

38. R. G. Steven, in "Plato and the Art of His Time," *Classical Quarterly*, 27 (1933): 149–55, suggests that the *klinê* (couch or bed) of *Republic* X (597ff.) has a precise visual analogue in an actual vase fragment on which an illusionistic image of a *klinê* is painted.

39. Trans. Stephen Halliwell, *Plato: Republic 10* (Warminster: Aris & Phillips, 1989), p. 39.

40. *Plato*, p. 119.

41. Cf. Hermann Wiegemann, "Plato's Critique of the Poets and the Misunderstanding of His Epistemological Argumentation," trans. Henry W. Johnstone, Jr., *Philosophy and Rhetoric*, 23 (2) (1990): 220: "When Plato, in the *Republic*, ranks art as at third remove from reality – still presupposing the skill of a craftsman, because art means *mimesis* of mere images – a determinate kind of *mimesis* is intended, perhaps that of the portrait artist (*Cratylus* 432b–d; cf. *Sophist* 236b). But the superior and real *mimesis* is that of Beauty (*Sophist* 236b, *Laws* 668b, *Timaeus* 80b, *Symposium* 205c), the representation designed with the help of the Muses."

42. Given the latitude in interpretive practices in much current literary criticism, one sympathizes with Plato's point. "Once a thing gets put into writing," Socrates says in the

Phaedrus, "the composition, whatever it may be, drifts all over the place, getting into the hands not only of those who understand it, but equally of those who have no business with it" (275e, trans. R. Hackforth, in *The Collected Dialogues of Plato*, Edith Hamilton and Huntington Cairns (eds) [Princeton, NJ: Princeton University Press, 1971], p. 521).

43. *In Search of Order*, p. 61.

44. The insight is from Eric Voegelin, *Plato and Aristotle*, pp. 52–62. See also Sallis, *Being and Logos*, p. 314. For a more extended revisionist discussion of Plato's critique of poetry, see Steven Shankman, *In Search of the Classic: The Greco-Roman Tradition. Homer to Valéry and Beyond* (University Park: Pennsylvania State University Press, 1994), chs. 1 and 14. For a recent discussion of Plato's literary response to the various genres of his day, see Andrea Wilson Nightingale, *Genres in Dialogue: Plato and the Construct of Philosophy* (Cambridge: Cambridge University Press, 1995). See also Christopher Janaway, *Images of Excellence: Plato's Critique of the Arts* (Oxford: Clarendon Press, 1995).

45. Schwartz, *The World of Thought*, p. 63.

46. Eno, *The Confucian Creation of Heaven*, p. 27.

47. "The Semasiology of Some Primary Confucian Concepts," *Philosophy East and West*, 2.4 (1953): 317–22; rpt. in *The Selected Works of Peter A. Boodberg* (Berkeley: University of California Press, 1979), p. 36.

48. See *Mencius* 6A.3.

49. *Confucius: The Secular as Sacred* (New York: Harper and Row, 1972), p. 37.

50. David L. Hall and Roger T. Ames, *Thinking Through Confucius* (Albany: State University of New York, 1987), p. 116.

51. See "'Virtue' in Bone and Bronze" and "The Paradox of 'Virtue'" in *The Ways of Confucianism: Investigations in Chinese Philosophy* (Chicago: Open Court, 1996), pp. 17–43, esp. p. 29.

52. See *agones* in *The Oxford Classical Dictionary*, ed. Simon Hornblower and Antony Spawforth (3rd edition; Oxford: Oxford University Press, 1996), pp. 41, 42. This contrast is one of the main themes of G. E. R. Lloyd's *Adversaries and Authorities*, esp. pp. 20–46.

53. See *Shi ji* 47.1943. On this topic, see also Durrant, *The Cloudy Mirror:* p. 62.

54. D. C. Lau, "Appendix 1: The Problem of Authorship," *Lao-tzu: Tao Te Ching* (1989; rpt., New York: Everyman's Library, Alfred A. Knopf, 1994), p. 89.

55. The story is first found in Sima Qian, *Shi ji*, ch. 63. The Keeper of the Pass becomes a Daoist hero because he is sensitive enough to recognize Laozi's greatness and is later provided with a Daoist biography.

56. "'The Poetical Parts in Lao-Tsï," *Göteborgs Högskolas Årsskrift*, 38 (3) (1932): 4.

57. We note this with some reluctance, fearing that we may spawn yet another translation of *Dao de jing*. The eighty or so already available are currently being supplemented at the rate of about two or three per year.

58. Laozi's articulation of the experience of a "return" to a lost state of oneness with the cosmos has an analogue in Greek philosophy; see the discussion on pp. 188–9.

59. The former graph is consistently used verbally in the sense of "to know," while the latter alternates quite freely with the former in the nominal sense of "knowledge" or

"wisdom." On this alternation in *Dao de jing*, see the different editions and readings noted in Shima Gunio, *Laozi jiaozheng* [*Corrected Readings of Laozi*] (Tokyo: Morimoto, 1973), ch. 3 (p. 58), ch. 18 (p. 88), ch. 19 (p. 90), ch. 27 (p. 108), and ch. 81 (p. 224). It is of interest to note that the graphic structure of *zhi* itself indicates its oral and, hence, intentional quality. On this structure, see *Shuo wen jie zi zhu*, p. 227.

60. For *yu* as meaning "to seek," see Ch'en Ku-ying, *Lao Tzu: Texts, Notes, and Comments*, translated and adapted by Rhett Y. W. Young and Roger Ames (San Francisco: Chinese Materials Center, Inc., 1977), p. 51. The same word is translated as "intending" by Chung-yüan Chang, *Tao: A New Way of Thinking* (New York: Perennial Library, 1977), p. 1.

61. "'An Epistemic Turn in the *Tao Te Ching*: A Phenomenological Reflection," *International Philosophical Quarterly*, 21 (2), issue no. 60 (June, 1983): 176. Eric Voegelin, like Laozi, sees intentionality as grounded in one's experience of consciousness as bodily located. "By its position as an object intended by a consciousness that is bodily located," Voegelin writes, "reality itself acquires a metaphorical touch of external thingness. We use this metaphor in such phrases as 'being conscious of something,' 'remembering or imagining something,' 'thinking about something,' 'studying or exploring something'" (*Order and History*, Vol. 5: *In Search of Order* [Baton Rouge: Louisiana State University Press, 1987], p. 15).

62. F. S. Couvreur, SJ, *Dictionnaire classique de la langue chinoise* (rpt., Taipei: Book World Company, 1966), p. 840. Chang translates *guan* as "contemplative seeing" (*Tao: A New Way of Thinking*, p. 3).

63. See, for example, Kato Joken, *Kanji no kigen* (Tokyo: Katokawa, 1974), p. 341.

64. So Edward Erkes (*Ho-Shang Kung's Commentary on Lao-Tse* [Ascona, Switzerland: Artibus Asiae, 1950], p. 164), following the Heshang Gong commentary, renders this line, "He does not regard himself. Therefore he is enlightened." Ellen M. Chen (*The Tao Te Ching: A New Translation with Commentary* [New York: Paragon House, 1989], p. 110), similarly, has "Not self-seeing, he is enlightened [*ming*]." The phrase *bu zi jian, gu ming* can also be translated, with Lau, as "He does not show himself, and so is conspicuous" (p. 79).

65. Ch'en Ku-ying, *Lao Tzu: Texts, Notes, and Comments*, p. 65.

66. *Lao Tzu*, p. 60. Of course, the equation of *di* with the "God" of the Western tradition is highly problematic. On this issue, see Robert Eno, "Was There a High God *Ti* in Shang Religion?" *Early China*, 15 (1990): 1–26.

67. The text is in dispute. The Wang Bi text has *wei*, the Heshang Gong text *zhi*. The Mawangdui text B, discovered in 1973, has *zhi*, which we follow here. See Robert Hendricks, *Lao-tzu: Te-Tao Ching: A New Translation Based on the Recently Discovered Ma-wang-tui Texts* (New York: Ballantine Books, 1989), pp. 206–7.

68. *The Myth of the Return in Early Greek Epic* (New Haven: Yale University Press, 1978), ch. 2.

69. *Disputers of the Tao*, p. 218.

70. See *Plato and Aristotle*, pp. 65ff.

71. *Disputers of the Tao*, p. 75. Recently Chad Hansen has challenged Graham's application of the term "reason" to the intellectual activities of this group of philosophers. Indeed, Hansen argues that there is no equivalent in Chinese philosophy to the Greek notion of "reason." See "Should the Ancient Masters Value Reason,"

Chinese Texts and Philosophical Contexts: Essays Dedicated to Angus C. Graham, ed. Henry Rosemont, Jr. (La Salle, IL: Open Court, 1991), pp. 179–208.

72. Graham believes that Huizi, like Zeno, might have been trying to make the point that "all things are one." If this is so, then he was essentially in agreement with Zhuangzi but had reached that agreement by following a quite different path from that of his Daoist adversary. It is also possible that Huizi, as a successful politician in a time when clever political argument was valued, was simply demonstrating his own immense cleverness and had no particularly philosophical goal in mind at all. Whatever the point of his paradoxes, their basis in a literalistic manipulation of language is quite clear.

73. *Zhuangzi*, Ch. 33. Cf. Zeno's famous paradox about the arrow. With their counterintuitive logic and manipulation of language, the Chinese and the Greek thinkers both obscure the very experience of oneness that their propositional language, at one level, wishes to reveal.

74. In Victor H. Mair's translation, *Wandering on the Way* (New York: Bantam Books, 1994), p. 346.

75. *Ibid.*, pp. 346–7.

76. Our own translation but with reference to *The Complete Works of Chuang Tzu*, trans. Burton Watson (New York: Columbia University Press, 1968), p. 269.

77. As A. C. Graham has observed: "Here Chuang-tzu's final stroke of wit is not necessarily mere exploitation of the accident that of the ways of asking 'How do you know?' in Chinese Hui Shih happened to ask with *an* 何以 'whence?' rather than for example with *ho-yi* 安 'by what means?' For Chuang-tzu all knowing is relative to viewpoint. There is no answer to 'How do you know?' except a clarification of the viewpoint from which you know, which relates to the whole of your concrete situation" (*Disputers of the Tao*, pp. 80–1).

   On the rationalism of Huizi in this passage, see Hideki Yukawa, "Chuangtse and the Happy Fish," in *Experimental Essays on Chuang-Tzu*, ed. Victor H. Mair (Honolulu: University of Hawaii Press, 1983), pp. 56–62, esp. p. 60.

78. For some comments on *ming*, "the 'ultimate' of ancient knowledge," see Kuang-ming Wu, *The Butterfly as Companion: Meditations on the First Three Chapters of the Chuang Tzu* (Albany: State University of New York Press, 1990), p. 200. For other instances of *ming* as "illumination" or "participatory awareness," see Zhuangzi, chs. 2. 8, 9, and 14. Zhuangzi's suggesting that "illumination" can resolve the antagonisms that result from purely intentionalist thinking has a parallel in Confucius, *Analects* 2.14, especially as translated by Waley: "A gentleman can see a question from all sides without bias [*zhou*]. The small man is biased and sees a question from only one side" (*The Analects of Confucius*, trans. and annotated by Arthur Waley [New York: Macmillan, 1938], p. 91). For Benjamin Schwartz, the Confucian passage, in asserting "the opposition of comprehensiveness versus one-sidedness," implies that "the Master's own vision is based on a synoptic *balanced* vision of the whole" (*The World of Thought in Ancient China*, pp. 129–30). Cf. also Philip J. Ivanhoe, who argues that Zhuangzi's perspectivism is a "therapy" that attempts "to free us from the confines of our cramped and narrow perspective and give us a greater and more accurate appreciation of our true place in the world" ("Was Zhuangzi a Relativist?" in *Essays on Skepticism, Relativism, and Ethics in the "Zhuangzi,"* ed. Paul Kjellberg and Philip J. Ivanhoe [Albany: State University of New York Press, 1996], pp. 209–10).

79. Cf. "Rationalism and Anti-rationalism in Pre-Buddhist China," *Unreason Within*

Reason: Essays on the Outskirts of Rationality (La Salle, IL: Open Court, 1992), p. 109, where A. C. Graham is explaining why he prefers the term "anti-rationalism" as opposed to "irrationalism" to describe the attitude of Zhuangzi: "Chuang-tzu, in his shifting usage for 'know,' sometimes derides the knowledge of one verbally formulated alternative [by which he probably means the verb *zhī*], and exalts ignorance; but he always has other words such as *ming* 'be clear about' for the sort of awareness which he prefers."

80. *Disputers of the Tao*, p. 176.

81. See the introduction to Kenneth Dover's edition of the *Symposium* (Cambridge: Cambridge University Press, 1980; rpt. 1989), p. 9. For this dating, Dover relies on Athenaeus 217b. See also D. Sider, "Plato's *Symposion* as Dionysian Festival," *Quaderni Urbinati di Cultura Classica*, 33 (1980): 41–56.

82. Walter M. Ellis, *Alcibiades* (London: Routledge, 1989), p. 58.

83. *A Historical Commentary on Thucydides*, 5 vols (Oxford: Clarendon Press, 1945–81), vol. 4, pp. 288–9. For a good vase-painting of a herm, see the name-piece of the Pan Painter (*c.* 460 BCE) in J. Boardman, *Athenian Red Figure Vases: The Classical Period* (New York: Thames and Hudson, 1989). See also Eva Keuls, *The Reign of the Phallus* (New York: Harper and Row, 1985), p. 386 (figures 328 and 329) and p. 389 (figure 330) for more vase-painting depictions of this statue; see p. 332 for a photograph of a mutilated herm head from the Agora.

84. See Ellis, *Alcibiades*, pp. 93–7.

85. So argues Dover, *Symposium*, p. 10.

86. We are grateful to Claudia Baracchi for pointing out to us this marvelously Dionysiac Platonic passage.

87. *Dionysiac Poetics*, p. 31. In a comic spoof of such lofty Athenian ambitions, and perhaps with special reference to the Sicilian Expedition, Aristophanes composed his play the *Birds*. The *Birds* was produced in 414 BCE, at the first Dionysiac festival after the Athenian fleet had set sail for Sicily in May, 415.

88. See, for example, A. W. Verrall, *Euripides, the Rationalist: A Study in the History of Arts and Religion* (Cambridge: Cambridge University Press, 1913).

89. *A Commentary on Homer's Odyssey*, 3 vols (Oxford: Clarendon Press, 1988–92), vol. 2, p. 119. See also M. P. Nilsson, *Geschichte der griechischen Religion* (Munich: 1967), C. H. Beck, vol. 1, pp. 228–9, as cited by Heubeck and Hoekstra.

90. *Euripides: Bacchae*, edited with introduction and commentary by E. R. Dodds (Oxford: Oxford University Press, 1944; rpt. 1960), p. 72.

91. See *The Birth of Tragedy* (1872), esp. ch. 12.

92. Trans. Francis Golffing (Garden City, NY: Doubleday, 1956), p. 79.

93. As Dodds translates in his commentary, p. 209.

94. *The Complete Greek Tragedies*, ed. David Grene and Richmond Lattimore, Vol. 4: *Euripides* (Chicago: University of Chicago Press, 1958), p. 549.

95. For a similar juxtaposition of the compassion of humans with the cruelty of the gods, see the ending of Euripides' *Hippolytus*.

96. See *Republic* 365b–e and *Laws* 906b.

97. As were the comedies, as well. Not only the spirit of tragedy, but the spirit of comedy as well, is present in the *Symposium*. Hence, at the conclusion of the dialogue, Socrates "was pressing" Agathon (a tragic poet) and Aristophanes (the famous comic poet) "to agree that it was possible for the same man to be capable of writing comedy and tragedy, and that the skilled tragedian could write comedy as well" (223d). These two realms of tragedy and comedy, both presided over by the spirit of Dionysus, thus are united in the *Symposium* and in Plato's literary art generally. This can be called a Dionysiac feat in the sense that, as Charles Segal has noted in *Dionysiac Poetics and Euripides' "Bacchae"* (Princeton, NJ: Princeton University Press, 1982; expanded edition, with a new afterword by the author, 1997), "Dionysus not only mediates contradictions, but exists in the midst of contradictions" (p. 30). See also Diskin Clay, "The Tragic and Comic Poet of the *Symposium*," *Arion*, 2 (1975): 238–61, and Martha C. Nussbaum, *The Fragility of Goodness: Luck and Ethics in Greek Tragedy and Philosophy* (Cambridge: Cambridge University Press, 1986).

98. See William H. Race, "Plato's *Symposium* and the Decline of Drama," unpublished paper delivered at the annual American Philological Meeting, 1989. See also Helen H. Bacon, "Socrates Crowned," *Virginia Quarterly Review*, 35 (1959): 415–30.

99. The metaphor of the Chinese box is drawn from Nussbaum, *The Fragility of Goodness*, p. 167. For an agile discussion of the complexities of the narrative frame and its philosophical implications, see David Halperin, "Plato and the Erotics of Narrativity," in *Plato and Postmodernism*, ed. Steven Shankman (Glenside, PA: Aldine Press, 1994), pp. 43–73. Halperin sees Plato's rhetorical practice as constantly questioning, even undermining, his efforts at putting his teachings into propositional, doctrinal form. Both Plato and Laozi knew that "the *dao* that can be put into words is not the constant *dao*." As his eulogy to Socrates indicates, Alcibiades can articulate in language the *dao* as spoken by Socrates, but he cannot live it. This fact does not, however, invalidate Socrates' insights into the nature of philosophical *erôs*, as R. B. Rutherford suggests it does (*The Art of Plato* [Cambridge, MA: Harvard University Press, 1995], pp. 203–4). It rather serves to emphasize the gulf between doctrine and practice, between the *dao* that can be put into words and the constant *dao*.

100. See Erwin Cook, *The Odyssey in Athens* (Ithaca, NY: Cornell University Press, 1995), esp. pp. 128–70, for a discussion of how performances of the *Odyssey*, in the context of the Panathenaia, encouraged Athenian citizens, from roughly the middle to the end of the sixth century BCE, to mold their characters in emulation of Odysseus' legendary metic intelligence.

101. For Plato's views on language in the *Cratylus*, see Shankman, *In Search of the Classic*, pp. 5–15.

102. See Shankman, *In Search of the Classic*, pp. 24–6.

103. Who, as Plutarch tells us, dreamed that he was dressed in women's clothes the night before he died (*Alcibiades* 39). "In the soul of this proudly aggressive man," Martha Nussbaum interestingly speculates, Alcibiades' dream "expresses the wish for unmixed passivity" (*The Fragility of Goodness*, p. 199). Plato symbolizes philosophical *erôs* – of which Alcibiades is finally incapable – as partaking of both activity and passivity. What Alcibiades could not achieve in reality thus expressed its repressed self, with a vengeance, in a dream. On *erôs* in the *Symposium*, see also A. W. Price, *Love and Friendship in Plato and Aristotle* (Oxford: Clarendon Press, 1989), esp. pp. 15–54 and 207–14.

104. Trans. Stephen Halliwell, *Plato: Republic 5* (Warminster: Aris & Phillips, 1993), p. 57. For a useful survey of the nature of Plato's feminism, see Halliwell's introduction, pp. 9–16.

105. Cited from the epilogue to Voegelin, *In Search of Order*, p. 116.

106. See G. E. L. Owen's essay "The Platonism of Aristotle," which can be found in *Logic, Science, and Dialectic: Collected Papers in Greek Philosophy*, ed. Martha Nussbaum (Ithaca, NY: Cornell University Press, 1986), pp. 200–20.

107. Trans. W. D. Ross, *The Basic Works of Aristotle*, ed. Richard McKeon (New York: Random House, 1941), p. 1105. For a remarkably analogous passage in Plato, see *Timaeus* 90c, in which human beings are said to be uniquely capable of "participating in" (*metaschein*) immortality.

108. *Lun yu yi zhu*, p. 164. Another contemporary Chinese scholar, who has published an English translation of the *Analects* in Beijing, expunges any transcendental overtones at all, "For I have understood quite a lot of fundamental truth through studying ordinary knowledge" (*Analects of Confucius*, trans. Cai Xiqin *et al.* [Beijing: Beijing Foreign Languages Printing House, 1994], p. 275).

109. The fragments from Parmenides are cited from Chapter 8, *The Presocratic Philosophers*, ed. G. S. Kirk, J. E. Raven, and M. Schofield (Cambridge: Cambridge University Press, 1995).

110. *The World of the Polis*, p. 217.

111. See Louis Orsini, "An Act of Imaginative Oblivion: Eric Voegelin and the *Parmenides* of Plato," in Shankman, *Plato and Postmodernism*, pp. 134–41.

112. This translation is indebted to that of Seth Benardete, *Plato's Sophist* (Chicago: University of Chicago Press, 1984).

113. *Chuang-tzu: The Seven Inner Chapters and Other Writings from the Book Chuang-tzu* (London: George Allen & Unwin, 1981). Zhuangzi, according to Graham, "never allows any of his characters to treat the Master disrespectfully to his face. Among the landmarks in his intellectual scenery Confucius stands as the great moralist" (p. 17).

114. For this difficult passage, we have chosen the lucid translation of F. M. Cornford in *The Collected Dialogues of Plato*, ed. Edith Hamilton and Huntington Cairns (Princeton, NJ: Princeton University Press, 1961), p. 1006. The passage in his *oeuvre* that should forever discourage the association of Plato with idealist absolutism is the description of the battle between the materialist giants and the idealist gods who maintain "with all their force that true reality consists in certain intelligible and bodiless forms" (246c). Real being, the Athenian stranger goes on to argue, exists in the "intercourse" (248b) between becoming and absolute being. The importance of this Platonic passage for the history of literary theory is well discussed by Wesley Trimpi in *Muses of One Mind: The Literary Analysis of Experience and Its Continuity* (Princeton, NJ: Princeton University Press, 1983), pp. 106–16. See also John McDowell, "Falsehood and Not-Being in Plato's *Sophist*," in *Language and Logos: Studies in Ancient Greek Philosophy Presented to G. E. L. Owen* (Cambridge: Cambridge University Press, 1982), pp. 115–34.

115. For a history of the term "participation," see M. Annice, "Historical Sketch of the Theory of Participation," *The New Scholasticism*, 26 (1952): 47–79.

116. *The Myth of the Return*.

Afterwords

What we have attempted in the preceding pages is to engage in a focused comparison of selected works of ancient Chinese and ancient Greek literature from the period of roughly the eighth through the second centuries BCE. As we stated in our introduction, we make no apologies for comparing works from two traditions so central to world civilization that they cannot *not* be compared. We believe that as long as human beings remain conscious of the past, and especially in the light of the current global situation of East–West partnership as well as competition, comparison of Greece and China will continue to be an irresistible and important scholarly endeavor. This does not mean, however, that we are untroubled by the skepticism, even scorn, that such study can provoke, especially among academic specialists. The pitfalls of a comparative study such as ours are numerous and we should confront these problems as directly and honestly as we can.

The first and most obvious temptation to be resisted is that of overgeneralization. Ancient China and ancient Greece are both immensely complex cultures made up of many different, sometimes contradictory, strands. The archaeological digs of recent decades have shown that the material and textual world of early China was much more varied than originally believed. Indeed, when generalizing about China, one sometimes fears that the next day's news will contain word of some discovery that proves one's blithely accepted assumptions to be entirely wrong. Moreover, it is the nature of any great tradition gradually to erase or assimilate those contrary voices that provide a challenge to what has become an orthodoxy. In China, for example, the so-called School of Names and the Mohists, particularly the Neo-Mohists, who elaborated ancient China's most refined language of logic, have tended through time to be relegated to the philosophical fringe, thus minimizing what must have been a formidable threat to those Masters whose concerns are today taken to be exemplary of the Chinese tradition. We recognize the fact that our book has privileged particular figures and certain texts and that our generalizations might well be different had we chosen to examine Herodotus, for example, rather than Thucydides, or *Songs of the South* (*Chu ci*) instead of the *Classic of Poetry*. We are aware that other scholars who will take up the comparative study of Greece and China might choose different texts for comparison than those we have selected and we recognize that such comparisons may well lead to generalizations different from our own.

The tendency to generalize, perhaps even to overgeneralize, is probably unavoidable in a book like this. Narrowly specialized studies, with carefully delimited aims and with conclusions that are rigorously and meticulously based on all of the available empirical evidence, are of crucial importance to comparatists. We have tried to build on such studies, and sections of this book are themselves attempts at contributions to the study of specific authors and texts. We entirely sympathize with the observation made by the great Renaissance art historian Aby Warburg, who remarked that "God is in detail." What we have attempted to do in this book is to emerge slowly out of our detailed, philologically grounded readings, and to ascend to an altitude from which we could take an "aerial photograph," in the analogy of the great comparatist Ernst Robert Curtius, of the relative contours of the traditions which are constituted, to a considerable extent, by the works we have analyzed.[1] We realize that, as Curtius has stated, "Universalism without specialization is inane." But we also recognize the validity of Curtius's parallel observation that "Specialization without universalism is blind."[2] We have chosen to rise out of our detailed readings to an altitude from which we could snap an aerial photograph because we are convinced that a broader study such as this will be provocative for other comparatists, and we hope that it will, as well, be accessible to general readers. Such a vantage point is, moreover, pleasantly unavoidable in the global world in which many of us live today.

Related to overgeneralization is the danger, in taking an approach as sweeping as our own, that such broad strokes can lead to the "essentializing" (to use a word frequently invoked these days) of Chinese or Greek culture. We have therefore emphasized the importance of the *experiences* of particular authors rather than reducing such experiences to the productions of something so abstract as "culture." "Essentializing" a "culture" in a study that compares two traditions can also raise the possibility that one of the two traditions being compared is, in fact, dictating the terms of the comparison. We are referring here to the troubling question of power or cultural "hegemony," a term and a concern which has been so prevalent in much postcolonial criticism.[3] When speaking of that vague and problematic thing called "culture," some essentializing is probably unavoidable. Even Edward Said, who was so justifiably critical of those who had essentialized the Orient, sometimes lapsed into his own brand of essentializing, as some of his most sympathetic critics have noted.[4] We do not believe that our comparison has asserted the superiority of one "culture" over the other. Indeed, the major paradigm that informs our comparison derives not from Greece but from a distinction we find expressed in the first chapter of the *Dao de jing* between "having no intention" (*wu yu*) and "having an intention" (*you yu*) and thus from the two different, but necessarily related, forms of consciousness that arise from each side of this distinction. Although we have paraphrased this distinction by using two terms – "participation" and "intentionality" – drawn from Western philosophy, we have done so, in part, because we are writing in the West and in English and we need a convenient way of speaking, in English, about a distinction that we find fully articulated in Laozi. Insofar as we find a perhaps stronger tendency toward the expression of the experiences of the intentional consciousness in Greece and of the participatory in China, this is only a tendency and not a hard and fast rule. We are, clearly, making no claim that the perspective of "intentionality" is in any way superior to that of "participation." Indeed, we have been careful to point out how Platonic philosophy itself emerged, in part, as a critique of the rationalist intentionalism so characteristic of fifth-century Athenian thought. Terms such as "intentional" or even "rational" do not necessarily imply an unqualified advance of consciousness in some kind of Hegelian, unidirectional, and ineluctably progressivist narrative. Surely many of us, in the wake of the passing of a number of the destructive mass ideological movements of the modern age, are deeply distrustful of such a belief in the allegedly undeniable benefits of the march of progress. If this book has one recurring theme, it is that "having no intention" and "having intention," to return to Laozi's terminology, both yield a dimension of vision that is a critical part of being human. In contemplating the *dao*, we would like both "to observe its wonders" *and* to "observe its manifestations."

The question of how comparative work might best proceed methodologically in this era of professionalized literary theory is an important one, but method is not an end in itself. Method in literary study is, rather, a mode of loving inquiry that should emerge from one's passionate responses to literary works. Our own research and writing did not begin with abstract concerns about methodology, but rather

227

with the experiences of excitement and enthusiasm about our Chinese and Greek texts and how juxtaposing them for our students created a palpable electricity in the classroom. Our research and writing began, that is, with the experience of wonder, the very experience that, according to Socrates, is the beginning of philosophy (*Theaetetus* 155d). Wonder is an emotion that, in our era of compulsive and rigorous demystification, tends to be discounted and even ridiculed in the more dour and self-congratulatory corners of the current academic literary world. The experience of wonder is, however, at the very heart of any scholarly endeavor, particularly in the field of literature, where our ancient Chinese and Greek texts are indeed often verbal miracles to be wondered at rather than reduced and distorted in order to be processed through this or that current ideology that is assumed to be the whole and final truth of human existence. The *dao* that can be put into such deadening words of ideological certainty is indeed not the constant *dao*.

Our collaboration began with the realities of pedagogy, of first reading ancient Greek and Chinese texts together with other scholars, and then sharing these texts with our students and marveling at their sense of wonder in coming to terms with the provocative juxtapositions of texts and authors. We hope that our focus, as we have written this book, has not strayed overly far from that initial engagement in the act of collaborative reading and teaching: teaching one another and then joining together in sharing our insights with others. This book, in other words, is a consequence of a truly participatory experience. All scholarship is, in truth, such a participatory enterprise, but we feel that this is especially true in the case of this book, which was in fact written as a collaborative effort between two very different intentional consciousnesses. In the summer of 1991, the two of us were participants in a National Endowment for the Humanities-sponsored faculty seminar that had the goal of integrating more Asian materials into the core humanities and social science courses at the University of Oregon. One of us (Durrant) was a teacher in that seminar and the other (Shankman) was one of the students. But the roles of teacher and student often reversed during classroom discussion and especially when the two of us met for lunch, as we often did, after a morning of exchanging views about Asian texts.

If the discussion of Confucius, Sima Qian, and early Chinese poetry contained much new for Shankman, certainly Homer, Plato, and Thucydides were hardly less "strange" to Durrant. Durrant never imagined that he would engage in this type of comparative study. His graduate training at the University of Washington was almost entirely in early Chinese literature, was primarily philological in nature, and was pursued under the direction of a professor whose reaction to the entire endeavor of comparative literature still rings in his ears: "Comparative literature? But what is there to compare?" – words, incidentally, from a man who had learned Greek and Latin thoroughly *before* he ever began the study that would eventually make him one of the world's leading experts on classical Chinese grammar.

Shankman was trained as both a comparatist and a philologist. He received his doctorate in Comparative Literature from Stanford, although at the time he was a graduate student Chinese literature was the furthest thing from his then firmly Eurocentric perspective. Interest in Asia was not discouraged in his Ph.D. program (one of his classmates, Pauline Yu, went on to become a distinguished authority on Chinese poetry), but neither was it particularly encouraged. Only after he returned from the East Coast to teach on the West Coast of the United States, which of course directly faces Asia rather than Europe, did Shankman feel compelled, in teaching introductory Humanities courses, to look seriously at Chinese literature. He recalls at that time experiencing an uncomfortable sensation, reminiscent of the less compliant prisoners in Plato's cave, of feeling a chronic crick in his neck from constantly and unnaturally looking over his shoulder toward the Europe that was situated across the Atlantic Ocean from his previous vantage point on the East Coast of the United States. Upon his return to the West Coast, it felt so much more natural to gaze straight ahead, at the magnificent Pacific Ocean and at the Asian continent that lay at its margins. And once he felt free to look ahead in that direction, as a trained comparatist he by instinct would again turn around in order to assimilate all this marvelous novelty into his previous experience, which had been largely shaped by his passion for Greek literature and for the Western classical tradition. Part of the effect of the infusion of all this novelty from across the Pacific was, suddenly, to defamiliarize what he thought he knew about Greece. The familiar (Greece), which had never really become totally familiar, was suddenly very strange once again. Once he first encountered Sima Qian, for example, and then returned to Thucydides, he was amazed by the brashness of Thucydides' tone at the opening of his great historical work. It was as if he had never really read Thucydides before, although in fact he had taught the text to university students for many years. The contours of the supposedly familiar became more clearly and more strangely etched when seen in juxtaposition to the great Chinese historian who emerged from an entirely different tradition. And Shankman's imagination was immediately engaged. He was reminded of the wisdom of Samuel Johnson's remark, in praise of Pope's poetry, that Pope had the ability to make the familiar strange and the strange familiar.

Durrant's initial inhibitions about comparative study, inherited in part from his teacher, have gradually diminished – but perhaps never really completely vanished – as he has worked on this collaborative project. This diminishing inhibition has, in part, resulted from the excitement he experienced as the two of us worked together and, in still greater part, from the enthusiasm of our students, who always seemed intrigued and enlivened by even the most modest attempts at comparison. Our students' enthusiasm was not the result, however, of an experience of comparing something they knew (Greece) with something they did not know (China). Today's first-year college students are as likely to have read the *Dao de jing* in high school as the dialogues of Plato, although they are most likely to have read neither. Certainly they find Plato no less strange than Confucius. One day, toward the end of a team-taught undergraduate seminar, we asked our students to rank the following three figures in terms of how "foreign" or "strange" they seemed: Confucius, Laozi, and Plato. That was their order – Confucius least strange, Plato most strange. And these students were all Westerners. We say this not to demean our students' educational background nor certainly their general intelligence, but simply to note that the world is converging. It is no longer certain that a comparison of Greece and China in a Western classroom – or even in a book such as ours, written largely for a Western audience – is a comparison of the allegedly known (Greece) with the allegedly unknown (China).

For Durrant, as for our students, Greek literature is very much a recent discovery, and he confesses to finding it much more exotic than anything he finds in ancient China. For Shankman, whose passion in college and in graduate school was for everything Greek, who memorized Greek poetry and chanted it as if each sonorous and luminous syllable were a sacred talisman, it is China that is the recent discovery, including the eye- and ear-opening experience of attempting to learn, in middle age, Mandarin and classical Chinese, languages whose principles of order and organization are so different from anything he had experienced before. The word "discovery" is the key. Students naturally respond in a lively manner to teachers who are themselves experiencing the freshness of new insights. One hopes that the insights reveal something about the reality of the subject being encountered, but a teacher's openness and eagerness to make the sympathetic leap outside of the closed circle of normal assumptions, routines, and responses is itself pedagogically stimulating. The quest to escape our own solipsism is contagious.

Shankman studied Latin for six years in a junior and senior high school just outside New York City, a most fortuitous occurrence in a public high school in the early to mid-1960s, and this experience introduced him to classical antiquity and inspired in him a love for classical languages at a relatively young age, but he recalls not a single moment of his education, from kindergarten through graduate school, that was devoted to China or to Asia. Durrant went straight from a mediocre high school education in Utah, where the Greeks were only one chapter in a world history textbook (the students skipped the Chinese chapter altogether) and one play (*Antigone*) in an advanced-placement English class, to an intensive experience in Taiwan and then an undergraduate and graduate career that focused almost entirely upon Asia. Durrant had read Confucius in classical Chinese long before he had read in English more than a dialogue or two of Plato. And later, during a time of personal crisis, Durrant turned to Zhuangzi and Sima Qian for consolation, not to the Greeks nor, for that matter, to the Judeo-Christian tradition which had nourished his own parents in their hours of distress. Patterns of influence, in our age, do not always follow neat ethnic and national lines.

This last point is an important one. While we would certainly not claim that racism and ethnocentrism are dead, it seems to us that the ease and speed with which we can now travel and communicate, as well as the increasing cultural diversity that exists in so much of the modern world, has made us all less certain of precisely what our own cultural grounding is. Surrounded and shaped by such remarkable diversity, perhaps we can now more easily appreciate cultural differences. Perhaps "we" can now regard the "other" more with a sense of wonder than with a need to dominate or to convert, for even "we" are ourselves often the "other." This is not a plea for the type of "multiculturalism" that is frequently encountered these days on university campuses. Some multiculturalists seem to believe that a primary educational goal should be to administer the proper doses of guilt to some and of self-pity to others and, in the process, to valorize all cultures as deserving of an equal amount of educational space in the curriculum. Certainly the serious study of many cultural traditions is a worthwhile academic endeavor, but cultures such as those of ancient China and ancient Greece (and others could be added here, such as India and Israel and Islam, for example) have had such a sweeping impact upon large segments of the world that we believe it is irresponsible for any institution to push any of these aside in the march to diversify cultural awareness in a blindly egalitarian manner. The great traditions, we believe, remain great and deserve our continued examination and appreciation. If we find in our explorations of these cultures many of the roots of the prejudice and violence that have characterized the history of both the East and the West, we will find ample antidotes to these practices as well.

231

Our enthusiasm for the comparative endeavor that we have attempted in this book is nurtured by the belief that such a comparative approach to the great civilizations of antiquity must highlight both the similarities and the differences between traditions. An appreciation of the cultural monuments of the past, whether they be products of East or West, demands a constant awareness of both difference and sameness. It is the ground of sameness that enables us, as readers far removed from the cultural configurations and the material world of antiquity, to reach across all the boundaries of time and space to say, as we all do when we read these texts, "Yes, I know what you are talking about."

In multicultural literary studies, examples from non-Western cultures are often used in order to exalt difference, to "honor diversity." What is less often stressed is a multiculturalism pursued in the spirit of establishing community rather than those oxymoronic "communities" founded upon the alleged absoluteness of cultural difference. As the Athenian stranger argues in Plato's *Sophist*, the forms of sameness and difference are interwoven throughout all of the other forms that comprise reality. Confucius has a parallel insight in *Analects* 2.14 when he says that "A gentleman can see a question from all sides without bias. The small man is biased and sees a question from only one side." For Plato, "the attempt to separate every thing from every other thing not only strikes a discordant note but amounts to a crude defiance of the philosophical Muse" and "this isolation of everything from everything else means a complete abolition of all discourse" (*Sophist* 259e–260a). For Confucius, it is the small man who cultivates differences for their own sake. Perhaps some measure of community can be achieved through a recognition, which is always accompanied by the experience of wonder, of the wisdom of such parallel insights drawn from very different traditions. It is this joyous and open-ended search for the discovery of similarity within profound difference that has challenged and motivated us in writing this book. We can only hope that these pages have captured something of the excitement we experienced in composing them.

Notes

1. *European Literature and the Latin Middle Ages* (New York: Bollingen Foundation, 1953), p. ix. See p. 35 for Curtius's attribution of the quote "God is in detail" to Aby Warburg.

2. *Ibid.*, p. ix.

3. The term "hegemony," so frequently used in cultural studies, is drawn from the work of Antonio Gramsci. By "hegemony," however, Gramsci, meant something very different from the way the word is used today. Hegemony, for Gramsci, was a positive

experience of common cultural currency, as Joseph Buttigieg, the editor of Gramsci's *Prison Notebooks* (2 vols. [New York: Columbia University Press, 1996]), persuasively argued in a recent lecture (as yet unpublished) delivered at the University of Oregon in June, 1997.

4. We are referring here to Edward Said's highly influential *Orientalism* (1978; rpt., London: Penguin, 1991). For a brief discussion of the conflict in Said between the notion of the Orient as a constructed space and as a real space which he himself essentializes, see Bart Moore-Gilbert, *Postcolonial Theory: Contexts, Practices, Politics* (London: Verso, 1997), pp. 41–2.

Bibliography

Adkins, Arthur W. H. (1960). *Merit and Responsibility: A Study in Greek Values*. Oxford: Clarendon Press.

Ames, Roger T. (1983). *The Art of Rulership: A Study in Ancient Chinese Political Thought*. Honolulu: University of Hawaii Press.

Ames, Roger T. and Henry Rosemont (1998). *The Analects of Confucius: A Philosophical Translation*. New York: Ballantine Books.

Annice, M. (1952). "Historical Sketch of the Theory of Participation". *The New Scholasticism*, 26: 47–79.

Aristotle (1951). *Aristotle's Theory of Poetry and Fine Art*. New York: Dover Publications.

Auerbach, Eric (1953). *Mimesis: The Representation of Reality in Western Literature*, Willard Trask (trans.). Princeton, NJ: Princeton University Press.

Auerbach, Eric (1965). "Sermo Humilis". In *Literary Language and Its Public in Late Latin Antiquity and in the Middle Ages*. Princeton, NJ: Princeton University Press.

Bacon, Helen H. (1959). "Socrates Crowned". *Virginia Quarterly Review*, 35: 415–30.

Basset, Samuel H. (1918). "The Second Necyia". *Classical Journal*, 13: 521–6.

Baxter, William H. III (1991). "Zhou and Han Phonology in the *Shijing*". In *Studies in the Historical Phonology of Asian Languages*, William G. Bolz and Michael Shapiro (eds). Amsterdam: John Benjamin.

Bérard, Victor (1931). *Did Homer Live?* B. Rhys (trans.). London: J. M. Dent.

Bielenstein, Hans (1980). *The Bureaucracy of Han Times*. Cambridge: Cambridge University Press.

Birell, Anne (1993). *Chinese Mythology: An Introduction*. Baltimore: Johns Hopkins University Press.

Bloom, Harold (1973). *The Anxiety of Influence: A Theory of Poetry*. Oxford: Oxford University Press.

Boardman, J. (1989). *Athenian Red Figure Vases: The Classical Period*. New York: Thames and Hudson.

Bodde, Derk (1981). "Dominant Ideas in the Formation of Chinese Culture". In *Essays on Chinese Civilization*, Charles Le Blanc and Dorothy Borei (eds). Princeton, NJ: Princeton University Press.

Boltz, William G. (1993). "Chou Li". In *Early Chinese Texts: A Bibliographical Guide*, Michael Loewe (ed.). Society for the Study of Early China and the Institute of East Asian Studies. Berkeley: University of California Press.

Boltz, William G. (1999) "Language and Writing". In *The Cambridge History of Ancient China: From the Origins of Civilization to 221 BC*, Michael Loewe and Edward L. Shaughnessy (eds). Cambridge: Cambridge University Press.

Bona, Giacomo (1966). *Studi sull' Odissea*. Turin: Giappichelli.

Boodberg, Peter A. (1979). "The Semasiology of Some Primary Confucian Concepts". In *The Selected Works of Peter A. Boodberg*. Los Angeles: University of California Press.

Brann, Eva T. H. (1966). "The Music of the *Republic*". *St. John's Review*, 39: 1–63.

Bremer, J. M. (1969). *Hamartia: Tragic Error in the Poetics of Aristotle and in Greek Tragedy*. Amsterdam: M. Hakkert.

Brooks, E. Bruce and A. Taeko Brooks (1998). *The Original Analects: Sayings of Confucius and His Successors*. New York: Columbia University Press.

Buitron, Diana *et al.* (1992). *The Odyssey and Ancient Art*. Annandale-on-Hudson: Edith C. Blum Art Institute.

Butler, Samuel (1967). *The Authoress of the Odyssey*. Chicago: University of Chicago Press.

Cai Xiqin, Lai Bo, and Xia Yuhe (trans.) (1994). *Analects of Confucius*. Beijing: Foreign Languages Printing House.

Campbell, David A. (ed.) (1982). *The Greek Lyric*. Cambridge, MA: Harvard University Press.

Chan Wing-tsit (1963). *The Way of Lao Tzu*. New York: Macmillan.

Chang Chung-yuan (1977). *Tao: A New Way of Thinking*. New York: Perennial Library.

Chen, Ellen (1989). *The Tao Te Ching: A New Translation with Commentary*. New York: Paragon House.

Ch'en Ku-ying (1977). *Lao Tzu: Texts, Notes, and Comments*, Rhett Y.

W. Young and Roger Ames (trans.). San Francisco: Chinese Materials Center.

Ch'en Shih-hsiang (1974). "The *Shih-ching*: Its Generic Significance". In *Studies in Chinese Literary Genres*, Cyril Birch (ed.). Berkeley: University of California Press.

Cheng Tsai-fa *et al.* (trans.) (1994). *The Grand Scribes' Records*, Vol. 1: *The Basic Annals of Pre Han China*, William H. Nienhauser Jr. (ed.). Bloomington: Indiana University Press.

Ching, Julia (1997). *Mysticism and Kingship in China: The Heart of Chinese Wisdom*. Cambridge: Cambridge University Press.

Chuang Tzu (1968). *The Complete Works of Chuang Tzu*, Burton Watson (trans.). New York: Columbia University Press.

Clay, Diskin (1975). "The Tragic and Comic Poet of the *Symposium*". *Arion*, 2: 238–61.

Clay, Jenny Strauss (1983). *The Wrath of Athena: Gods and Men in the Odyssey*. Princeton, NJ: Princeton University Press.

A Commentary on Homer's Odyssey (1988–92). 3 vols. Oxford: Clarendon Press, Vol. 1, Alfred Heubeck, Stephanie West, and J. B. Hainsworth (eds), 1988; Vol. 2, Alfred Heubeck and Arie Hockstra (eds), 1989; Vol. 3, Joseph Russon, Manuel Fernandez-Galiano, and Alfred Heubeck (eds), 1992.

Connor, W. Robert (1984). *Thucydides*. Princeton, NJ: Princeton University Press.

Cook, Constance A. (1995). "Scribes, Cooks, and Artisans: Breaking Zhou Tradition". *Early China*, 20: 241–78.

Cook, Erwin (1995). *The Odyssey in Athens*. Ithaca, NY: Cornell University Press.

Coulmas, Florian (1989). *The Writing Systems of the World*. Oxford: Blackwell.

Couvreur, F. S., SJ (1966). *Dictionnaire classique de la langue chinoise*. Rpt., Taipei: Book World Company.

Curtius, Ernst Robert (1953). *European Literature and the Latin Middle Ages*, Willard R. Trask (trans.). New York: Bollingen Foundation.

D'Arms, E. F. and K. K. Hulley (1946). "The Oresteia Story of the Odyssey". *Transactions of the American Philological Association*, 77: 207–13.

de Romilly, Jacqueline (1990). *La Construction de la vérité chez Thucydide*. Paris: Juillard.

de Romilly, Jacqueline (1947). *Thucydide et impérialisme*. Paris: Société d'Édition Les Belles Lettres.

Detienne, Marcel and Jean-Pierre Vernant (1991). *Cunning Intelligence in Greek Culture and Society*, Janet Lloyd (trans.). Chicago: University of Chicago Press.

Diels, Herman (ed.) (1922). *Die Fragmente der Vorsokratiker*. 3 vols (Berllin: Weidmann).

Doherty, Lillian (1995). *Siren Songs: Gender, Audiences and Narrators in the Odyssey*. Ithaca, NY: Cornell University Press.

Dover, K. J. (1973). *Thucydides, Greece and Rome: New Surveys in the Classics*, No. 7. Oxford: Clarendon Press.

Dover, Kenneth (1980). "Introduction". In *Symposium*, Kenneth Dover (ed.). Cambridge: Cambridge University Press.

Dubs, Homer H. (1944). "The Victory of Han Confucianism". In *History of the Former Han Dynasty*, Vol. 2. Baltimore: Waverly Press.

Durrant, Stephen (1994). "Ssu-ma Ch'ien's Portrayal of the First Ch'in Emperor". In *Imperial Rulership and Cultural Change in Traditional China*, Frederick P. Brandauer and Huang Chun-chieh (eds). Seattle: University of Washington Press.

Durrant, Stephen (1995). *The Cloudy Mirror: Tension and Conflict in the Writings of Sima Qian*. Albany: State University of New York Press.

Eberhard, Wolfram (1967). *Guilt and Sin in Traditional China*. Berkeley: University of California Press.

Edwards, Mark W. (1986). "Homer and Oral Tradition: The Formula, Part I". *Oral Tradition*, 1: 171–230.

Edwards, Mark W. (1988). "Homer and Oral Tradition: The Formula, Part II". *Oral Tradition*, 3: 11–60.

Edwards, Mark W. (1992). "Homer and Oral Tradition: The Type-Scene". *Oral Tradition*, 7: 284–330.

Eisenberger, Herbert (1973). *Studien zur Odysee*. Wiesbaden: F. Steiner.

Ellis, Walter M. (1989). *Alcibiades*. London: Routledge.

Eno, Robert (1990). *The Confucian Creation of Heaven: Philosophy and the Defense of Ritual Mastery*. Albany: State University of New York Press.

Eno, Robert (1990). "Was There a High God *Ti* in Shang Religion?". *Early China*, 15: 1–256.

Erkes, Edward (1950). *Ho Shang Kung's Commentary on Lao-Tse*. Ascona, Switzerland: Artibus Asiae.

Euben, J. Peter (1990). *The Tragedy of Political Theory: The Road Not Taken*. Princeton, NJ: Princeton University Press.

Euripides (1960). *Bacchae*, E. R. Dodds (ed.). Oxford: Oxford University Press.

Fang Zidan (1978). *Zhongguo lidai shi xue tonglun* [A General Discussion of Chinese Historiography across the Ages]. Taipei: Dahai.

Fei Xiaotong (1992). *From the Soil: The Foundation of Chinese Society*, Gary G. Hamilton and Wang Zhen (trans.). Berkeley: University of California Press.

Fenik, Bernard (1974). *Studies in the Odyssey*. Hermes Einzelschriften 30. Wiesbaden.

Fingarette, Herbert (1972). *Confucius: The Secular as Sacred*. New York: Harper and Row.

Focke, Friedrich (1971). *Die Odysee*. Stuttgart: W. Kohlhammer.

Frame, Douglas (1978). *The Myth of the Return in Early Greek Epic*. New Haven: Yale University Press.

Girardot, N. J. (1983). *Myth and Meaning in Early Taoism*. Berkeley: University of California Press.

Gomme, A. W. (1945–81). *A Historical Commentary on Thucydides*, 5 vols. Oxford: Clarendon Press.

Graham, A. C. (1981). *Chuang-tzu: The Seven Inner Chapters and Other Writings from the Book of Chuang-tzu*. London: George Allen & Unwin.

Graham, A. C. (1986). *Yin–Yang and the Nature of Correlative Thinking*. Singapore: Institute of East Asian Philosophies.

Graham, A. C. (1989). *Disputers of the Tao: Philosophical Argument in Ancient China*. La Salle, IL: Open Court.

Graham, A. C. (1992). "Rationalism and Anti-rationalism in Pre-Buddhist China". In *Unreason Within Reason: Essays on the Outskirts of Rationality*. La Salle, IL: Open Court.

Gramsci, Antonio (1996). *Prison Notebooks*, 2 vols, Joseph Buttigieg (ed.). New York: Columbia University Press.

Grene, David and Richmond Lattimore (eds) (1958). *The Complete Greek Tragedies*, Vol. IV: *Euripides*. Chicago: University of Chicago Press.

Grene, David and Richmond Lattimore (1965). *Greek Political Theory: The Image of Man in Plato and Thucydides*. Chicago: University of Chicago Press.

Gu Jiegang (1983). "Qi xing". In *Shi jing yanjiu lunji* [A Collection of Essays on the Study of the *Classic of Poetry*], Lin Qingzhang (ed.). Taipei: Xuesheng.

Hall, David L. and Roger T. Ames (1987). *Thinking Through Confucius*. Albany: State University of New York.

Hall, David L. and Roger T. Ames (1995). *Anticipating China: Thinking Through the Narratives of Chinese and Western Culture*. Albany: State University of New York.

Hall, David L. and Roger T. Ames (1998). *Thinking from the Han: Self, Truth, and Transcendence in Chinese and Western Culture*. Albany: State University of New York.

Halperin, David (1994). "Plato and the Erotics of Narrativity". In *Plato and Postmodernism*, Steven Shankman (ed.). Glenside, PA: Aldine Press.

Han Shu [Historical Record of the Han]. Beijing: Zhonghua, 1962.

Hansen, Chad (1991). "Should the Ancient Masters Value Reason?". In *Chinese Texts and Philosophical Contexts; Essays Dedicated to Angus C. Graham*, Henry Rosemont Jr. (ed.). La Salle, IL: Open Court.

Hansen, Chad (1992). *A Daoist Theory of Chinese Thought: A Philosophical Interpretation*. New York: Oxford University Press.

Hawkes, David (trans.) (1985). *Songs of the South, An Ancient Chinese Anthology of Poems*. Harmondsworth: Penguin.

Hegel, Georg Wilhelm Friedrich (1967). *The Phenomenology of Mind*, J. B. Baillie (trans.). New York: Harper Torchbooks.

Henderson, John B. (1984). *The Development and Decline of Chinese Cosmology*. New York: Columbia University Press.

Henricks, Robert G. (1989). *Lao-Tzu: Tao-Te Ching: A New Translation Based on the Recently Discovered Ma-wang-tui Texts*. New York: Ballantine.

Henry, Eric (1987). "The Motif of Recognition". *Harvard Journal of Asiatic Studies*, 47 (1): 5–30.

Heraclitus (1964). In *The Presocratic Philosophers*, G. S. Kirk and J. E. Raven (eds). Cambridge: Cambridge University Press.

Herington, John (1986). *Aeschylus*. New Haven: Yale University Press.

Herodotus (1983). *The Histories*, Aubrey de Sélincourt (trans.), rev. A. R. Burns. Harmondsworth, Penguin: rpt.

Herodotus (1996). *The Histories*. Loeb Library Edition, 3 vols, A. D. Godely (trans.). Cambridge, MA: Harvard University Press.

Heubeck, Alfred (1965). "KE-RA-SO. Untersuchungen zu einem Mykenischen Personennamen". *Kadmos*, 4: 138–45.

Heubeck, Alfred and Arie Hoekstra (1988–92). *A Commentary on Homer's Odyssey*, 3 vols. Oxford: Clarendon Press.

Hightower, James Robert (trans.) (1954). "The Fu of T'ao Chi'en". *Harvard Journal of Asiatic Studies*, 17: 169–230.

Hightower, James Robert (trans.) (1994). "Owl Rhapsody". In *The Columbia Anthology of Traditional Chinese Literature*, Victor Mair (ed.). New York: Columbia University Press.

Horkheimer, Max and Theodor W. Adorno (1996). *Dialectic of Enlightenment*, John Cumming (trans.). New York: Continuum Books.

Hornblower, Simon (1991, 1996). *A Commentary on Thucydides*, 2 vols. Oxford: Clarendon Press.

Hsiao Kung-chuan (1947). *The Logic of the Sciences and the Humanities*. New York: Meridian.

Hsiao Kung-chuan ((1979). *History of Chinese Political Thought*, Vol. 1: *From Beginnings to the Sixth Century A.D.*, F. W. Mote (trans.). Princeton, NJ: Princeton University Press.

Hsu, Cho-yun (1965). *Ancient China in Transition: An Analysis of Social Mobility, 722–222 B.C.* Stanford, CA: Stanford University Press.

Hu Shih (1922), *The Development of the Logical Method in Ancient China.* New York: Paragon, 1963 rpt.

Hu Shi, Shen Gangbo, and Dai Junren (1980). In *Zhongguo shixue shi lunwen xuanji* [A Selection of Essays on Chinese Historiography], Vol. 1, Du Weiyun and Huang Jinxing (eds). Taipei: Huashi.

Hurwit, Jeffrey (1991). "The Representation of Nature in Early Greek Art". In *New Perspectives in Early Greek Art*, Diana Buitron-Olivier (ed.). Washington, DC: National Gallery of Art.

Janaway, Christopher (1995). *Images of Excellence: Plato's Critique of the Arts.* Oxford: Clarendon Press.

Jaspers, Karl (1953). *The Origin and Goal of History.* New Haven: Yale University Press.

Jensen, Mina Skafte (1980). *The Homeric Question and the Oral Formulaic Theory.* Opuscula Gracolatina 20. Copenhagen.

Jin Dejian (1963). *Sima Qian suojian shu kao* [An Investigation of the Books Seen by Sima Qian]. Shanghai: Renmin.

Jones, P. V. (1988). *Homer's Odyssey: A Companion to the Translation of Richmond Lattimore.* Carbondale: Southern Illinois University Press.

Jullien, François (1995). *Le Détour et l'accès: stratégies du sens en Chine, en Grèce.* Paris: Bernard Grasset.

Jullien, François (1992). *The Propensity of Things: Toward a History of Efficacy in China*, Janet Lloyd (trans.). New York: Zone Books.

Kakridis, Johannes T. (1971). *Homer Revisited.* Lund: C. W. K. Gleerup.

Karlgren Bernhard (1932). "The Poetical Parts in Lao-Tsï". *Göteborgs Högskolas Årsskrift*, 38 (3): 1–45.

Karlgren Bernhard (1964). "Kuo Feng and Siao Ya." *Bulletin of the Museum of Far Eastern Antiquities*, 16: 204.

Kato Joken (1974). *Kanji no kigen* [The Etymology of Chinese Characters]. Tokyo: Katokawa.

Keightley, David (1978). *Sources of Shang History: The Oracle-Bone Inscriptions of Bronze Age China.* Berkeley: University of California Press.

Keightley, David (n.d.) "Death and the Birth of Civilizations: Ancestors, Art, and Culture in Early China and Early Greece". Unpublished paper.

Kennedy, George A. (1964). "Interpretation of the Ch'un-ch'iu". In *The Selected Works of George Kennedy*, Tien-yi Li (ed.). New Haven: Far Eastern Publications, Yale University.

Kennedy, George A. (1964). "The Monosyllabic Myth". In *The Selected Works of George Kennedy*, Tien-yi Li (ed.). New Haven: Far Eastern Publications, Yale University.

Keuls, Eva (1985). *The Reign of the Phallus*. New York: Harper & Row.

Kirk, G. S. (1962). *The Songs of Homer*. Cambridge: Cambridge University Press.

Kirk, G. S., J. E. Raven, and M. Schofield (eds) (1995). *The Presocratic Philosophers*. Cambridge: Cambridge University Press.

Knox, Bernard (1996). "Introduction". In *Odyssey*, Robert Fagles (trans.). New York: Viking/Penguin.

Knox, Bernard (1957). *Oedipus of Thebes*. New Haven: Yale University Press.

Kramers, Robert P. (1986). "The Development of the Confucian Schools". In *The Cambridge History of China*, Vol. 1. Cambridge: Cambridge University Press.

Laozi zhu (A Commentary on Laozi), Zhuzi Jicheng (ed.), Vol. 2.

Lau, D. C. (1963). *Lao Tzu, Tao Te Ching*. Harmondsworth: Penguin.

Lau, D. C. (1970). *Mencius*. Harmondsworth: Penguin.

Lau, D. C. (1979). *Confucius: The Analects*. Harmondsworth: Penguin.

Legge, James (trans.) (1994). *The Chinese Classics*, 5 vols. Rpt. Taipei: SMC Publishing.

Lesky, Albin (1967). "Die Schuld der Klytaimnestra". *Wiener Studien*, 80: 5–21.

Lévi, Jean (1995). *La Chine romanesque: fictions d'Orient et d'Occident*. Paris: Éditions de Seuil.

Levinas, Emmanuel (1995). *The Theory of Intuition in Husserl's Phenomenology*, 2nd edn, André Orianne (trans.). Evanston, IL: Northwestern University Press.

Lewis, Mark Edward (1999). *Writing and Authority in Early China*. Albany: State University of New York Press.

Liu Dalin (1993). *Zhongguo gudai xing wenhua* [The Sexual Culture of Ancient China]. Yinchuan: Liaoning chubanshe.

Liu Zhiji (1980). *Shi tong tongshi* [A Comprehensive Explanation of a Study of History]. Rpt., Taipei: Liren.

Lloyd, G. E. R. (1990). *Demystifying Mentalities*. Cambridge: Cambridge University Press.

Lloyd, G. E. R. (1996). *Adversaries and Authorities*. Cambridge: Cambridge University Press.

Loewe, Michael (1986). "The Former Han Dynasty". In *The Cambridge History of China*, Vol. 1: *The Ch'in and Han Empires, 221 B.C.–A.D. 220*. Cambridge: Cambridge University Press.

Loewe, Michael (1986). "The Religious and Intellectual Background". In *The Cambridge History of China*, Vol. 1: *The Ch'in and Han Empires, 221 B.C.–A.D. 220*. Cambridge: Cambridge University Press.

Loewe, Michael (1994). "Man and Beast: The Hybrid in Early Chinese Art and Literature". *Divination, Mythology and Monarchy in Han China*. University of Cambridge Oriental Publications 48. Cambridge: Cambridge University Press.

Longinus (1964). *"Longinus" on the Sublime*, edited with an introduction by D. A. Russell. Oxford: Clarendon Press.

Longinus (1965). *"Longinus" on the Sublime*, trans. W. Hamilton Fyfe. London: Harvard University Press and Heinemann.

Lun yu jijie [Collected Explanations of Analects]. SBBY edition.

McDowell, John (1982). "Falsehood and Not-Being in Plato's Sophist". In *Language and Logos: Studies in Ancient Greek Philosophy Presented to G. E. L. Owen*. Cambridge: Cambridge University Press.

Macleod, Colin (1983). "Thucydides and Tragedy". In *Collected Essays*. Oxford: Oxford University Press.

Mair, Victor H. (trans.) (1994). *Wandering on the Way: Early Taoist Tales and Parables of Chuang Tzu*. New York: Bantam.

Mair, Victor H. (1995). "Mummies of the Tarim Basin". *Archaeology*, April/May: 28–35.

Mao shi yinde [A Concordance to the Mao Odes] (1934). Harvard–Yenching Sinological Index Series, Supplement no. 9. Beijing: Harvard–Yenching Institute.

Martin, Richard P. (1989). *The Language of Homer: Speech and Performance in the Iliad*. Ithaca, NY: Cornell University Press.

Mengzi Zhao zhu [Mencius with the Zhao Commentary]. SBBY edition.

More-Gilbert, Bart (1997). *Postcolonial Theory: Contexts, Practices, and Politics*. London: Verso.

Mote, Frederick (1971). *Intellectual Foundations of China*. New York: Alfred A. Knopf.

Moulton, Carrol (1977). *Similes in the Homeric Poems*. Göttingen: Vandenhoeck & Ruprecht.

Murnaghan, Sheila (1987). *Disguise and Recognition in the Odyssey*. Princeton, NJ: Princeton University Press.

Nagy, Gregory (1990). *Pindar's Homer: The Lyric Possession of an Epic Poet*. Baltimore: Johns Hopkins University Press.

Nagy, Gregory (1992). *Greek Mythology and Poetics*. Ithaca, NY: Cornell University Press.

Needham, Joseph (1956). *Science and Civilisation in China*, Vol. 2: *History of Scientific Thought*. Cambridge: Cambridge University Press.

Needham, Joseph (1969). "Human Laws and the Laws of Nature". In *The Grand Titration: Science and Society in East and West*. London: George Allen & Unwin.

Nietzsche, Friedrich (1956). *The Birth of Tragedy*, Francis Golffing (trans.). Garden City, NY: Doubleday.

Nightingale, Andrea Wilson (1995). *Genres in Dialogue: Plato and the Construct of Philosophy*. Cambridge: Cambridge University Press.

Nilsson, M. P. (1967). *Geschichte der griechischen Religion*. Munich: C. H. Beck.

Nivison, David (1996). *The Ways of Confucianism: Investigations in Chinese Philosophy*. Chicago: Open Court.

Nussbaum, Martha C. (1986). *The Fragility of Goodness: Luck and Ethics in Greek Tragedy and Philosophy*. Cambridge: Cambridge University Press.

Orsini, Louis (1994). "An Act of Imaginative Oblivion: Eric Voegelin and the *Parmenides* of Plato". In *Plato and Postmodernism*, Steven Shankman (ed.). Glenside, PA: Aldine Press.

Owen, G. E. L. (1986). "The Platonism of Aristotle". In *Logic, Science, and Dialectic: Collected Papers in Greek Philosophy*, Martha Nussbaum (ed.). Ithaca, NY: Cornell University Press.

Owen, Stephen (1986). *Remembrances: The Experience of the Past in Classical Chinese Poetry*. Cambridge, MA: Harvard University Press.

Owen, Stephen (1992). *Readings in Chinese Literary Thought*. Cambridge, MA: Harvard University Press.

Owen, Stephen (1996). *An Anthology of Chinese Literature: Beginnings to 1911*, Stephen Owen (ed. and trans.). New York: W. W. Norton.

The Oxford Classical Dictionary (1996). Simon Hornblower and Antony Spawforth (eds). Oxford: Oxford University Press.

Plato (1961). *The Collected Dialogues of Plato*, Edith Hamilton and Huntington Cairns (eds). Princeton, NJ: Princeton University Press.

Plato (1989). *Plato: Republic 10*, Stephen Halliwell (trans.). Warminster: Aris & Phillips.

Plato (1993). *Plato: Republic 5*, Stephen Halliwell (trans.). Warminster: Aris & Phillips.

Price, A. W. (1989). *Love and Friendship in Plato and Aristotle*. Oxford: Clarendon Press.

Prusek, Jaroslav (1970). *Chinese History and Literature: Collection of Studies*. Dordrecht: D. Reidel.

Pucci, Pietro (1987). *Odysseus Polytropos: Intertextual Readings in the Odyssey and the Iliad*. Ithaca, NY: Cornell University Press.

Puett, Michael (1997). "Nature and Artifice: Debates in Late Warring States China Concerning the Creation of Culture". *Harvard Journal of Asiatic Studies*, 57 (2): 471–518.

Qian Mu (1983). *Liang Han jingxue jin-guwen pingyi* [A Critical Discussion of New and Old Script Schools in Han Dynasty Classical Studies]. Taipei: Dongda.

Qian Mu (1985). *Qin Han shi* [A History of the Qin and Han]. Taipei: Dongda.

Qian Zhongshu (1979). *Guan zhui bian*, Vol. 1. Hong Kong: Zhonghua.

Queen, Sarah A. (1996). *From Chronicle to Canon: The Hermeneutic of the Spring and Autumn According to Tung Chung-shu*. Cambridge: Cambridge University Press.

Race, William H. (1989). "Plato's Symposium and the Decline of Drama". Unpublished paper.

Raglan, Lord (1979). *The Hero*. New York: New American Library.

Raphals, Lisa (1992). *Knowing Words: Wisdom and Cunning in the Classical Traditions of China and Greece*. Ithaca, NY: Cornell University Press.

Raphals, Lisa (1998). *Sharing the Light: Representations of Women and Virtue in Early China*. Albany: State University of New York Press.

Reynolds, Sir Joshua (1969). *Discourses on Art*, Robert W. Wark (ed.). London: Collier Books.

Richardson, N. J. (1983). "Recognition Scenes in the *Odyssey*". In *Papers of the Liverpool Seminar*, Vol. 4. Liverpool: F. Cairns.

Robinet, Isabella (1991). *Histoire du Taoisme: des origines au XIVe siècle*. Paris: Les Éditions du Cerf.

Rocco, Christopher (1997). *Tragedy and Enlightenment: Athenian Political Thought and the Dilemmas of Modernity*. Berkeley: University of California Press.

Rose, Peter (1992). *Sons of the Gods, Children of the Earth: Ideology and Literary Form in Ancient Greece*. Ithaca, NY: Cornell University Press.

Ross, W. D. (1941). *The Basic Works of Aristotle*, Richard McKeon (ed.). New York: Random House.

Rozman, G. (1991). *The East Asian Region: Confucian Heritage and Its Modern Adaptation*. Princeton, NJ: Princeton University Press.

Rozman, G. (1992). "The Confucian Faces of Capitalism." In *Pacific Century*, M. Borthwick (ed.). Boulder, CO: Westview.

Ruan Zhisheng (1980). "Shi lun Sima Qian suoshuo de 'tong gujin zhi bian'" [A Preliminary Essay on Sima Qian's Statement "To Penetrate the Transformations of Ancient and Modern Times"]. In *Zhongguo shixueshi lunwen xuanji* [A Selected Collection of Essays on the History of Chinese Historiography], Du Weiyun and Huang Jinxing (eds). Taipei: Huashi.

Rutherford, R. B. (1995). *The Art of Plato*. Cambridge, MA: Harvard University Press.

Rutherford, R. B. (1996). *Greece and Rome: New Surveys in the Classics*. No. 26. Oxford: Oxford University Press.

Said, Edward (1991). *Orientalism*. London: Penguin.

Sallis, John (1996). *Being and Logos: Reading the Platonic Dialogues*. Bloomington: Indiana University Press.

Saussy, Haun (1993). *The Problem of a Chinese Aesthetic*. Stanford, CA: Stanford University Press.

Saussy, Haun (1996). "Writing in the Odyssey: Eurykleia, Parry, Jousse, and the Opening of a Letter from Homer". *Arethusa*, 29: 299–338.

Savage, William E. (1992). "Archetypes, Model Emulation, and the Confucian Gentleman". *Early China*, 17: 3.

Schwartz, Benjamin (1985). *The World of Thought in Ancient China*. Cambridge, MA: The Belknap Press of Harvard University Press.

Schwartz, Benjamin (1996). Review of Lisa Raphals's *Knowing Words: Wisdom and Cunning in the Classical Traditions of China and Greece*. In *Harvard Journal of Asiatic Studies*, 56 (2): 229–30.

Segal, Charles (1997). *Dionysiac Poetics and Euripides' "Bacchae"*. Princeton, NJ: Princeton University Press.

Seon-Hee Suh Kwon (1991). "Eric Voegelin and Lao Tzu: The Search for Order". Ph.D. dissertation, Texas Tech University.

Shang shu (1973). Shisan jing zhushu ed. Taipei: Yiwen.

Shankman, Steven (1994). *In Search of the Classic: The Greco-Roman Tradition, Homer to Valéry and Beyond*. University Park: Pennsylvania State University Press.

Shankman, Steven (ed.) (1994). *Plato and Postmodernism*. Glenside, PA: Aldine Press.

Shankman, Steven (n.d.) "*Katharsis, Xing*, and *Hua*: Aristotle and Confucius on Poetry's Affective Power". Unpublished paper.

Shaughnessy, Edward (1991). *Sources of Western Zhou History*. Berkeley: University of California Press.

Shaughnessy, Edward (1998). *Before Confucius: Studies in the Creation of the Confucian Classics*. Albany: State University of New York Press.

Shi Ding (1982). "Sima Qian xie 'Jin shang (Han Wudi)'" [Sima Qian's Writing of "The Present Emperor" (Emperor Wu of the Han)]. In *Sima Qian yanjui xinlun* [New Essays in Sima Qian Studies]. Zhengzhou: Henan renmin.

Shi ji [Records of the Historian] (1959). Beijing: Zhonghua.

Shigenori Nagatomo (1983). "An Epistemic Turn in the *Tao Te Ching*: A Phenomenological Reflection". *International Philosophical Quarterly*, 22 (2), issue no. 60, June.

Shima Gunio (1973). *Laozi jiaozheng* [Corrected Readings of Laozi]. Tokyo: Morimoto.

Sider, D. (1980). "Plato's *Symposion* as Dionysian Festival". *Quaderni Urbinati di Cultura Classica*, 33: 41–56.

Sivin, Nathan (1995). "Text and Experience in Classical Chinese Medicine". In *Knowledge and the Scholarly Medical Traditions*, D. Bates (ed.). Cambridge: Cambridge University Press.

Sse-schu, Schu-king, Schi-king (1864). In *Manduschuischer Uebersset-zung*. Leipzig; reprinted, Neudeln Liechtenstein: Kraus Reprints Ltd, 1966).

Stanford, W. B. (1965). *The Odyssey of Homer, with General and Grammatical Introduction, Commentary, and Indexes*. 2 vols. London: Macmillan.

Steven, R. G. (1933). "Plato and the Art of His Time". *Classical Quarterly*, 27: 149–55.

Stewart, Andrew (1990). *Greek Sculpture: An Exploration*, 2 vols. New Haven: Yale University Press.

Strassler, Robert D. (1996). *The Landmark Thucydides*. New York: Free Press.

Thornton, A. (1970). *People and Themes in Homer's Odyssey*. Dunedin: University of Otago Press.

Thucydides (1928–30). *History of the Peloponnesian War*, Charles Foster Smith (trans.). Loeb Library Edition, 4 vols. Cambridge, MA: Harvard University Press.

Thucydides (1982). *History of the Peloponnesian War*, Richard Crawley (trans.). New York: Modern Library.

Thucydides (1999). *The Landmark Thucydides: A Comprehensive Guide to the Peloponnesian War*. A newly revised edition of the Richard Crawley translation. New York: Simon & Schuster.

Tracy, Stephen V. (1990). *The Story of the Odyssey*. Princeton, NJ: Princeton University Press.

Trimpi, Wesley (1983). *Muses of One Mind: The Literary Analysis of Experience and Its Continuity*. Princeton, NJ: Princeton University Press.

Tu Wei-ming (1985). *Confucian Thought: Selfhood as Creative Transformation*. Albany: State University of New York Press.

Tu Wei-ming (ed.) (1996). *Confucian Traditions in East Asian Modernity: Moral Education and Economic Culture in Japan and the Four Mini-dragons*. Cambridge, MA: Harvard University Press.

Tuan Yi-Fu (1974). *Topophilia: A Study of Environmental Perception, Attitudes, and Values*. Englewood Cliffs, NJ: Prentice-Hall.

Van Zoeren, Steven (1991). *Poetry and Personality: Reading Exegesis, and Hermeneutics in Traditional China*. Stanford, CA: Stanford University Press.

Vandermeersch, Leon (1980). *Wangdao ou la voie royale: recherches sur l'esprit des institutions de la Chine archaïque*, tome 2: *Structures politiques, les rites*. Paris: École Française d'Extrême-Orient.

Verene, Donald Phillip (ed.) (1987). *Vico and Joyce*. Albany: State University of New York Press.

Verrall, A. W. (1913). *Euripides, the Rationalist: A Study in the History of Arts and Religion*. Cambridge: Cambridge University Press.

Voegelin, Eric (1957). *Order and History*, Vol. 2: *The World of the Polis*. Baton Rouge: Louisiana State University Press.

Voegelin, Eric (1957). *Order and History*, Vol. 3: *Plato and Aristotle*. Baton Rouge: Louisiana State University Press.

Voegelin, Eric (1987). *Order and History*, Vol. 5: *In Search of Order*. Baton Rouge: Louisiana State University Press.

von der Mühll, P. (1940). "Odysee". *Paulys Realencyclopädie der classischen Altertumswissenschaft*, G. Wissowa, W. Kroll and K. Mittelhaus (eds). Supplementband vii. Stuttgart.

von Falkenhausen, Lothar (1995). "Reflections on the Political Role of Spirit Mediums in Early China: The *Wu* Officials in the *Zhou Li*". *Early China*, 20: 279–80.

von Scheliha, Renata (1943). *Patroklos: Gedanken über Homers Dichtung und Gestalten*. Basle: B. Schwabe.

Waley, Arthur (trans.) (1960). *The Book of Songs: The Ancient Chinese Classic of Poetry*. New York: Grove Press.

Waley, Arthur (1996). *The Book of Songs: The Ancient Chinese Classic of Poetry*, Joseph Allen (ed.). New York: Grove Press.

Wang, C. H. (1974). *The Bell and the Drum: Shih Ching as Formulaic Poetry in an Oral Tradition*. Berkeley: University of California Press.

Wang, C. H. (1988). *From Ritual to Allegory: Seven Essays on Early Chinese Poetry*. Hong Kong: Chinese University Press.

Watson, Burton (1958). *Ssu-ma Ch'ien: Grand Historian of China*. New York: Columbia University Press.

Watson, Burton (trans.) (1989). *The Tso Chuan: Selections from China's Oldest Narrative History*. New York: Columbia University Press.

Watson, Burton (trans.) (1993). *The Records of the Grand Historian: Qin Dynasty*. Hong Kong: Research Centre for Translation, Chinese University of Hong Kong, and Columbia University Press.

Webb, Eugene (1981). *Eric Voegelin: Philosopher of History*. Seattle: University of Washington Press.

Whitehead, Alfred North (1929). *Process and Reality: An Essay in Cosmology*. New York: Macmillan.

Wiegemann, Hermann (1990). "Plato's Critiques of the Poets and the Misunderstanding of His Epistemological Argumentation", Henry W. Johnstone Jr. (trans.). *Philosophy and Rhetoric*, 23 (2): 109–24.

Wilamowitz-Moellendorff, U. (1927). *Die Heimkehr des Odysseus*. Berlin: Weidemann.

Wu Hung (1989). *The Wu Liang Shrine: The Ideology of Early Chinese Pictorial Art*. Stanford, CA: Stanford University Press.

Xiao Tong. *Wen Xuan* [Anthology of Literature]. Taipei: Commercial Press.

Xie Jinqing (1933). *Shi jing zhi nuxing de yanjiu* [A Study of Women in the Classic of Poetry]. Shanghai: Shangwu.

Xu Fuguan (1980). "Yuan shi – you zongjiao tongxiang renwen de shixue chengli" [The Original Scribe – From a Religious to the Establishment of a Humanistic Historiography]. In *Zhongguo shixue shi lunwen xuanji* [A Collection of Essays on the History of Chinese Historiography], Vol. 3, Tu Weiyun and Chen Jinzhong (eds). Taipei: Huashi.

Xu Shen (1962). *Shuo wen jie zi zhu* [A Commentary on Explaining Simple Graphs and Analyzing Compound Characters]. Taipei: Shiji.

Xunzi. SBBY edition.

Yang Bojun (1988). *Lun yu yi zhu* [A Translation and Commentary of Analects]. Rpt., Taipei: Huazheng.

Yang Bojun (ed.) (1990). *Chun qiu Zuo zhuan zhu.* 4 vols, revised edition. Beijing: Zhonghua shuju.

Yang Kuan (1986). *Zhanguo shi* [A History of the Warring States]. Zonghe: Gufeng.

Yip Wai-lim (1993). *Diffusion of Differences: Dialogue between Chinese and Western Poetics.* Berkeley: University of California Press.

Yu, Pauline (1987). *The Reading of Imagery in the Chinese Poetic Tradition.* Princeton, NJ: Princeton University Press.

Yukawa, Hideki (1983). "Chuangtse and the Happy Fish". In *Experimental Essays on Chuang-Tzu*, Victor H. Mair (ed.). Honolulu: University of Hawaii Press.

Zhang Dake (1985). *Shi ji yanjiu* [A Study of the Records of the Historian]. Lanzhou: Gansu Renmin Press.

Zhao Yi (1973). *Ershier shi zhaji* [A Notebook on the Twenty-two Dynastic Histories]. Taipei: Letian.

Zheng Haosheng (1956). *Sima Qian nianpu* [A Year-by-Year Chronology of Sima Qian], rev. edition. Shanghai: Commercial Press.

Zhu Xi (n.d.) *Shi jing jizhu* [Collected Commentaries on the *Classic of Poetry*]. Hong Kong: Guanzi.

Zheng Xuan. *Mao shi zheng jian.* SBBY edition.

Zhuangzi. SBBY edition.

Zürcher, Erich (1959). *The Buddhist Conquest of China*, 2 vols. Leiden: E. Brill.

Index

Achilles 20–1, 23, 34, 47, 91, 93
  and Patroclus 35, 43–4
Aeneid, compared to Homeric epics
  47
Aeschylus
  Oresteia 65, 114, 176
  Suppliants 165–6, 176
Agamemnon 23, 34, 65, 91, 93, 97,
  114
Agathon 193–4, 202–3, 205
agricultural motifs
  in *Classic of Poetry* 20, 27, 33, 48,
  51
  in *Odyssey* 30, 36–7, 41, 46, 48, 64
Alcibiades 113–15, 138, 165
Ames, Roger T. 6–7, 180
ancestor worship 24, 28–9, 82, 95,
  160–1
  in Greece 164
Antikleia 45–7
Aristotle
  as literary critic 2, 20, 52, 62–3,
  197
    on tragedy 111–12, 113–16,
    137, 172, 213
    aims of poetry and of history
    94, 110, 176, 213
  Metaphysics 207
  Nicomachean Ethics 207, 212

as *philosophos* 4, 7, 79, 111, 165,
  188
  on noetic participation 188,
  212, 207–8
Poetics 20, 52, 110–11, 166, 176,
  178, 197
Athena 36, 61, 65
Athens, fifth-century
  Athenian character 95, 111–16,
  137–45, 146, 166–9, 177, 189,
  194–5
  figures of 112, 113, 137–9,
  142–5, 146, 168, 194–5
  Piraeus 114, 167–9, 177, 194
  social, political, and intellectual
  climate 113–16, 137–45,
  164–9, 175–8, 227
  attitudes toward justice 142,
  166–9
  and emergence of philosophy 1,
  92, 164–9, 178, 212
  role of tragic theater in 165–7,
  193, 196–201, 202, 212
  self-identification of citizens 96,
  112, 139, 142, 165
  war with Sparta and Sicily 94–7,
  101, 103, 110–16, 122, 137–45,
  146, 157, 166–9, 177, 189,
  194–5, 212–13

249

Index

Index